WENDY D

Hot and Bothered

Men and Women,
Sex and Love in the 1990s

Grafton
An Imprint of HarperCollins*Publishers*

Grafton
An Imprint of HarperCollins*Publishers*,
77–85 Fulham Palace Road,
Hammersmith, London W6 8JB

Published by Grafton 1993
9 8 7 6 5 4 3 2 1

First published by
Key Porter Books Limited, Toronto, 1992

Copyright © Wendy Dennis 1992

The Author asserts the moral right to
be identified as the author of this work

The excerpts from "Betrayed" which appear in chapter seven are
copyright © Lisa Grunwald 1990. These excerpts are from an article
which first appeared in the June 1990 issue of *Esquire*.

ISBN 0 586 21440 2

Set in Caledonia

Printed in Great Britain by
HarperCollins Manufacturing Glasgow

Contents

5. *Sexual Etiquette for the Nineties* 133

For my parents

Acknowledgments

I WOULD NOT HAVE WRITTEN THIS BOOK IF I DID NOT HAVE A CHERISHED association with *Toronto Life* magazine. The idea for *Hot and Bothered* emerged from an article about sexual etiquette that the *Toronto Life* editors encouraged me to write in 1989; it took nerve to publish that piece—it wasn't a shy treatment of the subject—but *Toronto Life* has never been short on guts. *Toronto Life* is a writer's heaven, and I've been blessed to have had a long-standing relationship with the magazine. I particularly want to thank Marq de Villiers and Peter Herrndorf, who know a thing or two about journalists and the work they do. Their generosity and kindness, both personally and professionally, have touched me deeply.

The article would not have been transformed into a book had it not been for the tireless efforts and encouragement of my agent, Lee Davis Creal at Lucinda Vardey Agency, who was enthusiastic about the idea from the beginning, and who managed to get distinguished publishers such as Lester & Orpen Dennys, Key Porter Books, Viking Penguin, Harper Collins and Penguin Australia enthusiastic about it too.

A number of other people dreamed this book into being and nurtured its development. Malcolm Lester and Louise Dennys lent a tremendous amount of time, energy, and financial and emotional support. I'm grateful to them for the faith they showed and I'm deeply sorry that they were unable to see this project through to its conclusion. I also want to thank Anna Porter and Phyllis Bruce at Key Porter Books for the speed with which they rescued the book from near demise, and the patience with which they saw it through to publication.

I want to acknowledge Catherine Yolles as well, who no doubt suffered through the editing of many strange incarnations of the manuscript before it reached final draft, and Mindy Werner at Viking Penguin, who collaborated in the editing. Both of them trusted in the possibilities of this book, even when they had good reason not to. I also owe thanks to my U.K. agent, Carolyn Brunton, and my publishers in the U.K. and Australia: Ian Paten, Robert Sessions and Bryony Cosgrove. But this book would still be just an idea—and an incoherent one at that—had it not been for Stephen Trumper's unflagging encouragement, accessibility and extraordinary editing gifts. I'm indebted to him in countless ways, but mainly because he understands writers and all things writerly.

Several other people helped. I owe appreciation to John Wellwood for his invaluable research assistance and the many laughs he provided along the way, Charles Rowland for his meticulous fact-checking, and Gena Gorrell for her insightful copy-editing. Mark Donald of Dallas, Texas, opened his files and gave generously of his time, and Jane Hardy saved the project from catastrophe when she recovered a year's worth of research materials that were stolen from my car. Many professionals too numerous to mention also gave magnanimously of their time and expertise, and their contributions helped me enormously.

I'm also blessed with remarkably supportive friends, colleagues and family who held my hand through the darker moments: Marsha Chesley, Kirk Makin, Joyce Harris, Judy Gold, Sarah Murdoch, Debbie Bernstein, Sam Freeman, Jane Mussett, Lorraine Gane, Brad MacIver, Dana Hall, David Hayes, Ian Brown, Ian Pearson, Art Niemi, Douglas Pepper, Rebecca Young, Donna Cohen, Paul Cohen, Fawna Abraham, Brian Hogarth, Trevor Wickham, Bob Schneider, Ellen Neeman, Jane Cudlipp, Linda Leighton, Michael Leranbaum and the gang, my parents, Evelyn and Irving Dennis, my sisters and brothers-in-law, Joan and Clifford Lax and Nancy Dennis and Ted Seligman, and the many other relatives, friends and acquaintances who showed interest and offered encouragement. I owe a particular debt of gratitude to my dear friend Ellen Vanstone. Not only did she fly to my door (or meet me at The Mars) at ungodly hours to pore over the manuscript, she kept me marginally sane and laughing when the going got tough.

There are two other people who saw me through: Ben and my daughter Sara. Ben came on board in the latter stages of the project and he's the best argument I can make to a woman who's disheartened about the possibilities of finding the love of a good man. Sara was nine years old when I began this book and eleven when I finished it. With a wisdom and maturity far beyond her years she understood what I was trying to accomplish, tolerated me when I was intolerable trying to accomplish it, and cheered me on. Everyone should have a kid like this.

Finally, I want to formally thank the men and women who opened their hearts so I could write this book. They had everything to lose and nothing to gain when they let a reporter snoop around in their sex lives. I hope I have been true to their trust.

"Don't let that little frankfurter run your life."

—BRUCE JAY FRIEDMAN

"Who wrote the Book of Love—and what the hell were they thinking?"

—LYNDA BARRY

Introduction

IN THE SIXTIES, WHEN I DISCOVERED SEX, THERE WAS NO SUCH THING AS a politically correct blowjob. Men could still admit they liked a woman on her knees, and get off on their lovely phallic power trip. And women could still admit they sometimes liked to submit, which meant that most were good sports about the knee-burns.

There was also no such thing in my teenage years as Women Who Loved Too Much, romance brokers, serial monogamy, the New Male, sportfucking, fear of commitment, quizzes about sexual history, video dating, Smart Women Who Make Foolish Choices, a man shortage, sex-role chaos, orgasm angst, commuter marriages, designer condoms, penicillin-proof sexually transmitted diseases, transitional relationships, Significant Others or sexual ennui. Celibacy happened to other people, and it was not something you could catch. Most of the men I knew would hit on a woman they found divine, and happily share her bed if the occasion demanded; often they would even fall in love. And most of the women I knew would fall in lust or in love right back.

In the mid-seventies (like many of those men and women) I met a Significant Other. We set up housekeeping and, some years later, got married. In 1984 (like many of those men and women) we split up. At that point, single again after nine years, I found myself catapulted into a world that felt lunar in its unfamiliarity. Certainly it was a world of male-female relationships light-years away from the ones I had known as a young woman discovering guys and sex in the sixties.

I soon came to realize that I was not alone. Most of the men and women I knew—whether they were single, divorced or struggling to stay together—were confused and anxious in their romantic dealings with the opposite sex. They were stymied trying to figure out how to behave with each other in a world where many of the ground rules of dating, mating and relationships had changed. If they were alone, or in troubled unions, they longed for a lasting, intimate connection; they just didn't know how to forge one, and they didn't understand why they didn't know how. There were, of course, the enviable couples who were managing to succeed in love; legions of hapless others, it seemed, were keen to discover their secret.

In many of the heterosexual relationships that I was observing from about the mid-seventies on, the story went like this: you would (if you were lucky) meet someone. Then you would go out, have fun, talk about The Relationship, fight, get tired of talking about The Relationship, hurl insults at each other—and break up. Or you would meet someone, go out, have fun, talk about The Relationship, get married, fight, get tired of talking about The Relationship, hire lawyers to hurl the insults for you—and break up.

Sex, romance and love, which had once fallen into the category of Fun Things to Enjoy in Life, were now falling into the category of Aggravating Things to Make You Crazy in Life. Sex had become maddeningly complex. Finding, establishing and maintaining a meaningful relationship had become a frustrating endeavor. And I'm talking about a Sisyphean sort of endeavor.

For one thing, it became a lot harder to meet a suitable mate. If you were lucky enough to connect, there were strange new mating rites to figure out. And then you had to deal with all the strategies, power plays, manipulations, crossed signals, hidden agendas, confusions and conflicts arising from the tyranny of contemporary sexual politics. What's more, there was the charming reality that you could pick up a killer virus in the process.

At first, I thought it was only my contemporaries who were having problems with the opposite sex. Many of them were yearning for the easy sexual rapport they had known in the sixties, when it had been as simple as "You're a man, I'm a woman, let's make love." (Or so it seemed through the haze of nostalgia. We were wistful, I suspect, because sex was a whole lot simpler in those days. Everybody wanted to sleep with you, and you wanted to sleep with everybody, and, generally speaking, you did.) But once I began checking around, I heard similar complaints from men and women in their early thirties and even in their twenties. They didn't seem to be faring much better. The sexual angst was pandemic.

Anxious to make some sense of these problems, in 1989 I wrote an article called "Sexual Etiquette for the '90s" for *Toronto Life*, a sophisticated city magazine. The piece was a straight-shooting, upbeat, ironic look at dating, mating and bedroom rites in the age of sexual apprehension.

To research the piece, I asked around for the names of people who were heterosexual, anywhere from their late twenties to late forties or older, single, single again, or involved, for better or worse, in marriages or relationships of some duration. Then I made cold calls to strangers, guaranteeing them anonymity if they would talk to me about the intimate details of their sex lives. No one refused. I met them in bars and restaurants, asking questions I clearly had no right to ask, and was utterly amazed at the eagerness and candor with which people spoke. Over and over again I was told that this was an important article I was writing, because sex was so damn complicated these days.

There was a good deal on the minds of these men and women: how to learn to love condoms, whether it was still okay to go all the way on the first date, what to do if your mate hardly ever wanted it, whether it was possible—or even advisable—to flirt anymore. Often, the stories I heard revealed that the traditional courtship roles had completely reversed. Men, for instance, now had to figure out how to deal with women who were asking them out. And women had to develop techniques for talking reluctant men into the sack. Several people were highly vocal about what they loved and hated in bed, about their methods for enduring torturous blind dates and about the mortifying fact that they were whacking off or privately diddling their privates more than they wanted to. Some of the stories people shared were poignant, some dramatic, some infuriating and some hilariously funny. I've incorporated them into this book.

Soon after the magazine article appeared, I got letters. Boy, did I get letters! They came from as far away as San Francisco and Vancouver, from teenagers and forty-year-olds, from singles and from those safely settled in long-term relationships.

I heard from a 33-year-old man who confessed he'd been a "reluctant celibate" for four years; the personal stories in the article, he wrote, assured him that he was not a freak. I heard from an eminent journalist who remarked that, twenty-four hours after reading the section on equipment failure (not ordinarily an amusing subject), he was still giggling. I heard from a single lawyer who wrote that she'd had many frustrating and puzzling encounters with the opposite sex, and had been close to losing her sense of humor; my story had allowed her the opportunity to laugh once more at the otherwise "pathetic state of affairs."

The huge response convinced me to press on and write a book. I wanted to know why so many people had wound up in a troubled state and—if such a thing was possible—how they might get out of it. Consequently, I began traveling to urban centers throughout North America, talking to hundreds of men and women in cities such as New York, Calgary, Dallas, Montreal, Toronto, Chicago, Vancouver and San Francisco. They too matched the selection criteria for the subjects of the magazine article and were hip to what was going on and willing to talk intimately and honestly for a couple of hours to a stranger. And they too had many tales to tell: of lust and love and social change and broken hearts and dangerous liaisons and sublime marriages and sexual boredom and dates from hell. You will hear their voices in these pages.

By this time I had garnered a reputation as something of an "expert" on yearning issues, and my phone started ringing. Pretty soon I took to answering, "Relationships Hotline..." and fielding one bizarre question after another. One woman called begging me to run a search of my computer for the file on blowjobs, to give her an up-to-the-minute report on technique; I located the file and read her the pertinent information. (For the latest on this subject, see chapter five.) Another woman called to confess that although she had three guys on the go at once, she was thinking of bringing a fourth one on deck. "Does that," she asked tentatively, "make me a nympho?" "Nah," I reassured her. "We don't use that word anymore." I suggested that perhaps "air traffic controller" would be more appropriate.

I also had many conversations with men and women who were not, shall we say, getting it as regularly as they wanted to. "I find I'm having sex with myself a lot," one wistful Sad Sack male confided. When I reassured him that he was by no means an isolated case and inquired solicitously how he was coping through the drought, he replied that afterwards he smoked two cigarettes and asked himself, "Was it good for you?"

I learned about how one woman had marched smartly up to a drugstore pharmacist, condoms and K-Y jelly tucked under her arm, anxious to do "the informed consumer thing" but puzzled as to why some condoms cost so much more than others. As the female pharmacist coolly explained that some people were "really picky" about quality, pointing out that "we have some boxes of condoms back here for $30 a crack," a guy waiting in line kindly offered a male perspective on the perfectly acceptable mid-priced purchase. He drew the line, however, at her teasing request that he model one.

I heard from a fortysomething woman who had just savored her first-ever threesome. After I shared this story with some of my married friends, who claimed that their sex lives were pretty humdrum, many of them confessed that the dirty details had kept them cranked up for days. "A threesome? Really? This happened to someone we know?" asked the husband of a friend of mine, who was dying to know names and specifics. "Shut up," said his wife. "You're lucky I told you that much."

One evening, attending the International Festival of Authors in Toronto, I was settling expectantly into my plush theater seat to hear Richard Ford read from his latest novel when a guy to whom I had just been casually introduced leaned over from the row behind and whispered sotto voce in my ear, "Talk dirty to me, baby.... C'mon, baby...write dirty to me."

And so it went. What had begun as a magazine article on sexual etiquette for the nineties quickly grew into something much more: a book about contemporary sexual mores and the state of the heart. Because in order to talk in more depth about what was "right" about sexual manners, I had to talk about what was wrong. And a lot was wrong.

The ironies were overpowering. So often during my interviewing I sat and listened to men and women telling me their yearnings, and so often their yearnings were the same: to put an end to the sexual strategies, the frustrating guessing games, the debilitating manipulations and power plays, and achieve some level of comfort and intimacy with each other. Frequently I was aware that I was the first person to hear an intimate disclosure. Sometimes the confessions were potentially devastating—like the revelation of an affair—but more often they were just the simple truths, wants and needs that lovers ought to share. I came to realize how much the unspoken but lethal nuances of sexual politics have become distancing mechanisms, stony barriers to intimacy, and I observed how oppressively they are keeping men and women from finding each other, falling in love and galloping off into the sunset together.

I realized, too, how much men and women are repressing what they secretly think and feel and need in the well-intentioned cause of political correctness. In the aftermath of feminism, most of the people I've met believe that it's important to move with the times and live up to politically correct notions about what it now means to be a man and a woman. And the majority dearly wish—and are struggling, with varying degrees of success—to shed the worst, most confining aspects of maleness and femaleness. In their hearts and loins, however, many still long for the lovely, primal edge sometimes engendered by those former roles; and that tug-of-war is taking its toll. For the truth is that we now desire in each other a *blend* of the past and the present, a subtle melding of the most alluring aspects of maleness and femaleness culled from our understanding of those words at this moment in history *and* from the days before the meaning of those words irrevocably changed. That yearning has a powerful erotic hold on many of us—and it haunts us in the bedroom whether we have the courage to confront it or not. The trickiest task for everyone is trying to find a comfortable modern balance between the old and the new.

Indeed, a sense of some innocence lost, a wistful harking back to the days when men were men and women were women, informed many of the conversations I had. Yet many people don't feel free to voice their yearnings. They fear that expressing certain needs, desires and expectations will be viewed as unsophisticated, sexist, passé or disloyal to their sex—like leaking privileged information to the enemy. And so they censor their feelings, and often wind up lying to the two people they are in bed with: themselves and their lovers.

We are paying dearly for our denial, I think, because our unexpressed needs and desires don't just go away. They fester and start making us behave erratically, or we project them onto others and start making *them* behave defensively. And erratically and defensively is a fairly accurate assessment of the way men and women are behaving with each other.

I also discovered that many of the questions of sexual etiquette that I first encountered while writing the magazine article—seemingly banal questions that were causing widespread confusion, such as whether a man should call a woman after he had slept with her, or whether a woman should admit to a man with "commitment" jitters that she truly cared for him—were simply matters of common sense or common human decency; they could easily be resolved with a little forethought or empathy about how one's behavior might have an emotional impact on another vulnerable human being. Because let's face it—when it comes to matters of sex and love, we're all vulnerable little bunnies, aren't we?

Many times, as I sat at my word processor writing about these questions of sexual etiquette, large and small, I found myself staring at the words on the screen, blinking in disbelief, thinking that this was absurd: surely I didn't have to say these things. And yet I knew that I had to, because so many men and women had told me, over and over, that they needed to be said.

A lot of people have come to a place where nothing surprises them anymore. Affairs happen. Marriages break up. Lovers leave. They are hip to it all. They *know*. They have become so inured to the casual brutalities of modern loving that many of them cannot even muster the energy to be outraged any longer. What that says about our future, and what we might do to fix things, I'll discuss as their stories unfold.

One of the most illuminating discoveries I made while working on this book was an understanding of what men are going through during this time of sexual turmoil. Their story, I believe, has received short shrift, and I have tried to tell it fairly.

After all, I had an opportunity most women would kill for. I got to talk, at length, with interesting, introspective, articulate men about women and sex. There was no need for subterfuge or game-playing or politically correct but insincere pronouncements. I was female, but I was not sexually involved with them, nor was I going to be. I gave them the chance to talk about their dreams and hopes and fears, and talk they did. In fact—and this may surprise many female readers—I discovered that they were hungry to talk, hungrier even than women.

I have always had an affection for men despite (like most women) being baffled and exasperated by them from time to time; while working on this book I discovered a deep empathy for the male point of view on much of what is happening between the sexes. It is an empathy I would never have developed had I just hung out with The Girls. For I have come to realize that women all too often have their guns out of the holster when they encounter men, and those guns are getting in the way. Women need to listen to men more often; like women, men are hurt and confused right now, and they have something valuable to say about their hurt and confusion.

Although this book primarily addresses the romantic tribulations single people face, in chapters six and seven you'll hear from those in longer-term relationships and marriages. Many of the men and women I met were contentedly coupled, and they too have confided their pressures, pleasures and success secrets. They have been remarkably forthcoming on several subjects: how they cope when the passion goes (and how they get it back); the role of fantasy and porn in their sex lives; what they do when the urge to sleep with someone else hits. Some also divulge how they're conducting their extramarital affairs, and the price they're paying.

And so this is a book about men and women and where I believe their sexual relationships are headed—where I dream they *should* head through the nineties. I did not conduct a scientific study. I did not compile statistics and extrapolate from them. I did not write a scholarly tome. During a period of two years I asked questions, listened, observed and consulted many sexperts. I always changed interviewees' names and I occasionally altered a minor detail of description to guard the anonymity of a subject; in all cases, however, I have related people's stories as they were told to me.

In addition, I have included stories and information about heterosexuals and AIDS. It is impossible to tackle the subject of sex in the nineties without addressing AIDS; I've looked at how that disease is transforming what goes on behind our bedroom doors. In chapter five, for instance, you'll find out what questions people are posing to each other at the bedside to ferret out sexual histories, how they're springing condoms on each other, and whether swallowing is on or off the sexual agenda these days.

While there is a serious purpose behind this book, I hope it also entertains. Many of the people I met said they needed a good laugh on the subject of sex and relationships right now, and I've done my best to accommodate them. As well, there's lots of how-to information in the following pages—like the current thinking on how to handle the dreaded sexual brontosaurus, how to deal with sexual politics on a date, and how to elegantly introduce the desire for back-door (anal) sex. In contrast to most other treatises on sex and relationships, however, the "how-to" portions of this book are written with a certain irreverence. I've had some fun with the material because, to me, sex is a raunchy, riveting, hilarious subject. I mean, just thinking about the act itself makes me laugh. After all, if you're doing it right—even if you're doing it wrong—it's supposed to be fun. (Woody Allen was on to this long ago when he observed that sex without love was a meaningless experience, but that as meaningless experiences went it was one of the best.) And yet, for a lot of people, sex isn't that much fun anymore. And this, I ask, is what we are supposed to view as social progress?

I have to wonder if there is any way for men and women to find their way back to each other. Because if I learned nothing else while I worked on this book, I learned this: men and women miss each other. They miss each other a lot. They *long* to reconcile.

"I'm hopeful," one man told me, "because people need each other and nobody likes this stuff that's going on. So we'll have to put our heads together and work it out. We're feeling pressured from all sides right now, and that's why I'm hopeful. I mean, *something*'s gotta give, doesn't it?"

It does indeed.

Part One

Disconnection

1. The State of the Heart

I WON'T DIVULGE *ALL* THE DIRTY DETAILS OF MY SEXUAL FANTASIES HERE, just a few choice tidbits. I will confess up front, however, that they're not even marginally politically correct. They're not exactly original, either. Although women don't like this sort of thing to get around, lots of them are having fantasies they're not supposed to be having.

The important thing to keep in mind about my fantasies is that they have virtually nothing to do with my actual life. In real life, I'm a fairly typical woman of the nineties. I have a rewarding career, my own home, a passable income, a healthy debt load, a kid, no husband and a hard-won sense of independence. And, as with most women of my generation (and younger women too, although often they are loath to admit it), feminism has had a lot to do with the person I have become.

I tell you all this because I have had a tough time, over the years, reconciling my fantasies with my vision of the contemporary woman I'm supposed to be: a plucky, powerful, assertive human being—not a replica of man, but his equal. In my fantasies, however, I'm a sex slave. In the juiciest variations, I willingly submit while Mongol hordes of broad-shouldered, masterful, slavering men do unspeakable things to my body.

It behooves me to report that men are not exactly kneeling before the goddess of sexual propriety in *their* fantasies either. They're out there doing what a man's got to do, exercising their inalienable right to phallic mastery of women. In many male fantasies, the man is sticking it every which way to a woman (better still, a couple of women), and of course the woman (or women) is lying there begging for more. In masculine erotic imaginations, guys are powerful, potent, piggy, macho men—something men are less and less allowed to be in the real world these days.

I've chosen to expose these naughty little secrets because there is no way to begin a book about contemporary heterosexual relationships without addressing what I see as one of the biggest stumbling blocks to men and women enjoying great sex and its longed-for companion—true love. What I see is this: as men and women, we're a little confused about our sexual roles. Never does the magnitude of that confusion strike me more compellingly than when I'm getting off on a politically incorrect fantasy.

———————————

First, a few words about cataclysmic social change. The good news is that in the past twenty-five years or so men and women have moved farther and faster in terms of sexual equality than they have at any other time in human history. In fact, John Naisbitt, author of *Megatrends*, told *Time* in 1984 that the readjustment of sexual roles has probably been *the* most significant trend of the twentieth century. The not-so-good news is that men and women have had to pay for all this wonderful social progress, and pay dearly. Indeed, what the sexes have been through is your basic nightmare.

That accident of history affectionately known as the sixties left them in the unenviable position of having to unlearn everything they thought was important in the business of being male and female. The sexual revolution and the women's movement blew the lid off all the familiar rules and roles and left this gaping hole where those rules and roles used to be. And so both sexes have had to inch their way through the rubble of their razed expectations and figure out what it means to be a man or woman all over again.

Trying to cope with this tricky business of becoming sexual equals in the aftermath of what one man called "the freedom and flowering of whatever the hell that was—that mess that has gotten us to where we are now" has turned out to be a not inconsiderable task. We are, after all, talking about ground-breaking work here, and half the time people had to make up the rules when they didn't know what in God's name they were doing. They are still making up the rules, an exercise that has taken guts, patience, fortitude and a great deal of idealism.

It has also taken its toll. According to Reay Tannahill in *Sex in History*, "The people of medieval Europe had twelve generations during which to adjust to the idea that women were worthy of respect, the Victorians three generations to accept that they were worthy of the vote. The modern world has tried to adapt to the idea of almost complete legal and sexual equality in a couple of decades. Predictably, the results have been chaotic, and the psychological penalty is still having to be paid."

You don't have to be a member of Mensa to figure out what the psychological penalty has been: bewilderment, anger, emotional shell-shock, power struggles, blame-throwing, name-calling. It's not a pretty sight. Naturally, a lot of people are having a tough time getting laid through all this.

How Are Women Doing?

Women are not in the most cheerful of moods these days. In fact, I think it's safe to say that most educated, thinking women are in a state of, at best, wistful ambivalence and, at worst, dazed shock, about how they see their futures, and what they want of themselves and of men.

Either they are depressed because they can't find any men, or they are frustrated because if they do manage to scare one up, and things look promising, he gets jittery and they can't get him to hang around for very long. Men come, men get scared, men start behaving strangely and men go. And so women find themselves sleeping with the hot-water bottle again, wondering, "Who *was* that masked man?"

"These are strange times," one woman in her late twenties told me. "I grew up believing that one day Prince Charming would arrive at my door and he would fall madly in love with me. He wouldn't show up and say, 'Well, sorry, love, but maybe this isn't the best time for me, and I've got to work some things out, and I've got a problem with commitment, and I've been burned before, you know, and I mean, I really like you, but I'm not interested in a relationship right now.' It's kind of sad, isn't it?"

There's also the small matter of the mixed feelings many women have about where feminism has brought them. When women survey their land-mined relationships with men, or their harried lives, which many are living without the emotional sustenance a partner or children can provide, they see a yawning gap between what the women's movement promised and what it delivered. For, although most thinking women will happily admit that equality is wonderful as a goal, turning feminism's shining ideals into practice has been quite another matter.

Oh, they like all the perks feminism has bequeathed to them over the years—stimulating careers, disposable incomes and, at least in the early stages, multiple sex partners. They're just tired of waiting for this plodding social revolution to hand over what feminism has so far failed to bestow—that elusive thing called true equality. Said one, "It was inevitable, and I wouldn't have it any different, but I say it in the full and sad realization of the price we have paid. The parameters that drove our mothers' lives societally—I wouldn't want those. But what I think of as a simple concept—people meeting as equals—may indeed be a radical concept for this generation."

One of the major ways feminism has turned out to be an albatross for many a contemporary thinking woman is that it has left her somewhat schizoid on the subject of men. One part of her brain—the part that feminism has irrevocably remodeled—is crammed with glossy, high-minded notions about the gentle, sensitive, supportive qualities she's supposed to admire and desire in a man. The other part of her brain, however—the part that's working overtime to decode signals from her pussy—has so far eluded renovation. *It* is filled with a whole lot of fluttery, centuries-in-the-making, decidedly politically incorrect desires for a more "masculine" model of manhood, with considerably more sex appeal. And so an epic battle ensues in the modern woman's head.

One woman who at least had the self-awareness to realize the Catch-22 of this conflict, and the impossible demands it placed on men, admitted shamefully that she once dated a guy she found quite attractive until she went to use his john and discovered a *Ms.* magazine. The experience totally snuffed out any prospect of carnal desire; while she chastised herself for this instinctive reaction, she felt bewildered and powerless about how to alter it.

"We keep telling men we want them to understand our experience," she said, "and a man who buys and reads *Ms.* magazine is certainly trying to do that. And yet, when I saw *Ms.* in his bathroom, it was a total turnoff! You don't want to see *Ms.* in a guy's bathroom," she said, sighing. "You want to see *Road & Track* or *Esquire* or—I can't believe I'm saying this—even *Playboy.* Somehow that would be more normal, more what you expect a guy to be about. And I remember how that guy also talked a lot, that night, about his relationship with his mother, and I kept thinking to myself, while he was going on and on, that I didn't need another girlfriend. So we get on their case because they're not in touch with their feelings, and then we meet a guy who is, by all evidence, a 'feeling' sort of guy, and we wind up secretly thinking that he's totally devoid of sex appeal!"

Sometimes women get so burned out trying to cope with their ambivalence and male ambivalence and the crossed signals that inevitably result in their love lives that they figure the only smart thing to do is to take a sabbatical from sex altogether, and seek satisfaction in other pursuits.

In *Burning Desires: Sex in America*, for instance, feminist visionary Germaine Greer admitted to authors Steve Chapple and David Talbot that she has "found sexual love extremely exhausting, riddled with tensions and hostilities and jealousies and insecurities. I spent most of the best years of my life trying to get it right, and I'm just delighted not to be worried about it anymore. I really couldn't care less. I am much happier to see that my house...is running well, that friends are well and happy, that we're eating well and the garden is flowering, that the animals are healthy and the trees are growing. I love all that. I can actually wake up in the morning and feel good. And my feeling good does not depend on somebody else's fucking mood."

She was also, she said, trying to "lose interest altogether in the penis," although it maddened her to think it was still so "fascinating." Unable to surrender this fixation altogether, Greer had at least been able to simplify her emotional and sexual life (again, like so many women of her era) by falling into bed with younger men. "But at least I prefer boys to men," she quipped, "so I'm not entirely lost." Heterosexual desire had become, in her view, just an irritating nuisance.

Greer's stance, or versions of it, is echoed by many women of her generation. They are as worn out as she, having been forced to come to similar unpalatable conclusions about their lives and the place of men in them.

One fortyish woman I spoke to shrugged as she told me that she'd rather stay home with a good book than deal with men. "I don't want them anymore if they can't make nice," she sighed. "Let the 25-year-olds deal with them." Another berated herself, like Greer, for not having mastered her fascination with the penis: "Why do I still put up with all their bullshit?" she wondered. "I guess because I still want a poke once in a while."

Or, being a pragmatic sex, often they make pragmatic choices— as did the woman who told me that she felt she was choosing her involvements with men the way she used to be chosen by men years ago. Unable to find men who were suitable as companions or mates, she opted to sleep instead with guys she viewed as lesser mortals—just for the sex: "I'm choosing to stay out of real relationships," she said. "My work is my focus and they are incidental to that. I'm choosing them based on the physical. They are my connection to the idea that there are real and decent men around, but they're not the ones I'm sleeping with."

Far from being happy about failing to find a way to embrace men as equals and keep their sanity at the same time, women are often, like Greer, caught between their desire and their better judgment. Many of them retreat from men and seek a safe harbor in their work or their friendships, not out of embittered man-hatred, but out of weary resignation: it's the only way they can think of to cope.

How Are Men Doing?

The men are in pretty rough shape too. Like women, they're a tad depressed about the opposite sex. For feminism has had its way with men as well. After all, this feminist learn-to-love-an-equal business was not their idea in the first place, and even if they are prepared to buy the idea in theory—which many of them are graciously doing—in practice they're still trying to work out a few glitches. One of the big glitches for men is that they sort of like the notion of an equal partner, but then, they sort of don't.

"Men will tell you they have this Dream Woman, and they'll say they want an equal," one man told me. "I bet a lot of men have told you that, right? But most men are not willing to let down their guard to have true equality. A lot of men are afraid of a woman who's equal to them. They're very competitive and they're still carrying around the notion that they should be better. It's all so primal, really. Nothing's changed since the caveman days. I know a lot of guys, well-educated guys, who are appealing to the women they're dating because they do their own laundry and they invite them over and cook meals for them, and then they get married and that's it! It's over! They expect all the same stuff men have expected of women for centuries."

You've got to feel for men on this count. I certainly do. Basically, they were sitting around minding their own business when the world turned upside down on them; the women in their lives marched through a door, came out the other side unrecognizable and started barking orders at them to hurry and catch up. Women have been reading them the riot act, in one way or another, ever since.

What men have absorbed from the experience of feminism is that they did something terrible and now they have to make reparations. What they have not yet absorbed is precisely *what* it was they did, and *how* they're supposed to repair the damage. Naturally, this leaves them feeling somewhat confused and, on a bad day, somewhat hostile. I remember vividly the way one man spoke to me of the tensions in his encounters with women, because there was fury, puzzlement, frustration and hurt in his voice, all at once. "My relationships are going backwards, not forwards," he said. "What's going on? And what did *I* do?"

It often seems to men that women have become so preoccupied—with themselves, their work, their pressures, their schedules, their five-year-plans—that they have stopped giving a damn about men. They no longer have time to nurture them, nor are they prepared to deal with their foibles—their otherness.

"Men are like St. Bernards," one man told me. "Women love the fact that we lick their faces, but they hate the saliva. They love cuddling us, but they hate taking us for a walk. We shed, we need some exercise, we shit, we get horny and we knock stuff over. That's the deal. Give us a break already."

Many men feel that, in the collective female scheme of priorities, they have been relegated to the bring-forward file—to be dealt with later, when there's time. For now they are merely the means to an end—be that end an orgasm, a relationship, a baby.

Women want it all in the nineties—the career, the committed relationship, the family—but if (as it so often turns out) they have to choose, if they can have, let's say, only two of the Big Three, then the career and the child become the non-negotiable items. The relationship is the most easily dispensable, the man most readily sacrificed. Not the sperm, necessarily, or even the penis—just the human being who happens to come along with the package.

In Chicago, for instance, I talked to the president of a $35-million company, who told me he had been dating a successful businesswoman for a few months when she gave him an ultimatum. "She actually told me I had an option to buy before June 1. Those were her words. She's a heavy-duty strategizer and she wants a father for her kid, so she told herself, 'I'm gonna give this guy one year.' I told her, 'I can tell you right now, I'm not going to exercise my option.'

"I meet a lot of women who seem in a real hurry to close the deal. Between the biological time-clock issue and confusion about their values, it's a mess. You can be cruising along, having fun, laughing and joking, and then you get the sense they're in a big hurry. There are a lot of desperate women out there."

Another man became completely depressed when a woman he had met at a New York club (and with whom he hoped to get something going) climbed onto the roof of a car outside the club and began writhing in orgasmic ecstasy. "She actually came, sitting on the hood of a car," he told me, rolling his eyes heavenward. "She had a real roof-burner. Jesus, women are finding ways to get off without men these days. Hip, hip, hurray. Safe sex without condoms, messy jellies, awkward IUDs. And guys are going home with surfboards in their shorts."

Most men long for intimacy and connection (exactly as most women do), but if they've been bruised in love they grow too wary to risk another involvement. Involvement would mean intimacy,

intimacy would mean emotional exposure, and emotional exposure would mean taking a terrifying risk.

Eventually, one too many difficult or incomprehensible encounters and, just like women, men decide to give up on the opposite sex, to seek, as one man put it, "an oasis of relief in this world." Escaping into the Valhalla of No Complications seems the only solution while they wait out this sexual slump.

"Women confuse me right now," one man put it. "And it's very easy to get used to living on your own. So you retreat. And that's the cruelest irony. You want a woman in your life but you can't find the right one, so you retreat from all women. You avoid an opportunity if it presents itself. You don't take the chances you once took."

Why Does It All Fall Apart in the Bedroom?

The idea of the man pursuing and the woman being pursued is still deeply embedded in both sexes' archetypal imaginations, and it has been a bit arrogant or naive of us to think that in the blink of an eye, historically speaking, we could have completely reinvented the rules of the game.

However, roles have shifted to such an extent that some women are brashly on the make, and some men are having a tough time coping with their bold sexual overtures. The anxiety engendered by this role-reversal is wreaking havoc with the contemporary male's vision of himself as the sexual predator. It's also wreaking havoc with his erections.

"I don't like sexually aggressive women," one man told me. "It turns me off. A subtle clue is okay, but there's something about the challenge, the pursuit, that I like. If a woman is sexually overbearing, it'll give me Inverted Penis Syndrome. I'll lose it."

In 1989, *GQ* magazine invited six men in their late twenties and early thirties to participate in a free-for-all discussion on what they wanted from their sexual relationships with women. The reporter turned on a tape recorder and let the men go to it. One of them, Ted, a single magazine-publishing executive, lamented the fact that women had turned into "pigs...like us."

"This is one of the bad things about feminism," he said. "Women have kind of joined us in the gutter. I go to baseball games with friends of mine—women—and they're looking at Jack Clark's dick. Most of my friends want to go steady. Guy friends. They just want to go steady, because we've sportfucked for a decade and a half now. Dating *is* a drag, but there are a lot of women now who have joined us in this sort of sportfuck merry-go-round. The roles are reversed. I want to go steady and they want to fuck. I want a meaningful relationship, and they just want to have at it."

As a defensive measure, many men are simply refusing to unzip their flies. I heard endless rants on this theme from women. Try as they may, they're having a hard time getting guys to go to bed with them. Either the guys they meet wrongly assume that every woman wants sex with commitment—and flee. Or they realize, to their horror, that some women will cheerfully use them for their cocks—and flee. "I'm seeing more men who start off with assumptions about what I'm looking for," one woman said. "In the sixties, nobody made assumptions. You just went to bed and that was that. Now they're reluctant to go to bed. You have to talk them into bed. You have to seduce them."

Confronted by this skittishness, women often become so frustrated that they wind up in the completely counterproductive position of deciding that, despite their oh-so-sophisticated claims of being progressive nineties men, all guys are stalled somewhere in the fifties.

"I go out with these New Men," one woman told me. "They go to men's groups and they're environmentally active and politically correct, and you get them into bed and they just can't cut it. I made an effort to perform oral sex on one guy and he left with an anxiety attack. They tell me it's related to my powerful stance. So strip away the rhetoric, and what I'm dealing with here are basically traditional guys."

Many of these women, who have beaten their own good girl/bad girl ambivalence about sex into submission and who have come to cherish and enjoy the admittedly limited but nonetheless pleasurable benefits of lust without love, suddenly find they can't even get laid anymore. To them this is hideously cruel punishment. Men never complained about sportfucking as long as *they* were the fuckers and not the fuckees. What is particularly galling to women is that men are now co-opting what for centuries has been a female prerogative: withholding sex—in dating and in marriage—as a means of control.

"Shit," one woman moaned, going straight to the heart of what has to be one of the most absurdly ironic flip-flops of the age: "Now *they're* onto it." (For a further exegesis on this matter, see chapter six.)

"I was involved in an exclusive relationship with a guy," another woman related, "but a few months into it he said that he couldn't be so committed and he wanted it non-exclusive. Then he said he didn't want to be just friends, so he didn't see any basis to continue. So I said, 'Well, we could have a relationship based purely on sex.'

" 'Really?' he asked. 'How would that work?'

" 'Well,' I said, 'we could just call each other up and say, "Hey, d'ya wanna fuck?" '

"He just backed right off. He couldn't handle it. He said, 'No, we'll go out for dinner. I want to date, just not have it as intense.'

"So we went out a few times after that, but for various reasons he kept making dates and getting the times wrong, doing this whole ambivalence thing. And when we did go out, all he ever wanted to do was discuss The Relationship. I didn't want to talk about *the problems*. If he refused to be 'committed,' then I just wanted to get laid. I swear, there's been this whole reversal between men and women.

"Then one night he said, 'Okay, these are the terms: we have a non-exclusive relationship. Don't expect me to reserve Fridays or Saturdays. No holidays. No meetings with friends. Don't think of us as a couple.' He talked the whole thing into the ground. I just wanted to scream, 'Shut up!' At 2:30 a.m. I finally said, 'Paul, I think our time would have been much better spent in bed.'

"A week later he calls me up in a state of high anxiety. 'I just can't have sex outside of a committed relationship.' So you tell me—what the hell is going on? I guess I confirmed his worst nightmares about women, that we are sexually rapacious creatures. In their fantasies they want us to be that, but if we are, they run like rabbits."

More than two decades of social progress, and we've arrived at the point where talking about sex seems to have replaced actually having sex as our favorite recreational pastime. There is—or so many complained to me—altogether too much talking and not enough fucking going on. Talk has become the fashionable erotic experience. Talk, after all, is the safest sex.

"You want to know what a modern romance is?" one woman told me, her voice shrill with exasperation. "Talk. Talk. Talk. It used to be boy meets girl, boy falls in love with girl, boy marries girl. Now it's more likely to be boy meets girl, boy retreats from feeling of falling for girl, girl phones girlfriends to figure out what he's doing, boy and girl discuss feelings, boy and girl decide they're not going to sleep together. This offers the thrill of the precipice, and the intensity, without the commitment."

Add in the "baggage factor" and the mess gets even messier. The "baggage factor" is particularly rampant in the over-35 set. Anyone who is single or single again by that age has likely logged a series of doomed relationships. Each time the dust clears, a heart has been broken and expectations have been dashed. Picking yourself up and brushing yourself off to skip merrily back into the fray is nobody's idea of a fun time. You have to be a masochist to want to do that.

"It's so ironic," one woman told me. "You yearn for connection, but run from it the minute it rears its head—the minute the experience resonates with some triggers from past relationships. It's like acid flashbacks. Your first response is, get me outta here, I've been here before. You retreat to safer ground. You don't have time to be fucked up twelve weeks out of the year. You need emotional equanimity to get through life. There are a lot of men out there who are fundamentally positive human beings but who are also damaged goods. So you have enough dismal experiences and they have a numbing effect. You start to feel cynical and you get hardened against the possibility of a great love."

The climate has grown so wary, in fact, that the word "love"— once evocative of sweet hope and erotic promise—has become dangerous. And this is true for both sexes. Everybody is standing around waiting for the other person to cough it up first. Some people have incredibly rigid rules for the stage at which they're prepared to say they're "in love." Ironically enough, it's almost become a badge of honor not to utter the word at all. "You don't use 'love' in the first couple of months," one man told me, in complete seriousness.

"Even if that's how you're feeling?" I asked.

"No way," he said. "It would destroy the currency of the word to say 'I love you' so soon. You don't want to scare someone away. Also, you don't want to lead them on. And you're not going to finish making love and say, 'Gawd, I respect you.' You have to go on your own assumptions about love unless you know what 'I love you' means to her. It's a suffocating term. It's almost presumptuous to say it."

At this point, he began mocking the phrase by repeating it, derisively, over and over: *"I love you, I love you, I love you.* See? That's only going to dilute its meaning. Let's face it, eighty percent of the time you really mean you're in lust with her, and maybe twenty percent of the time you mean you adore her. You have to reserve the word 'love' for people you really do care about. 'Love' is a grossly misunderstood word."

That "love" has become "a grossly misunderstood word" is probably the greatest understatement I heard in several months of interviewing. Almost everybody I met yearned, on some level, to be in love. But the idea of love has become so scary that a lot of people can't even get the word out.

How Has AIDS Affected the Mating Game?

In the eighties, another wild card entered the already high-stakes game of sex and love: fear of sexually transmitted diseases. That fear—which by 1987 had spiraled into paranoia due to AIDS—gave vent to some grandiose theorizing about our sexual future. By mid-decade the mainstream media were proclaiming the sexual revolution dead. More than anything else, the media declared, the AIDS virus had written its epitaph.

Time's alarmist cover story on herpes in 1982 ("The New Scarlet Letter") was only the first of many media pieces to trumpet the death of sex and the rebirth of chastity; the stories predicted that those few lunatics who were still brave enough to copulate would be doing so using rubber dams and sterile gloves.

By 1984, *Time* was reporting in boldfaced type: "The Revolution Is Over." Other phrasemakers soon followed: "Fear of Sex—a deadly threat is changing the rules of the dating game," proclaimed *Newsweek*; "The New Sexual Morality," announced *Ebony*; "Once upon a time, there was a thing called sex," lamented *Cosmopolitan*.

Private investigators began reporting an increase in clients—predominantly female—who were hiring them to check out prospective lovers' résumés, and to ensure that their inamorati did not have sexually transmitted diseases (STDs).

For the lawyers, of course, the paranoia was a beautiful thing. In *The Futurist*, Edward Cornish suggested that, given the way things were going, prospective lovers might want to sign a dating contract and hire a lawyer to go along on dates. "So lovers of the future will have to watch every step," he warned. "It may not be romantic,... but love has gone through a lot of strange changes in recent years."

Indeed, a new litigiousness did develop in relations between the sexes. Lovers (again mainly women) didn't hesitate to sue the bastard if they awakened one dark morning with some creepy sores. One 29-year-old New Yorker lost her virginity to a married lover whom she later sued for the gift of genital warts. Some complainants won huge settlements. In 1989, for instance, a woman sued an ex-boyfriend who had given her herpes, and walked away with a six-figure sum.

By this time, although the disease was still on the increase, the widespread paranoia around AIDS had settled down somewhat. In January 1989 *The Washington Post* reported that the media's gloomy predictions that sex had gone out of style might well have been "the most misbegotten prognoses since the Great Herpes Panic of '82, when *Time*'s cover story predicted that the gregarious virus would bring a 'grudging chastity back into fashion' and help 'bring to a close an era of mindless promiscuity'. Several billion random copulations later," the *Post* wryly observed, "that obituary seems somewhat premature."

The *Post* based its perceptions on compelling evidence from a variety of studies, sources and telltale cultural signs. In New York, for instance, "so often a harbinger of our carnal customs," *The Village Voice* (the *Post* cited) was reporting that the club crowd was "starting to rebel against repression with little explosions of drunken, guilt-free pleasure." The *Post* also pointed out the following: the youngest married women had overtaken men in the speed with which they were having affairs. Fifty percent of new marriages were breaking up. The average adult's sexual repertoire had expanded to include practices unthinkable outside Tijuana twenty years before. Fellatio—once regarded as degrading to women—had become commonplace, doubling in frequency since Kinsey's studies in the forties and fifties. The paraphernalia of sex—like garter belts and sexy lingerie—was making a fashion comeback.

Against all odds, people were clearly still doing it, and raunchy sex—solo or otherwise—was hot again. The new sexual smorgasbord included "dirty dancing" parties, proliferating computer chat lines with blatantly autoerotic import and explicit late-night TV ads pitching telephone sex to suit every fantasy.

While it must have come as a great relief for many *Post* readers to learn that the sexual revolution was by no means dead, the fact remains that fear of AIDS had upped the ante in the already fragile relations between the sexes. One man told me jokingly that he sometimes thought it was going to take a lifetime to figure out all of love's complications, and by that time "we'll all be too old to do it." And a woman wisecracked that "all this makes me want to get married immediately and have twins by Thanksgiving. I don't want to go through all the rigmarole you have to go through to have a relationship. I want to fast-forward it. It's enervating just thinking about it."

Now there was not only a higher emotional price to be paid for engaging sexually with another human being; now people were reduced to doing actuarial math to determine the risk-factors involved. Now, if they had unprotected sex with the wrong person, they could die.

In its halcyon days, the sexual revolution gave my generation the chance to rewrite the Book of Love. We experimented wildly with the newfangled idea of equality between the sheets, and by and large found the experience to our liking. Free love, we called it then, and a fetching phrase it was.

More than two decades later a lot of us have discovered that love ain't free. This realization leaves us scratching our heads and wondering how such a grand idea could fail so miserably. How did the job get botched? Where, we plaintively ask, did it all fall apart?

It's a long story, but women are the protagonists, so I'll let them tell their side first.

2. Why Are Women Confused?

IN THE EARLY DAYS OF THE WOMEN'S MOVEMENT, BACK IN THE SIXTIES, feminism decreed that women were good and men were bad. Women were still allowed to forgive men for being bad, however, and sleep with them. Oh sure, the radical feminists were saying that the penis was a tool of oppression and that sex with the male beast was, by its very definition, degrading. But the pill had taken the fear out of sex, and the women's movement had taken the guilt out of sex, and most women were so happy to be able to get in on the action without fear or guilt that they weren't about to limit their newly discovered options by staying celibate as a political statement. A tool of oppression the penis might be, but it was better than no tool at all.

In those heady early days, feminism was making women an offer they couldn't refuse—the chance to have sexual equality with men plus a crack at having it all—and women practically trampled one another rushing to get in on this extraordinary deal. Now women could have everything men had always had: carefree casual sex, fulfilling work, supportive mates and adoring kids. The twin notions that women might be equal to men and have it all gripped my female contemporaries with an unrelenting, almost mystical force. Certainly I believed in the possibility of achieving those worthy goals, and most of the women I knew believed in the possibility too.

In their enthusiasm to sign on the dotted line, few women took time to read the fine print. By the late seventies, however, the fine print was a lot more noticeable. There were, as it turned out, a few kickers to this bargain. By this time, disenchantment had surfaced and women were grumbling that maybe they'd been taken. By then women were pulling their weight in previously "male" domains—like the workplace—but men weren't exactly picking up the slack in "female" spheres—like the home. In *Heartburn*, for instance, Nora Ephron observed that during the seventies women all over America nagged their husbands to do some housework, with the result that their husbands agreed to clear the table, acted "as if they deserved a medal," and then prayed the women's movement would disappear. "And it did. The women's movement went away, and so, in many cases, did their wives. Their wives went out into the world, free at last, single again, and discovered the horrible truth: that they were sellers in a buyers' market, and that the major concrete achievement of the women's movement in the 1970s was the Dutch treat."

Indeed, by the eighties, any woman with even one functional brain cell had discovered that the realistic possibility of achieving her goals was a whole lot of crapola: you could hire a nanny for the kids, but a nanny was not exactly going to parent them. You could convince your boss to agree to part-time work at home, but you'd kiss the fast track goodbye. You could become a *Fortune* 500 CEO, but you'd die a lonely old woman with cats. You could hold out for a "supportive" man, but you'd wind up having a meaningful relationship with your VCR. You could put all kinds of gluey emotional energy into your relationship, but it wouldn't necessarily stick. You could become an accomplished, successful, well-rounded human being—but your husband would dump you for a gum-popping bimbette named Bethany.

Throughout the eighties, on the political front, women watched in collective disillusionment as many of the dreams they had dared to weave began to unravel. Women's rights—rights a generation of feminists had fought for in the personal and political realms at the cost of their sleep, sweat and marriages—didn't advance or began to be rolled back. Women continued to lag significantly behind men in wages, conservative governments hacked blithely away at funding for "women's" causes such as daycare, and hard-won gains on abortion rights were mercilessly undone.

These external disappointments reverberated endlessly within. Growing cynical about bringing their sweet vision of equality to a world where men continued to call the shots, waiting for political progress that was still far away, watching despairingly as the same battles had to be fought over and over, wondering how the reality of their lives had fallen so far short of their dreams, many women began to question whether what often seemed like puny progress had been worth the losses. And so they were caught—on the one hand wistfully nostalgic for what they had surrendered, on the other hand impatient for what remained still to accomplish.

By the late eighties it was no longer possible for thinking women to ignore the fact that feminism had made some grandiose promises that wouldn't be fulfilled in their lifetimes. Although it had brought women closer to the brass ring of sexual equality than any previous generation, it had done so by taking their emotional lives on a rocky ride. By this point, especially in their relationships with men, women were mostly practicing damage control.

Nothing revealed the extent to which women were dissatisfied with their love lives—and the degree to which the grenades were flying in the erogenous zones—more than the publication, in 1987, of *The Hite Report: Women and Love*, the third book in Shere Hite's trilogy on contemporary sexual mores. When it hit the marketplace (on the same day the stock market crashed—all in all a black day for the male member), the author was almost uniformly savaged in the media.

One of the most vitriolic detractors was *Time*. The magazine's cover featured warring male and female symbols—the former looking like a bewildered, pussy-whipped chump, the latter like a hot-headed shrew—and the text accused Hite of slipshod methodology, grasping commercial motives and, of course, man-hatred.

Whether readers bought Hite's statistics or some of her unflattering conclusions about men, they could not ignore the book's litany of passionate, pained female voices. *Women and Love* was a cry from the female heart. It documented exhaustively what most major women's magazine surveys had been consistently turning up since the mid-seventies, and what any woman who hadn't been on sabbatical in Papua New Guinea was discussing over lunchtime Perriers at the time with her girlfriends: that her relationships with men were deeply troubled; that she was tired of fighting with them; that she couldn't get them to talk to her; that now she was expected to be nurturer and breadwinner too; that if she had an affair or two to deal with her isolation, she (like many men) didn't feel particularly guilty; and that her relationships with these, exasperating beings no longer took center stage in her life.

Indeed, doctrinaire feminism had not exactly been clairvoyant on the subject of how men would react to the aftershocks of the women's movement. Feminism had led women to believe that if they doggedly plugged away, eventually men would be good sports and hand over the keys to the clubhouse, dutifully do the dishes and agree to letting the woman be on top sometimes. There was never the slightest indication in the grand feminist plan that, as women started to get demanding, men would get surly, sullen and withdrawn, or that as women blossomed sexually, men would get confused, or that as women judged them as lovers, men would get threatened, or that as women nudged them aside in the workplace, men would get angry. Nor was there the tiniest suggestion that men would try to win back some sexual control by retaliating against women, or by simply taking a pass on them altogether.

How Have Women Reacted to the So-Called Man Shortage?

Alas, the perception of the dreaded man shortage became—and remains—the number-one obsession of the well-educated career woman. In the mid-eighties, *Newsweek* was reporting the cheery news that, if you happened to be female, college-educated and over thirty-five, your chances of meeting Prince Charming (according to the latest Yale-Harvard study) were a seriously lousy 5 percent. If you were forty and still hadn't tied the knot, you had a better chance of being shot by a terrorist.

The man shortage seemed so acute, one 28-year-old told me, that if one of her girlfriends actually managed to land a date, the news immediately went out on the female yak lines. "You know what we say? We say it's one small step for woman, one giant leap for womankind."

Of course, even men who *appear* to be eligible sometimes aren't. Estimates of the number of single males who are gay hover around 15 percent. In cities like New York, San Francisco and Toronto, ferreting out an upwardly mobile guy who also happens to be presentable, available and heterosexual is no small task. One woman became utterly discombobulated when she finally found a guy worth falling for, only to have him confide that his last love affair had been with a man.

"There was all this sexual energy between us," she moaned. "And then he laid this bombshell on me. And all I kept thinking was, shit, haven't I got enough to deal with already? Now I've got to deal with a guy who wants to go to bed with another man? I told myself that the up-side was that at least I didn't have to be jealous of another woman. But then I started thinking, well, I can't be a man, and *that* threw me into a tailspin. I wound up in one of those horrible self-loathing things where I kept asking myself, 'What's wrong with me?' Christ...there's always something."

In some urban centers the situation is so grim that Ron Powers, writing about the hit television series "Beauty and the Beast" in *GQ*, quipped: "[The show] costarred Linda Hamilton as Catherine, the Beast's mane squeeze, the ultimate Eighties career-woman–criminal-lawyer–rich-girl–princess type who can't tear herself away from the big lug. (Which just goes to prove that if you're single and straight in New York, the women will overlook just about anything.)"

The man shortage, however, is really more a problem of failed feminist expectations and urban lifestyle than a dearth of straight, single guys in the population. In *Erotic Wars: What Happened to the Sexual Revolution?* Lillian Rubin observed that you could take the Yale-Harvard statistical data on women's marriage prospects, interpret it somewhat more rosily than *Newsweek* had and conclude that by age forty over 90 percent of all American women would be married. What's more, according to Martha Farnsworth Riche, director of policy studies at the Population Reference Bureau in Washington, the ratio of men to women in America has held more or less constant for the last forty years. The census figures show more single men than women in all ages of the American population until the age of forty. Between forty and fifty-five, the balance shifts slightly, and women begin to overtake men.

After that, because men tend to die about seven years earlier than women, the odds become increasingly skewed. Until then, however, Riche believes that the so-called man shortage is actually more a perceived than a real problem. The difficulty is not so much a shortage of male bodies as a shortage of a certain highly targeted breed of eligibly straight men—with the right job, the right income, the right wardrobe, the right address and the right feminized mindset—on whom women, with their recently improved status, have set their sights. "Women are better employed and pickier," she says, "and so they're redefining their needs. There's a shortage of men women consider marriageable because they're doing a far more in-depth cost/benefit analysis than they were twenty years ago."

To complicate matters further, even if women could scare up more hetero guys who meet their rigorous standards, they would still have to deal with another discouraging problem: how on earth do they meet them?

For women who came of age during the most turbulent days of the sixties and early seventies, the problem of finding Mr. Right is particularly critical. If they want to "mate up" with men somewhat older than themselves whose net worth exceeds their own (as they've always been expected to), they have to choose from a smaller pool of men who were born before the population explosion of the baby-boom and whose consciousness, therefore, often remains largely unaltered by feminism. According to many women, sensibility-wise, a lot of these guys might as well be their fathers.

What's more, if women divorce, their chances of mating with simpatico divorced male contemporaries are lousy too. In 1985, Barbara Finlay, Fausto B. Alvarez and Charles E. Starnes published a telling study on this subject in a journal called *Sex Roles*.

Now, you don't read a journal like *Sex Roles* unless you absolutely have to—which is just as well, really, because if this study had leaked into the larger female population, it would probably have prompted mass suicide.

What the researchers found, among other things, is that whereas divorce tends to radicalize women, it has the opposite effect on men. What this means is that a divorced woman will sooner burn in hell than hook up with another reactionary, it's-your-job-to-wait-on-me-hand-and-foot control-freak like her ex. If a man is divorced, however, the chances are good that the experience has left him, shall we say, somewhat more traditional in his thinking. The chances are also good that he is looking for less aggravation this time around—and to a divorced man of a traditional bent, the quest for less aggravation generally means he is looking for a younger, more pliable mate. Moreover, since men have greater social sanction to choose from a wider range of partners (who are younger, for example, or who make less money), and because they feel more comfortable than women in doing so, they wind up in what the researchers call a "much better market position."

Women in their forties, who are operating at a tremendous disadvantage in this marketplace, often wind up enduring months—sometimes years—of celibacy. In such a chilly climate, they've pretty much given up on finding long-term love and will often happily settle for short-term sex. Finding even that, however, is tough. Lamented one woman, "The same men who were readily available to me when I had extramarital affairs continually for twenty years, while I was married to the vice-president of a brokerage firm, are no longer available to me. Now they see me as a danger. I might want or need. I might have expectations of them. I might want a commitment. Before, the fact that I was married was a built-in safeguard for them."

Yet another forty-year-old sighed as she related a conversation she'd had with a former male friend she met at a high school reunion twenty years later. "He asked me how come a nice, attractive girl like me had never married. He thought maybe I was being too picky. I told him that I had a long and short list, that I wanted to be with someone who was emotionally honest, first with himself, and then with others. He stared at me and said, 'Oh well, that explains it. No wonder you're still single.'"

In the end, the hard lesson women take from the apparent man shortage is this: by trying to live up to the lofty ideals of feminism, by elevating their expectations of themselves and of men, they have relinquished the chance for love and set themselves on a collision course with loneliness. Men will punish them for their ambitions, and they will punish them in the cruelest way imaginable: by not wanting them anymore.

How Have Women Reacted to the Ambivalence Disease?

Fear of commitment is the most bandied-about relationship buzz phrase of the day. The C-word crops up in every self-help book, in every women's magazine, on every talk show, and is the number-one theme of endless, frustrating heart-to-heart yaks women have among themselves: "At least I'll put my heart on the line," said one woman who'd had a bellyful of male nervousness. "I hate guys who just ride off into the sunset. Guys back off at the moment of truth, or at least when it becomes apparent that the moment of truth might come. Guys in their thirties at least address it. But guys in their forties will say, 'You are somebody I've been looking for all my life, but I can't get involved anymore.' And I'm left wondering, was it something I said?"

Men are clearly the main carriers of what one woman called "the ambivalence disease," but it's a contagious condition and women can catch a nasty case of it too. One woman was dating a man who told her up front that he had three reservations about entering into a relationship with her: she was two years older than he, not Jewish (as he was) and living in another city. "Well, I said, one and two I can't change. But what he's saying to me is that his image of who he should be with is a younger Jewish woman. I kind of rationalize, well, he'll fall in love with me and it won't matter. What I want to do is give myself over to a man and fall madly in love. But do I want to walk into a situation where I'm three down already? These things are barriers, the early warning signs. He's got the heebie-jeebies, and his ambivalence gives me ambivalence." Were it not for the fact that all this skittishness is causing a lot of people a lot of heartache, it would provide endless material for a hilarious black comedy, as Linda Sunshine demonstrated in *Harper's Bazaar*. Describing a scenario in which a man and woman proceeded cautiously from lunch, to drinks, to dinner and eventually into the sack, she noted that each time the two spent the night together and actually enjoyed the experience, it took the guy longer to call back for the next date. "This is popularly known as 'parry and retreat,' " wrote Sunshine. "The closer you become, the longer it takes for him to get back in touch. Just your luck: he falls madly in love with you and never calls again."

Sooner or later, men start playing out their ambivalence in the bedroom. That's when the dissemblings and distancing games heat up and the accusations really start flying, and that's when even the most patient and forgiving women become inarticulate with confusion or rage.

"I met this law professor," one woman related, "and we're having a good time together—good enough that I'm interested in sleeping with him. He gets into a trip with me. We should spend the night together but not sleep together, he says. He's not owning up to whatever is holding him back. The deal is that we sleep together but we don't make love. So of course the minute we're in bed, it all blows up. You have to agree to buy a ticket in, but once you're in bed it all goes to hell. I said we had to talk about this. He couldn't stand that. He said, oh my God, why do we have to talk? Why are you making this into a heavy thing? *He's* doing a totally bizarre thing and *I* get nailed for being the heavy!"

Another woman got upset when a guy with whom she was sexually involved, from another city, invited her to fly to his ski chalet for New Year's week, but then refused to sleep with her once she got there. "He came on really strong at the beginning," she said, "called me several times a week and then invited me, but when I arrived he kept making these excuses for why he didn't want to sleep with me. He was tired, he said, or anxious, or 'just not into it.' And I said, well, what's going on here? He kept telling me I was making too big a deal about it. But if you're sexually involved with a man and he invites you to spend the week with him, I think it's reasonable for you to have certain expectations. Only he kept trying to make me feel as if my wanting to sleep with him was *my* problem, and as if by asking what was wrong I was being overly sensitive. So the whole week was tense and awkward because of what wasn't being said. At the end of it I gave him an out and asked him if he wanted to wind the affair down and he said no. So I went home with nothing resolved and I still don't know what he's doing. I have the feeling he's simply keeping me on the hook until something better comes along.

"I'm open to the possibility that my assumptions about his behavior are completely erroneous. But how the hell am I supposed to know what he's feeling if he won't tell me? Honesty is always so much better than phony excuses and game-playing. With honesty, even if it's bad news, you suffer for a while but then you get over it. This way you're second-guessing all the time, and you just keep on suffering."

How Have Women Responded to the Revisionist Slut Theory?

Inevitably women take a lesson from all this masculine sexual withdrawal. If they hope to lay eyes on a throbbing male member again, they too must resort to game-playing. For, like the ambivalence disease, game-playing is a contagious malady and tends to breed quickly in others. The coy stance women feel compelled to take is one they thought the women's movement had liberated them from feigning a long time ago—acting like chaste teenage girls, or (as one woman on an NBC documentary dubbed "Second Thoughts on Being Single" put it) "born-again prudes."

Indeed, in scrambling to regain some lost ground in the aftermath of feminism, men are unknowingly forcing women into the untenable position of having to act like virgin princesses again. For, as one woman put it, "Even when you jokingly tell a guy, 'If I don't get laid soon there's gonna be big trouble,' he laughs, but he's uncomfortable with it. He doesn't want to know about your sexual needs, particularly if they seem voracious."

For many women who have come to enjoy their sexual autonomy, this turn of events is a low blow. "Whereas once it was 'bingo and off to the races,' " one woman told me, "now the leftover guys are into 'nice girls' don't and 'bad girls' do. They're into this madonna/whore thing in a big way."

Another woman was having drinks with a male friend when she realized how ingrained—even in the most culturally sophisticated men—the double standard can be. "He's a pretty hip guy and we're good friends and we were sharing stories about past sexual encounters," she said, "and so I told him about the time I walked into the kitchen at a party in university and realized I'd slept with every guy there. He looked at me in amazement and said in this really sarcastic voice, 'Jeez...that must have made you feel great!'

"The thing is, it did make me feel great. I had a sweet feeling about every one of those guys. But his comment assumed that I must have felt like a slut or something, and you know what? It worked. Suddenly I felt cheap, as if I'd done something wrong. And my whole Catholic upbringing and all the guilty feelings around sex that I've spent a long time trying to get over came welling up inside of me.

"That incident made me realize how little has really changed. Men still have the power to judge our sexual behavior and call us sluts. They may say they're in favor of sexual equality, but there's just all this talk woven into the exchange now, and the moral judgments have gone underground. In a way, that's even worse than before. Because when those judgments go underground, you can't deal with them. You can't name the double standard and call it what it is. And what it is, in fact, is *their* problem—not ours."

It's in the next generation, however, that feminist values have taken the most brutal flogging. Men and women in their twenties appear to have returned, in their erotic encounters, to the blatant double standards, perverse role-playing and phony sexual strategizing of the fifties. In *Erotic Wars*, Lillian Rubin reported results of a questionnaire she distributed to six hundred students in eight colleges around the United States. Almost 40 percent of the sexually active women ("sexually active" often translating into fewer than twelve sexual encounters) said they would understate their sexual experience because "my boyfriend wouldn't like it if he knew" or "people wouldn't understand" or "I don't want him to think I'm a slut."

Most of the women were angry that they had to dissemble about their sexuality, observed Rubin, but some seemed to have accepted the inequity without much reaction, as one of the realities of life. Rubin found corroborating evidence of this reversal of feminist values among the college men she interviewed. "In reply to a question about what they expected of the woman they might marry," she wrote, "well over half the men commented that they wouldn't want a woman who had been 'around the block too many times'; that they were looking for someone who didn't 'sleep around'; that a woman who did was 'a slut'—the definition being what it has been for most of this century, a woman whose sexual activity is no more, and most likely far less, than a man's."

In her chapter on teenage sex, she observed that while she did not believe that men consciously set out to control female sexual behavior, or that any given man was even aware he was doing it, "it's so deeply ingrained a part of the social fabric that it seems almost as natural as breathing." And while, among the American teenagers Rubin interviewed, "male condemnation of girls who violate the norm of monogamy is ubiquitous," she did not once hear anyone speak about a boy with equal disparagement.

This revisionist slut theory—the worn assumption that men can fuck as they please but women who do likewise are sluts—cropped up with depressing regularity in several student surveys. In 1985, sociologist Arthur Jacoby and statistician John Williams, at the University of North Dakota, polled two hundred college students about their range of sexual experience and willingness to date others with varied experience. To be sure, nobody ever accused North Dakota of being New York, but this study turned up some fairly astonishing results. What Jacoby and Williams found was that both sexes, regardless of their own sexual history, preferred virgins as marriage partners! And lest anybody had any misbegotten ideas that college campuses were still hotbeds of sexual experimentation and social change, *Glamour* magazine's

1987 poll of 1,200 college students across the U.S. destroyed those illusions. The magazine declared that "students today are surprisingly traditional—much more so than in a similar survey we conducted in 1980...." Male students were more "erratic and extreme" in response to questions on casual sex, mating and lifestyle, and—get this—*felt more pressured to have sex than women*.

Are the Yes-You-Can Fix-It Books Helping?

Naturally, all these problems have left women desperate for answers. Enter the morally proscriptive fix-it books in which the ineffable subtleties of male-female relationships are reduced to a perky twelve-step to-do list, usually including such helpful suggestions as working on your relationship by going outside together to make angels in the snow.

If the dust-jacket sales figures are to be believed, people—millions of people—are buying these books. Often they do so out of sheer desperation for some insight into what, in God's name, is going on. One woman whose literary tastes do not usually lean in such directions embarrassedly admitted to me that she had finally succumbed to purchasing *If I'm So Wonderful, Why Am I Still Single?* even though "it's the kind of book you want to wrap in brown paper before you take it on the subway."

Fix-it books about sex and romance are targeted almost exclusively at women, who now have more so-called advice on this subject than they can possibly sort through in a lifetime. Men, I can only conjecture, are assumed to be perfectly content with their sexual relationships and are out playing racquetball.

The how-to tomes tend to divide by genre: Woman-As-Jerk (*Smart Women, Foolish Choices/Women Who Love Too Much*); Men-As-Saps-or-Swine (*Cold Feet: Why Men Don't Commit/Successful Women, Angry Men/Men Who Can't Love*);

Woman-As-Slow-Learner (*How to Make Love to a Man/How to Keep a Man in Love with You Forever/How to Love a Difficult Man*); I-Give-Up (*Why Women Shouldn't Marry*) and, finally, Wishful-Thinking (*The One Hour Orgasm*).

Many fix-it books distinguish themselves with psychobabble masquerading as writing, and regressive attitudes masquerading as thinking. Often the writers simply leech onto the one element of the culture readers are certain to understand in the Age of the Schedule—brisk, brutal, efficient time-management—and tart up what are essentially creepy, outmoded 1950s notions about romance in the guise of a take-charge philosophy. Men are portrayed as such jerks, a critical reader begins to question why women are so hot to land one. Often the subtext suggests that a man's Pavlovian responses can (and should) be manipulated by a cleverly dissembling woman. In the bestselling *How to Make a Man Fall in Love with You*, readers are advised to get a man by drawing up a "Man Plan." *Why Women Shouldn't Marry* begins with the hostile assertion "Today there are only two basic reasons for a woman to marry: sperm and support."

An enterprising San Franciscan who saw a window of opportunity in all this romantic hunger is Rebecca Sydnor. Sydnor calls herself a Romance Manager, and is the author of a self-help book called *Making Love Happen*. She told *Harper's Bazaar* in April 1989 that, in order to find husband number three, she had "put together a game plan based on psychological strategies" and then "conducted a full-scale manhunt in the Bay Area." Sydnor markets her technique, "The Smart Love Approach," in seminars and "private practice," to San Francisco professional women who happily fork over $100 an hour for her brand of enlightenment.

The Smart Love Approach is based on the assumption that waiting for a man to parachute into your life is bad, but using "executive search methods" to meet one is good. Smart, successful career women, the thinking goes, would never walk into a boardroom expecting to close a deal without a game plan. Why, then, are they such nitwits about their romantic lives?

The strategy is simple. You compile "data" on the traits you want in a man. You fill out questionnaires. Once you have completed the questionnaires, you know all about the nasty neurotic patterns that have sabotaged your previous relationships. Then you fix the problems.

Devotees of The Smart Love Approach also "screen" or secretly interview their dates. (Men with "fear of commitment" don't make the cut. Men with whom there is "chemistry" and "power" do.) Having winnowed out the undesirables, clients then offer "inconsistent positive reinforcement" to the chosen ones. IPR means that, at this stage, a woman does not offer a man unconditional love. According to Sydnor, laboratory rats are more loyal to those keepers who give them food inconsistently. *Ergo*—since it is not that tough to convince a certain percentage of the female population that men, too, are rats—it logically follows that an overindulged man will act like a complacent rodent. Instead, the desired tactic (as in all successful business ventures) is to "diversify" (date other men), then to "unfold slowly" and, above all, withhold sex. "Sex," says Sydnor, is "an incentive to a man for continuing to date a woman. Satisfy his curiosity too soon and he'll lose interest."

Naturally all these stratagems can be frightfully unnerving to many of Sydnor's clients, who fancy themselves sophisticated women and who ditched their coquettishness, with their falsies, a long time ago. They too need reinforcement. So she gives them reminder stickers for their compacts and diaphragm cases that read, "Don't tell him, tell your therapist," or "Have you bonded with him yet?"

Lest all systems fail and clients lose it in mid-date, they can call their romance manager on her beeper for advice. "What am I supposed to do now, Ms. Sydnor?" one imagines the bewildered creatures blubbering into their cellular phones. "He just put his penis on the dessert plate."

Preying on the massive insecurity in the air, the fix-it books (and many women's magazines) also churn out chipper (or deadly earnest) advice suggesting that their readers respect the laws of supply and demand and move where the men are—like Alaska. Failing that, they are admonished to enroll in manly extra-curricular pursuits like trekking in Nepal, or to signal a guy like mad over the cantaloupes in the supermarket. Despite the fact that such advice leaves one wondering what sort of man cruises for women in the grocery store, or how any self-respecting woman is supposed to maintain her dignity while waving her tits down the tinned goods aisle, the reality is that many savvy women *who should know better*, but who haven't had a date in a couple of years, actually start believing this stuff. At any rate, it gives them something to do besides wait haplessly by the phone.

Such "strategies" usually fail, however, and only make those who attempt them (and are already wallowing in self-pity) feel worse. One woman who took such advice to heart headed on vacation to a dude ranch in Wyoming. What she found upon arrival was a stable full of horny cowgirls like herself. "We wound up calling it the dudeless ranch," she told me archly.

Is There a "New" Traditionalist Woman?

Even as women were struggling to assimilate contradictory feelings and desires, to deal with the disappointments and downside of feminism and to rethink their roles and their relationships with men, the media tapped into their ambivalence, exploited it and made them feel even worse.

Take what happened to the media's image of the ideal New Woman, for instance. The feminized New Man was supposed to be stepping haltingly into the future, but the New Woman (if one believed the almost unanimous point of view offered by the mainstream media during the eighties) was doing some furious backpedaling.

Whereas, in the early days of the women's movement, TV producers and the editors of women's magazines and "family" newspaper sections zealously ran stories on female fast-trackers and overachievers—those brave challengers who were defying sex-stereotyped career choices—now they started assigning pieces on "The Mommy Track" and "The New Chastity." For more than a decade the message to women had been "Get on with it, girls, keep marching"; in the eighties it subtly shifted to "Burn your draft cards, you've been sold out. You've all made a dreadful mistake. Come home and Daddy will forgive you."

Such revisionist phrase-making had a ripple effect. Women began to do strange about-faces, to recant in print the ideals and feminist values that had led them to the place they now were. Even major-league feminists like Germaine Greer, whose *Sex and Destiny* was brimming over with a keening baby-lust, were turning in their medals, chanting, "Hell no, we won't go!"

During the latter part of the eighties, in the nostalgic, misty eyes of the media, the ideal New Woman was no longer to be an independent, gloriously single, career-focused, sexually adventurous creature, or even a woman who, if married, "had it all." In many magazine spreads, the "new" New Woman smiling into the camera was a well-dressed, attractive, late-thirtyish woman blissfully relaxed in a countrified living room, her smiling, well-kept kidlets at her side. Oh, in an earlier life she'd gotten that career nonsense out of her system (the veiled implication was that choosing a career had been an oh-what-the-hell-why-not? decision, like deciding between fusilli and grilled salmon), but fortunately she'd come to her senses. Now she was a good old-fashioned girl who cooked "comfort food" and chauffeured her kids. Now she opted to find fulfillment in "traditional values." This imagery was dangerously misleading, however, because it denied the reality of most female lives.

What roles are women actually playing? In fact, more than 60 percent of women with children under six are in the labor force; three out of ten American families with children are headed by single parents, which means that tens of thousands of women in the labor force are single mothers whose jobs are their sole means of support; many of them are eating beans out of cans and struggling desperately to keep hearth and home together while they chase down the scandalously high three-quarters of ex-husbands who renege on child support payments. Households now require two incomes even to hang on by their fingernails to the middle-class standard of living of a generation ago. Many women who might dearly wish to take a breather from the fast track to embrace marriage and family are simply not meeting suitable men, while by far the majority of women in the upper echelons still find their careers tremendously gratifying and are not about to give them up to go bonkers at home.

In real life, most coupled career women (or so studies on household division of labor reveal) are managing their careers, their relationships, their personal lives, their social arrangements with their mates, their kids' lives, their households, and maybe even caring for an ailing parent or two, all the while getting a few hours of "help" each week from their partners.

After years of being stretched to the limit, many women may well be fantasizing about cashing out and escaping to some suburban or rural Happy Isle to watch their kids grow up (as indeed may an increasing number of men). But that fantasy is one the overwhelming majority can never hope to realize. The truth is, if the New Woman is sometimes nostalgic for the past, it's not because she is tired of having it all. She's just burned out from having to do it all.

Women were feeling swamped during the eighties and the mixed feelings many were expressing were a desperate plea for help. For most, going back to the "good old days" was neither a desire nor an option, but they could envision no way to move forward. They were crying out for workable solutions to help them reconcile with men, enlist men's help in shouldering a more equitable share of life's burdens, and balance the demands of career and family so that they could enjoy *both*. What they got were moral judgments to chuck it all and turn back the clock. The "new" traditionalist woman was an image of themselves that exacerbated already-seething doubts and fears about their roles and relationships, and it served only to confuse them more.

Are Women Chaste Again?
On the sexual front, with AIDS creating tremendous anxiety about the perils of sex with a "stranger," the dominant impression in the media was that a single woman now wanted "commitment," not carnality; "courtship," not casual sex. Indeed, another prim moral lesson began to emerge from the culture during this conservative backswing: casual sex, especially for women, was a low-life activity.

In the early days of liberation, for the average woman just discovering its pleasures, sex had implied hope, adventure and freedom. By the mid-eighties, sex outside of a conventional monogamous relationship had turned into something many people now named "mindless promiscuity." In other words, sex was bad for women again.

Club Med, for instance, where members had always been expected to carouse, had some particularly sticky promotional problems to address in the middle of all this backpedaling. Cleverly, the organization opted to take the middle road. According to Richard Goldstein, writing in *The Village Voice* in December 1986, in a Club Med ad at that time a "desirable young woman swims, sails, reads a novel—and meets no men. At its most salubrious, this suggests self-sufficiency: a freedom from dependence on unhealthy substances and obsessive desires. But it also affirms that there's something unmentionable—if not unhealthy—about a woman who would come to Club Med to do what it's famous for."

Back in the real world, however, the "New Chastity" and the "New Sexual Restraint" hardly meant that women had suddenly donned chastity belts and checked into a nunnery. I met many women who were experiencing long periods of celibacy (anywhere from several months to several years), but in most cases they were not having sex as often as they wanted to because sex was simply no longer as available to them. Most were desirous of establishing a long-term relationship with a compatible man, but had so far been unable to meet one. In the meantime, they were decidedly unwilling to deny themselves the pleasures of occasional sex with a man who might be here today and gone tomorrow.

"As a single person," said one woman, "I've been happy for intermittent sexual intimacy. I've always been capable of having sex with someone even if I'm a far cry from being in love with him. If

I feel as if something sweet is going on, even if I know it's only going to go on for a short time, I will go to bed. We're both here and we both need some tenderness, so what the hell?"

One forty-year-old woman told me she was "so horny she was ready to pick a guy out of a police lineup." Many other women said they would gladly sleep casually with the occasional man if only they could find one. Remarked one, "I'm not picky, really. All I'm looking for is a pulse. A guy with a pulse."

All of these strains chipped away at female self-esteem until, by the early nineties, women were in a mean or despairing mood. As they saw it, they had finally got the hang of guilt-free sex and now everybody was wagging a finger at them again. They had finally figured out what they wanted in bed and now there was nobody to whisper their longings to. They had finally decided to settle down and now there was no one to father their children.

No suitable men. Only commitment-fearing men. Emotionally damaged men. Men who want bimbos or virgins or women half their age. Who are these monster guys? And what role, dare one ask, did women play in creating them?

3. Why Are Men Confused?

THE NEW WOMAN DEFINED HERSELF THROUGH FEMINISM, AND AL-
though most thinking men will readily admit that they have much
to thank her for in this regard, they also admit that they've been
paying for her little personal adventure ever since.

The New Man was skeptical about this liberation business at
first, but over time he's grown to appreciate the blossoming of the
New Woman. She has turned out to have many charms—savvy and
sex appeal, class and style. She's also fun to hang out with, has
disposable income and knows a few tricks in the sack. He owes her
as well for convincing him that there's more to life than work—like
the simple pleasures of spending more time with his kids. No
question—she's a challenge, and life would be simpler if she weren't
so opinionated. But he concedes that she never bores him, and that
he truly respects the woman she's become.

Still, it hasn't been easy, because the New Woman can be a
royal pain in the ass. Even though he's been bending over backwards to adjust to her ever-changing needs, over the years he's
taken a fair bit of flak for behaving like the male creature he was
raised to be. He has also heard—and endured in manly silence—
interminable lectures about how he must mend his ways. In fact,

the story of his life in the aftermath of feminism has largely been a story of censure, blame, belittlement and distaste for the male person that he is.

For one of the implicit, if unadmitted, tenets of feminism has been a fundamental disrespect for men. Nowhere is that disrespect more obvious—or ironic—than in the person of the contemporary woman who complains bitterly about men, and then wonders why none of them will fall in love with her. If the New Woman isn't altogether thrilled with the New Man in her midst, she can't deny the fact that she has had much to do with creating him.

Throughout the eighties in particular, men suffered many slings and arrows at the hands of feminists, becoming increasingly repugnant in their eyes. The women's magazines and relationship fix-it books vilified men, analyzed their faults and failings, and put them on war crimes trials, fueling in women what was already a dangerous and surly us-against-them mood. One runaway bestseller bore the charming title *Men Who Hate Women and the Women Who Love Them*, but the title that left the least room for debate about men's alleged inadequacies was *No Good Men*.

At the same time, feminists were working diligently to expose the widespread problem of male-perpetrated crimes such as child abuse, wife-battering and rape. Often, however, feminist discussion and media reportage about those crimes implied that *all* men were evil creatures with naturally debased impulses. By the end of the eighties, feminism had left a lot of men with the lingering, sour impression that women believed men were contemptible—as a sex. Even if a particular man was decent, honorable and innocent of the things men were collectively being accused of, he wound up being tarnished by association, and eventually he grew weary of listening to the litany of his shortcomings.

What has been glaringly—and shamefully—absent from feminist ideology, however, is any understanding of the degree to which feminism has unseated and disoriented men. A man who has been subjected to the insistent barrage of feminism has been asked to stop thinking of himself as the center of the universe, to unlearn everything he thought was important in the business of being a man, and to stop expecting to be needed by women, at least in any familiar sense.

As Michael Blumenthal commented in *The New York Times'* "About Men" column, "the analogy made by feminists between men and [America's] patriarchal nation itself is...rather apt. Because, as men, we have been like America itself—and still often are. Accustomed to immediate respect, attention, deference, flirtation when we walk into a room full of women...it still comes, I think, as a shock to many of us that we are, in some measure, 'no big deal'...."

Countless men I spoke to told me that there were no clear guidelines or rules of appropriate masculine behavior anymore, that they simply didn't know how to behave around women as a result and that women weren't exactly making life any easier.

"Most of the men I know want to be in relationships," one man told me, "but they no longer know how to be in relationships, and they don't understand why they no longer know how. And women aren't helping them to understand." Said another, "Ever since I was little, I put myself to sleep dreaming of rescuing the damsel in distress. But all that stuff is warped now."

How Have Men Reacted to the Feminist Makeover?
In response to changing female expectations, the New Man has also been asked to execute a complete renovation of his psyche. He has been directed to transform himself from dull but dutiful breadwinner, in the Ozzie Nelson mold, to androgynous danger-boy, in

the Mick Jagger mold, to caring-sharing-and-relating soul-mate, in the Phil Donahue mold, to risk-taker with a vulnerable heart, in the Bruce Willis mold, to sensitive but sexy man-boy, in the Kevin Costner mold. And for the most part he has tried valiantly—according to the mood of the moment—to overhaul himself, despite the fact that not one of the models of manhood held up for him has been generated by male thinking, or in any way reflects what he himself may actually wish to be. For although the nineties man has certainly become more feminized through feminism, he has never (unlike his female contemporaries, whose definition of themselves has been virtually reconstructed from the ground up) undergone a collective mind-altering process of deep internal reflection, metamorphosis and transformation of his own making.

For instance, vanguard feminists such as myself were big on the idea of androgyny. We rejected the idea of traditional sexual roles and thought the world would be a better place if we blurred their boundaries. In setting out to redefine masculinity and femininity, we vehemently rejected the argument that biology was destiny. In our version of Utopia, impoverishingly rigid sex roles would self-destruct and in their place a rich, ultimately more multifaceted New Man would rise, like a phoenix, from the ashes.

Our plan was that the New Man would "get in touch with his feminine side," trade in a little "masculine" power for some "female" sensitivity and wind up a better person for it. He'd shed his unseemly "masculine" aggression, gain some superior "feminine" soul and march, an androgynously corrected person, into the future.

We knew this was a brilliant plan because we were obviously better equipped than men to decide what an ideal man should be. Maybe men had the power but, as women, we had the advantage of possessing a genetically inbred moral superiority.

Eventually pop culture picked up on this theme that androgyny was now seductive to women; Mick Jagger, David Bowie, Michael Jackson and Prince, to name only a few, strutted their stuff onstage. If a pop icon embodies, at any given moment, the projections of a culture's *Zeitgeist*, it was not hard to see how the winds had shifted.

The idea that sexual ambiguity was now attractive to women and that, if you acted like a woman, you could also get one was a bizarre concept to most men, who had been weaned on other definitions of manhood, and a lot of them had trouble with it. There was the small matter, for instance, that this androgynous ideal was hardly a compelling or sexually masterful role model for them. As author Ken Kesey commented to author Robert Stone in an article entitled "Blows to the Spirit," in *Esquire*'s 1986 special issue on The American Man (1946-1986): "[Jagger's] got lips like a woman's, and he moves like a woman, and he sings in a kind of insinuating voice.... A lot of people, looking around for something besides this stiffening [big dick, macho] American image, pick Mick Jagger, who's pretty limp."

Despite the fact that this fashionable new ideal of manhood confused men, many of them tried to be sporting about adapting, but sometimes they forgot themselves, slipped back into ingrained habits and acted too much like men.

For instance, sometimes they said or did the "wrong" thing, or didn't do enough of the "right" thing, or they eventually managed to figure out what the "right" and "wrong" things were but didn't manage quickly enough, and women got on their cases. For women had come so far so fast, and were so transfixed with their own precious concerns, that they simply didn't have the patience left to grasp why men were taking so long to get this. How can men still have the nerve, they muttered contemptuously among themselves, to act so damn male?

Certainly I was an expert at trashing men for being men. Around the mid-seventies, for instance, I was reading Susan Brownmiller's groundbreaking treatise on rape: *Against Our Will*. The book had such a stunning impact on me that I called the Rape Crisis Center the day I finished it, to volunteer my services. There were a lot of poorly paid young women in that shabby downtown office, trying to mobilize their anger to move mountains. It was hard to get funds. Everybody was exhausted. Sometimes there was nothing to do but turn men into voodoo dolls and viciously stick pins into them.

Then I would go back home and attend dinner parties where all the women, including me, were clearing the tables where men sat discussing life and art. If I made an issue out of this, I knew, the men would accuse me of overreacting—of being a hysterical female. All the other women seemed to know *their* place. Those were the moments I got so weary, so tempted to just give up, even though I knew in my heart that giving up wasn't even an option anymore.

One night, however, I did make an issue of it. I rose and delivered a stinging oration. I longed for the men to leap from their chairs, throw off years of cultural conditioning, shout, "I believe!" and dutifully begin carrying plates into the kitchen. Instead, their eyes just glazed over. I wanted to hack them to bits with the carving knife. All of them.

Eventually men had had one too many here-we-go-again encounters with impatient, directive, lecturing women like me, and they started to get pissed off. No matter what they did—and by the eighties they were doing a whole lot more than *their* fathers had ever done—it never seemed to be enough. Try as they might to please women, they still couldn't do anything right.

By the mid-eighties they were really fed up and, in increasing numbers, they were pulling back. That is why, throughout a good part of that decade, the women's magazines were whining incessantly about the fact that men were hopeless Peter Pans who refused to "commit."

Of course, another factor in the much-discussed failure of men to commit was the fact that they were no longer under the same social pressure to marry and define themselves as breadwinners. Because many had become more feminized, they were pretty good now at selecting their own ties and whipping up a decent meal in the wok. In becoming, at women's urging, more *like* women, men seemed to have carved out a comfortable niche where they were doing just fine without having to "commit" to them. So much for the visionary plan of androgyny.

What was even more of a problem, as far as harmonious relationships were concerned, was that by then women were having some serious second thoughts about where feminism had brought *them*, and they were unconsciously telegraphing this ambivalence to men.

By the nineties, not only did men no longer have the energy to try to do what was "right," they didn't have the foggiest clue anymore what *was* "right." So often they just said, "Fuck it!"

"It's really bleak out there, boy," one 28-year-old man told me. "All my male friends are having a terrible time with women. It's just like what Norm on 'Cheers' says: 'Boy meets girl. Boy drinks beer.' I'm confused by women because they tend not to know what they want a lot of the time. Or maybe they know, but they're unwilling to say. But how are we supposed to know if they don't? I'm so bewildered by everything going on right now that I've found myself exhibiting a lot of aggressive behavior toward women, to the point where I've felt the need to withdraw completely. At times I've felt as if there were a Greek chorus in my head saying: *This can't be done. You must have your will.* The idea that relationships can be gained by imposing your will is absurd. That's not how humans work. You have to behave with decency and hope your will will be honored. But people are trying to assert their will and see what happens, so relationships are taking shape in an atmosphere of poison and malice.

"In most of the relationships I know, women are calling the shots. But they're calling the shots out of their confusion. Men go along with women putting up the boundaries, but the boundaries aren't clear anymore, and the result is so much confusion between the sexes. If women get confused, they say they need some time to think and sort things out. But men just walk away."

"Look," another man put it, "I think most men will concede that they have to change. Women have changed and now we have to change. But women have been putting a lot of pressure on men to change and we're not dealing with it very well. We're confused and so we're retreating. We have a word for what women do to us. We call it mind-fucking."

"Mind-fucking" is one of the more delicate descriptive terms men used. Another man put it even more plainly: "Listen," he said, "if somebody shoves something down your throat long enough, eventually you just want to vomit it up."

Is There a New Man?

In March 1989, *Psychology Today* asked its largely liberal, upscale, educated readership to define the ideal New Man. From the analysis of the responses published later that year, it seems that the ideal nineties man was a bit of a schizo. He would jump into a Superman suit if the occasion demanded; if a diplomat was required, he would fill those shoes too. In other words, he was sort of competitive, sort of sensitive, but not too much of either. Narcissism was definitely an undesirable quality, as was an interest in power politics or a self-definition that came primarily through work. No one offered any brilliant suggestions as to how these contradictory qualities were supposed to reside within the same psyche.

Much to the editors' surprise, men and women had almost identical views of how the ideal New Man saw women. Significantly, even though he was far from traditional in most ways, both sexes believed he was still carrying around relatively traditional notions about women. He believed women were more nurturing and intuitive than men, less aggressive in bed and in general.

Broadly speaking, he was committed to personal growth and family; he would leave the world a better place than he had found it and he was definitely more "feminine" in his receptivity. And although 69 percent of the respondents believed he should have the traditionally admired "masculine" qualities, such as being a "doer" or taking charge, those characteristics cropped up at the very bottom of the list of his attributes.

On the other hand, the ideal New Man was no wimp either. He lay, both male and female responses indicated, somewhere between a sweet, sensitive guy and Dirty Harry. Where women were concerned, he enjoyed equality and didn't "panic" when they took the sexual lead. But although men generally professed that he would be more turned on by powerful, accomplished women than by those who were merely drop-dead gorgeous, even in their fantasies women were skeptical that he could evolve to that degree.

However, in gaining all these sterling, feminized qualities, the ideal nineties man was no longer the sort of guy who would get a girl's lust-meter ticking. Indeed, in shedding his macho "insensitivity" and becoming kinder, gentler and more politically correct, he appeared to have lost a little bit of his edge. Not only did he no longer go in for one-night stands, but only 58 percent of the respondents thought sex was an essential source of pleasure for him! On the list of his imagined qualities, only thirteen women (and not a single man) characterized him as "sexy." And when the magazine asked its readers to list famous men who best embodied his qualities, both men and women picked Jesus as their number-one role model—nobody's idea of the kind of guy going to get a woman all hot and bothered.

Some women confessed that, even if they could find this Uto-pian creature out there in the real world, he probably wouldn't get them horny. And "in a more troubled vein," *Psychology Today* observed, other women admitted that the guys who really turned their cranks had many qualities they judged to be inferior, if not downright evil.

"Ideals are distant stars by which we can set our compass," the editors concluded. "If we never reach them, they nevertheless help us travel more wholeheartedly in the direction we desire to go." What they didn't add was that, since the compass needle was flickering all over the map, men had ahead of them one hell of a journey.

The flesh-and-blood New Man of the nineties who wishes to emulate the currently fashionable model of manhood certainly has his work cut out for him. If he is savvy and wants to get the girl, he has to walk an impossibly fine line. He has to be gentle but not weak, malleable but not limp, masterful but not macho, sensitive but not sappy and stylish but not shallow. He has to cook! He has to clean! He has to garden and decorate! If he's married, he has to chauffeur the kids and pontificate knowledgeably on the subject of fatherhood. In his leisure time, however, should he experience a moment of heaving desire, he has to radiate the animal magnetism of a Tom Cruise, do a me-Tarzan, you-Jane routine and (with her lusty consent, of course) pin Jane against the fridge, remove her panties and make the earth move for her.

On the sexual front, executing this delicate balancing act poses some tricky dilemmas. For instance, if men come on to women as they were expected to do in the good old days, they're now pretty sure they'll get kneed in the groin.

"There are very few postures left for men," one man said. "A lot of men feel that most women want them to be less sexually driven and more emotionally sensitive. Men have reacted to the feminist agenda by pulling back from women, because they now think that to come on to a woman overtly sexually is bad manners. You hesitate to come on to a woman because you don't want to be perceived as totally insensitive. You don't want to get that look that says, 'Don't start acting like every other jerk who ever tried to make me.' "

On the other hand, they've found out that if they *don't* come on to a woman, but do their best to behave like the sincere but sexless ideal New Man in the *Psychology Today* survey, it's the best way to ensure that they'll never get laid again. "Women go on and on about how they want us to be open and sensitive and bleed emotionally like they do," one man said. "Then you take them at their word and open yourself up and have talks with them about your own feelings and fears, and they turn on you. Now you're a wimp! You try to be a sensitive man and they run the other way. Then they fall for the macho pricks who treat them like shit."

I met many men who expounded at length on this theme, but none expressed his confusion quite as succinctly as the one whose voice was riddled with contempt as he told me, "Listen, women don't want to be pursued and they don't want to chase. Well, you tell me: what the fuck do they want?"

Where Do Men Turn?
Should men wish to glean some understanding of what it means to be a man in the nineties, or a few insights into how to find their way through their confusion—as some of them are now starting to do—they have few places to turn for help. In two years of reading everything I could find on the subject of male-female relationships, I found few reflections by men, about men, in the aftershocks of feminism. There is, of course, Robert Bly's bestselling treatise on manhood—*Iron John*—which has become the bible of the men's movement (as it is being called), but it leaves out all those men who don't find practicable, as a solution to these problems, the idea of wearing masks and searching for their Wild Men or Inner Kings while dancing naked in the forest.

Almost exclusively, women are doing the talking. "Like a husband who sullenly withdraws to his tool shed to escape his wife's temper and misery," wrote the authors of *Burning Desires: Sex in America*, "American men simply opted out of the cultural dialogue."

In the media, female writers authoritatively interpret and analyze men to other women, as if men are aliens who speak an unintelligible language of grunts and snorts and can't be counted upon to speak, with any clarity, for themselves. Women preach, proselytize, diagnose and deliver the final verdict on the inarticulate gender. And, with a few noteworthy exceptions, the verdict is that men are arrested adolescents, recalcitrant little boys, emotional slow learners or verbal Neanderthals. If women only *do* something, take the matter into their own hands, improve this or that, practice some behavior modification techniques on these turkeys, then eventually men will come around.

What's more, a man who fancies himself sympathetic to feminist concerns and is doing his damnedest to assimilate them, but who occasionally feels the tug of what are now considered reprehensible sexist impulses—or who simply wishes to voice, without fear of censure, the conflicted feelings churning within him—has very little outlet for those feelings.

One doctor in his early thirties, for instance, admitted to me that he happens to think there is "more valor involved in staying home and educating a child. I think women are totally out of sync with their biology. I think we'd have a better society if women did the maternal work of having kids and raising them. But you can't voice that view right now. It's taboo. You'd be castrated."

Inevitably, the savvy man who wishes to travel in "civilized" circles learns the wisdom of muzzling his authentic feelings and repressing any comments of dubious acceptability. Otherwise he runs the risk of being slam-dunked by Big Sister, and having women—whose radar for such transgressions is by now finely tuned—land on him with such force that he's made to feel like a chastened child. Unless he wants to risk embarrassment and have to apologize for his feelings, his choice is to either second-guess and offer a phony version of them, or to maintain a stony, Clint Eastwood silence.

I especially realized how much the cultural pressure to be politically correct had become a burden for men—and a barrier to fluid relationships between the sexes—in June 1990, when *Esquire* published a theme issue entitled "The Secret Life of the American Wife." When it hit the stands, an outraged chorus of feminists claimed it was riddled with demeaning caricatures and female stereotypes. It was, or so they claimed, sexist to the max.

I was puzzled by this reaction because I thought—and I say this as a feminist—that the issue was at once an insightful portrayal and a clever parody of the way *Esquire*'s well-educated, urbane male reader saw the woman with whom he now, for better or worse, shared his life. And, given that I had come across very little *male* commentary on what such men were actually thinking, it was a rare opportunity to see—in print—what was actually going on in their heads.

With considerable irony and wit the magazine went straight to the heart of what one particular breed of American male was feeling, at that moment in history, about the woman he had taken to be his wife. The tone was at once wistfully nostalgic and frankly contemporary. Its message was: *this is who she is, boys, and although she sometimes surprises, scares and irks us, she ain't so bad after all. Better get used to her, though, because she's here to stay.*

At times (the subtext of the articles and visuals telegraphed) this woman was baffling, annoying, dangerous, exasperating and a million light-years away from the girl who married dear old dad; nevertheless, her husband looked upon her with a certain bemused fondness, admiration and grudging respect. Even if turning back the clock were within his power—which it clearly wasn't—in his heart of hearts he didn't *really* want to go back in time. His newly found maturity, however, didn't preclude indulging in a deeply satisfying fantasy, now and then, about the good old days when men were men and women were understandable.

Shortly after the issue hit the stands, a female friend attended a dinner made up of several prominent magazine writers and editors of both sexes. Someone raised the *Esquire* controversy, and a discussion ensued. "Not one man at that table would admit that he liked the issue," my friend confided later, "although they were all saying as much to each other in quiet little huddles. Not until I said that I thought it was a smart, witty and honest portrayal of the way men are feeling right now, and that I had found it a fascinating insight into the contemporary urban male's take on women—through their caricatures—did they feel they had permission to express what they actually believed. My God, men are so afraid."

Indeed, they are often so jittery about opening their mouths and saying the "wrong" thing that one hapless *Playboy* columnist who said he was "just trying to stay alive" in the middle of a revolution wrote that being labeled sexist in America was as dangerous as being labeled Communist in the fifties. Men like him had been "scared into silence."

"Men now feel ashamed of certain feelings and impulses that they have," one man told me, "because women have made them feel ashamed. But there is this little secret compartment in their brains that they never let women into, because they think women would be appalled at what they're thinking, and they're right— women would be appalled. Like sometimes they really do lust after women with blonde hair and big tits. Like sometimes they really wouldn't mind being waited on hand and foot. So men tell themselves, hey, I better be careful not to think this way. They're secretly ashamed, yet they are acculturated to think this way. There's a dialectic going on in them all the time."

Why Are There So Many Angry Men?

If you confuse men about their sexual roles, tell them to rein in their erotic impulses and then advise them to shut up when they're having a few problems adjusting, it's a pretty safe bet that sooner or later some of them are going to get a little testy. Eventually that anger will find a way to express itself in a deformed manner. Sure enough, throughout the eighties there were many troubling manifestations of increasing male anger toward women. All of them were set against the larger political canvas of a conservative and anti-feminist backlash. Although they were disturbing signs of disturbing times, and did say something unsettling about the generalized frustration and anger men were feeling, they hardly spoke for the overwhelming majority of thinking men, most of whom—in their troubled relationships with women—were stoically carrying on, trying to make the best of a bad situation.

"Since I came of age in the sixties," one man told me, "most of the hopes and dreams of those years have been smashed in a conservative backswing. What came about in the sexual revolution—the idea of sexual equality—is nowhere near being realized. The abortion issue is still flaming and there are terrible setbacks. I live in Dallas, the buckle of the Bible belt, and a local candidate running for governor said that God made women to stay home and take care of the family. That's how far we've come. The sexual revolution was about power. Until men are willing to share it, there's going to be some static."

In Canada, the static flared in a grotesque form. In December 1989, a 25-year-old man carrying a semiautomatic rifle entered an engineering classroom at the University of Montreal's Ecole Polytechnique. "You're all a bunch of feminists, and I hate feminists," he shouted, and then opened fire on the female students, whom he had instructed to gather separately from the men. Over the next twenty minutes he methodically hunted his "feminist" quarry in the corridors and classrooms of the school. Of the twenty-seven students struck, fourteen died, and all of the dead were women. Then he turned the gun on himself. In his suicide note, the man, whose name was Marc Lépine, blamed "feminists" for ruining his life.

Many observers believed the Montreal Massacre—as it came to be called—was a "random act," that Lépine was a "madman" and that to see in the tragedy any larger implications about male resentment and retaliation was a feminist overreaction. Police and social scientists in both Canada and the United States, however, were picking up on a worrisome trend which suggested the Montreal Massacre made horrible sense as an example—albeit extreme—of a widespread social problem.

What they were observing was that many men now felt inferior in their relationships with the opposite sex and that those feelings were starting to surface in the form of wife abuse, family violence (where estranged husbands or lovers came home one last time to blow away their ex-mates, their children and sometimes themselves), incest and sexual assault. As well, there were reports of troubling increases in the number of women who were suddenly "disappearing" or meeting with gruesome "inexplicable" deaths.

According to the social scientists studying these incidents, male resentment was a common thread running through many of them. The feminization of society, and the resultant threat some men were experiencing to their manhood in its wake, appeared to be spawning some malcontents, to say the least.

Rosemary Gartner, a sociology professor at the University of Toronto, conducted a study of homicides of women in eighteen industrialized countries, including Canada and the United States, between 1950 and 1980. Gartner told *Maclean's* (Canada's weekly national newsmagazine) that she had discovered that, in the cultures where women moved into nontraditional roles, their murder rates rose significantly. One of the motives, Gartner argued, was that as women made forays into the more lucrative, previously male preserves, their inroads were perceived, consciously or unconsciously, as a threat to the traditional male-dominated order. This increase in murders, she believed, might indicate a sort of "backlash violence."

As well, there were other signals, all across North America, that in some maladjusted men, particularly when they traveled in packs, male anxiety had gone haywire and turned inside out into aggression. When a campus women's group at Queen's University in Kingston, Ontario, mounted a "No means No" poster campaign about date rape, some male students altered the wording to say, "No means tie her up" or "No means kick her in the teeth" or "On your knees, bitch. No more Mr. Nice Guy."

In the U.S., reporter Lisa Olson told reporters that she suffered "nothing less than mind-rape" when she attempted to interview a player in the New England Patriots' locker room. Patriots tight end Zeke Mowatt, along with several other undressed players, Olson alleged, encircled her during an interview, sounding the all-she-needs-is-a-good-lay theme.

What these incidents indicated was that some of The Boys were feeling antsy and threatened and needed to kick some ass again—and kick ass they did. Although such incidents were almost always passed off as boys-will-be-boys behavior, there was a serious—and telling—undercurrent, a psychopathology that spoke volumes about the upset in the balance of power between the sexes.

The incidents were symbolic rapes, power plays masquerading as boyish antics. They were reminders to women that men were still calling the shots, and would continue to whenever the mood struck. You can get your passkeys to the boys' clubhouse, the incidents telegraphed, but don't forget who's boss.

It was only a matter of time before the repressed anxiety many men were feeling bubbled up in the popular culture as well. It erupted in the U.S. in the mutant form of Andrew Dice Clay. Self-described as The Brooklyn Bad Boy, Andrew Dice Clay began as a comic who left Sheepshead Bay for Hollywood in 1980, where he languished in relative obscurity, playing small clubs until he tapped into the sexually dissonant mood of his generation and hit the big time. Given the rage (sexual and otherwise) festering just beneath the surface of North American culture, he was an accident waiting to happen.

By 1988 he had his own HBO special—"The Diceman Cometh" (later to become a best-selling video). A year later he was doing a 27-city tour, filling 17,000-seat arenas and grossing more than $4 million—a staggering amount for a comedy act. His debut LP reached the top hundred and was followed by a double comedy album, and by the summer of 1989 he had a three-movie deal with Twentieth-Century Fox. Clay's career faded soon afterwards—almost as quickly as it had blossomed—but his brief mega-success was a significant cultural marker.

Clay's schtick was in the genre of the Comedy of Hate and his targets were all the liberal establishment's sacred cows: gays ("get the fuck back in the closet"), Asian immigrants ("Chink bastards," "slanty-eyed cocksuckers"), the homeless ("fuckin' bums,") and women ("pussies"). Only blacks escaped Clay's venom, not coincidentally because they were "proud of their penises" and needed a "fitting just to wear a condom." Strutting onstage, dragging on a cigarette, with his biker jacket and James Dean swagger, Clay was the epitome of the nastiest motherfucker in the neighborhood. Behind his swagger and the vitriol that spilled from his mouth was a message: the white North American male has had the shit kicked out of him and I, the Diceman, am here to give him back his balls. What better place to begin than by reducing women to cunts again?

In Clay's "comedy," women were only sexual slot machines, cocksucking "sluts," "plastic fuck-dolls." Often they were evil tempt-resses who wore "fuck-me pumps" and "little cut-off shorts creeping up their fuckin' asses," thereby begging men to treat them like the "pigs" they were. Sex (translation: date rape) was a male prerogative; a woman's role was merely to spread her legs and service a man. ("*So I say to the bitch, 'Lose the bra—or I'll cut ya.' Is that a wrong attitude?*") Tenderness and female pleasure were nowhere to be found in this sexual universe. You did to women "things you wouldn't do to a farm animal," and then you dumped them. Sometimes Clay segued into wildly unwitty nursery rhymes. His fans—the women as much as the men—cheered loudly and chanted along, word for word.

In June 1990, Clay, who had refused all interviews for almost a year because of the heat he was taking in the media, told a *Vanity Fair* reporter what had prompted the "sexual material" in his act. When he first came to Los Angeles, he said, the "promiscuity" of women amazed him. "I always had a steady girlfriend like since I was sixteen, but I'm not going to say that every chick I met in Brooklyn, I would nail her. Because I didn't. But I come out to L.A. and it's like any girl you meet, they're goin', 'Hey, why don't you come over?' I just couldn't believe it. They were filthier than the guys." One time he awakened handcuffed to his window, and the woman in his bed was laughing "like some real sicko."

Clay had been turned into a sexual object by the women he was meeting and, clearly, he didn't like it much. *He* was supposed to be calling the shots. *He* was supposed to be "nailing" them, not the other way around. Such misadventures, he said, led to the birth of "the Diceman" in 1983. Indeed, at one point in the act the Diceman proclaims derisively that "Oh, women love the one-night stand, but they just can't face the fact that we *own* it." Only by reducing women to pussies again could a man make his sexual universe unfold as it should.

Clay's anxiety that he was now expected to be the sexual object was echoed by a lot of men I met, and they didn't like the feeling much either. "I don't like sexual aggressiveness," one man told me. "A too sexually aggressive woman is a double-edged sword. The positive side is, hey, she wants me. The negative side is, oh Christ, now I have to make it happen. Maybe I'll disappoint her."

Another man admitted that while he had, unbeknownst to the woman with whom he lived, enjoyed the occasional fling on the side, he would have great difficulty accepting the possibility that she had done likewise. "I don't know how I'd deal with it," he said. "Probably not very well. I'd like to say that I'd have no problem with it but I think I would. It's the double standard, I admit it. Maybe I'd even use that fact as an excuse to get out of the relationship."

The fact that women were now sometimes the sexual adventurers or predators, were capable of finding men, fucking them and forgetting them, were often in the game for the sexual jollies and nothing else and were behaving as callously as men often had, was extremely disturbing to men. Had that anxiety (along with the other "random rage of the decade," as *The Village Voice* so aptly put it) not been so widespread, Clay would have remained just another no-name comic struggling to make it in L.A.

What Do Men Want?
In some men I met (as in some women), anxiety manifested itself in bitter words. Most, however, are quietly and patiently philosophical about women and matters of the heart. What they want is a relationship of consequence, or the tools to make one work. Above all, I think, they long to understand what's expected of them as men, and how to conduct themselves in a brave new world.

Often I came away from their interviews with the lingering sense that they are searching to know who they are. I also saw how deeply they need to process what's confusing them, and how genuinely they desire connection.

The irony of those observations—and their apparent contradiction of what so many women were telling me about men—struck me time and again. How could it be that what men appeared to desire most—to end their confusion and get close to women—was precisely what women accused them of recoiling from?

I asked them if they were telling women what they were telling me. Often they shrugged and said that was a tricky thing to do. Partly because talking about emotional issues is not easy for them at the best of times—and these are far from the best of times—but partly because women have other things on their minds. Nurturing men or shepherding them through their doubts, many said, is not high on a woman's priority list these days.

"Men have had a rough shake," one man told me. "They can't kid themselves that they're superior to women anymore. All they have to do is look around them and see how successful women have become. So they feel they've lost an edge. They can't fall back on any of the traditional ideas about being a man—those ideas just don't hold anymore. A lot of women are making good money and they're taking care of themselves. They're so independent now. You go on a date and they're ordering the wine and instructing the maître d'—you don't even know if you're supposed to be the gallant gentleman anymore, and so you're second-guessing yourself all the time. You feel completely at sea.

"I think men look at women these days and they start asking themselves what men are good for anymore. And maybe they do get up the courage to turn to a woman for an answer to that question. Lots of women will give them the feeling that they're not good for much—except maybe to romance them when they're in the mood, or take care of them, on their terms, or fuck them once in a while.

"You know, back in grade school, there was always a kid on the team who was lousy at sports. There was always this one kid who was uncoordinated and all the other guys got impatient with him. They didn't want him on the team because he'd wreck the team's chances. Sometimes, though, there was one guy who'd take that poor kid under his wing and give him a little encouragement, show him a move or two.

"I think a lot of men are feeling just like that uncoordinated kid. They can't get it right, no matter what they do, and they have no confidence or past triumphs to fall back on. So they look to women to be the wise ones and to take them under their wing, because they've always looked to women for emotional guidance, and in the past women have usually been there for them.

"But right now, women are saying, 'Fuck you, buddy, I've got enough on my plate. Now I have to mother *you too*?' Or they're contemptuous of men when they fumble. So men don't have anywhere to turn. They don't know how to share their fears with other men, and they no longer have any illusions to hide behind. Men are feeling terribly threatened on so many levels. That's why I think that now, maybe more than ever, they need women's help. They need to see women as their allies."

Part Two

Connection

4. Getting Men and Women Together

THE QUESTION OF THE MOMENT IS HOW TO GET AMBIVALENT MEN AND confused women back on track so they can go out with each other, have fulfilling relationships and start having fun in the sack again. Casual sex just isn't cutting it anymore for a sizable segment of the population and—despite the press it's been getting—celibacy is not, for most, an ennobling experience.

But before you can figure out how to have great sex and true love that lasts, you have to figure out how to feel kindly disposed toward the person you're in bed with—a not inconsiderable task in these troubled times. And before you can tackle that small matter, you have to date so you can meet a person with whom the potential to enjoy both great sex and true love exists.

Can the Romance Brokers Help?

One way men and women are increasingly seeking mates is through romance brokers. The search for love has become the quest of the day as stressed, lonely people wave hard cash in the face of anybody offering a quick-fix solution. Everywhere you look there's someone or something purporting to be the answer: the relationship fix-it books, the talk shows, computer chat lines for the lovelorn, "meeting" cards engraved with titillating messages, telephone love-connection lines, land-a-date home shopping programs, video dating services, highly targeted (and increasingly bizarre) mainstream and alternative press personal ads, matrimonial agencies, executive matchmakers, intimacy workshops, car decals and wearable pendants declaring marital status, flirting classes, singles' clubs and so on....

Although occasionally the romance brokers succeed in match-making, generally speaking they tend to market a superficial brand of compatability ("I like Bach, moonlight walks and dining alfresco"), but fail miserably at addressing the chemistry factor. (This distinguishes them from the bars, which rely on chemistry to the exclusion of just about everything else.) Consequently, the brokers only slightly improve the odds of finding true love. True love is—and always has been—an amalgam of both.

In the age of computers, many hopefuls are raising their eyes heavenward to the God of High Tech. "American enterprise," wrote James Bennet in a trenchant piece in *The New Republic*, "is doing an impressive job of harnessing information technology to romantic desperation. The deep, anxious urge to mate, stirred by the sexual revolution and then dammed by growing fear, growing workloads, and various other modern obstacles, has overflowed the traditional channels and is spilling into every available conduit."

Bennet surveyed the various high-tech services available to American lovelorn in 1989: Aline, the first computer-to-computer communications system where lonely hearts could log on to "cruise the integrated circuits"; CompuServe, a multi-channel computer network on which a user had to lure a prospective mate away from the party line to a private channel, risking the humiliation of having the desired one politely excuse herself or himself to log back onto the main line; 976 numbers—telephone personal ad boards that allow a woman like Karen, who is interested in a "mistress-type relationship," to break a lot of ice fast; Great Expectations, a nationwide video dating service in the U.S. that charges between $1,200 and $1,850 for memberships that last until marriage.

Bennet found that the big sell of the more expensive high-tech matchmakers was their offer of "quality" (the screening out of undesirables with no cash and bad clothes, let's say) and "efficiency" (the avoidance of dead-end dating, with its waste of time, energy and money)—virtues devoutly to be wished for in a time-is-money culture. And he discovered that time-management considerations (not to mention superficial ones) determined the making or breaking of most high-tech liaisons. Since, on the general-purpose networks, users have only seconds between question and response, suitors have to "rise or fall on the sharpness of their wit."

Although Great Expectations' promotional hype said the service offered members the deep background on "fine quality singles" at "a time when commitment is more important than ever," a study by psychologists Stanley Woll and P. Chris Cozby of California State University, Fullerton, concluded that members chose their dates largely on those timeworn standbys, looks and age. Usually members flipped through books from back to front, since photos appeared on the reverse of profiles—and although they were paying top dollar, they repeatedly refused to take the few minutes to check a video if a photo was less than compelling. In other words, reported Bennet, the same hasty, superficial selection process prevails in the video library as in the bars.

Ultimately, Bennet reports that Woll and Cozby estimate the service's success rate to be a "not particularly impressive" 10 to 15 percent. "Great Expectations builds a stage, assembles a troupe," observes Bennet, "and leaves them to act out the same old brutal, clumsy black comedy about mating, while paying extra for sneak previews."

Most of the testimonials I heard from those who'd gone the route of dating services or personal ads echoed Bennet's observations. Usually people had some terrible dates, some so-so dates, some decent dates or some wonderful dates, the latter developing into dating relationships that added sexual spice and/or companionship to their lives. Even though they failed to find their dream mates however, most people viewed the experience as a positive one. One female executive in her late forties who spent three months garnering the courage to place an ad, and who mistakenly assumed that only "social misfits" would answer it, received an avalanche of responses from men whose professions ranged from stockbroker to artist, doctor to body-builder. What she discovered was that "dating through the personals is an adventure. I think that's the best way to view it. Yes, you meet some people who are totally inappropriate for you, but you also meet some interesting ones and broaden your social contacts. I developed one warm relationship that lasted for several months, and if I'd wanted to pursue several other relationships I could have. More importantly, though, I got back on my feet emotionally after the end of a love affair. You can wait forever to be asked out these days, and I didn't want to have to wait around. I needed to feel in control of my life. I wanted some male attention and I needed to feel attractive again, so I figured I had nothing to lose and went after what I needed."

Those with long-term success stories say that the best way to meet—especially in the nineties—is still the oldest way: introductions through family or friends. And they strongly advise you not to reject out of hand those set-ups arranged by your mother.

My 35-year-old sister can attest to the advisability of this method. For many years she was the consummate single woman. She had a glamorous career, a room at the best hotels, an enviable expense account, a drawerful of shoulder pads and a rocky history of blind dates with psychopaths. Then my mother fixed her up on a blind date, whereupon she promptly fell madly in love and got married. (Wisely, she hung onto the expense account.)

Dance parties—in the forties style—also work wonders. One woman said she and her friend threw a party at which they played only Frank Sinatra records. "My friend is totally obsessed with Frank Sinatra and that's all he would play, so people were forced to touch when they danced. Several hot romances came out of that party. A lot of my married friends showed up later, when the thing was in swing, and they said they'd never been to such a volatile, sexually charged party. If we hadn't played Sinatra, it wouldn't have worked. Playing Sinatra made everyone touch again."

In a world where it's tough to connect, the already-paired-off can also play a role in bringing people together; instead of just sitting around and gloating that they don't have to deal with this nonsense, they have a moral responsibility to set up their single friends with worthy eligibles they know. (And, while I'm ranting here, they ought to be inviting them to dinner parties too—even though a single person screws up the table setting.) The problem of meeting in the nineties is so confounding, it requires a collaborative effort to solve.

Is There a Place for the Lost Art of Flirting in the Nineties?
In 1985, Thomas E. Murray, an English professor at Ohio State University, visited fifty singles' bars in the St. Louis area, and, in what must have been an extreme fit of masochism, collected some 3,000 opening lines. He published his research in *American Speech*.

Murray found that compliments were the least common form of ice-breaker. Leading the pack in the compliments category was "I like your [article of clothing]." It's an innocuous enough way to kick things off, but running a close second, alas, was "Best boobs I've seen all night." The "advertisements" and "declarations" were even more pitiful. Next to a simple (albeit dull) introduction ("My name is...,") the let's-not-mince-words declaration "I'm hot" was a favorite opener. And one raconteur sought to ingratiate himself by announcing that his "dong" was two feet long. In the question-as-opener category, "Wanna bang my wang?" "Wanna honk my horn?" and "Wanna collar my bishop?" were among the popular bons mots, as was the timelessly elegant "Wanna fuck?" Such is the state of flirtation in the singles' bars of America.

Even among those whose opening gambit is unlikely to be "Wanna honk my horn?" flirting has fallen on hard times. Most of the people I met confessed that they simply didn't know how to flirt. What's more, a good many of them don't even know if they're *supposed* to flirt these days.

Why Won't Men Flirt Anymore?

Any guy schooled in Feminism 101 believes that it's now considered insulting for a man to come on to a woman. If he hits on her, he reasons, she'll think he's less interested in *her* than in having sex with her. Mind you, about 90 percent of the time he *is* interested in having sex with her—feminism has made few inroads in that department. All that's changed is that now a man who wishes to be considered sophisticated can't be frank with himself about his desires, can't be too overt with the object of his desires and gets queasy about actually acting on them.

A man who, in a previous life, would have felt comfortable

chatting up a woman to jump-start proceedings, now instinctively holds back. "I'd never come on to a woman," one man said. "I always wait until she makes the first move. I don't want to set myself up to be perceived as some macho asshole."

In the workplace—where men and women most often meet and where the balance of power in the sexual dynamics may be tipped by seniority issues—men are worried about a good deal more than being perceived as having loutish sexual manners. They're worried about engaging in what they intend as innocuous friendly flirtation and being slapped with a sexual harassment suit. (The degree to which men are anxious and confused about what now constitutes the difference between friendly flirtation and sexual harassment was thrown into high relief in 1991 by the intense public debate over the Anita Hill/Clarence Thomas U.S. Congressional hearings.)

And so all the energy that should be going into good, old-fashioned, harmless sexual intrigue (as opposed to soul-destroying sexual harassment—a distinction most women understand) is getting short-circuited in men's minds by political correctness, which, so far as I can tell, never gave anyone a libidinal rush. Having lost the fluency of the courting language, a generation of men are slowly going insane; like Hamlet, they're tortured by fear and introspection. "I wish I could flirt with a woman," one man lamented. "I used to be able to flirt, but I don't have the confidence anymore. You have to be receptive to the clues, the language spoken and unspoken, but my head keeps getting in the way!"

Monkeys, in fact, are far more adept at figuring out when a woman is hot to trot than most men are. Sexologists have discovered that when a woman is in the excitable state of estrus or heat, if researchers smear scrapings from her vagina on female rhesus monkeys, male monkeys go ape-shit with desire. Unfortunately, human males don't have the same refined sense to know when a woman wants it.

Alas, when humans started to walk upright, they lost their finely tuned sense of smell; men just don't get off on these aromas anymore. When they started standing on two feet it was too much of a stretch between their noses and girls' privates—and since it's now considered unseemly, in polite company, for men to do a bum-sniff, it would be hard for them to get a satisfactory reading anyway. Instead of picking up the scent and doing his business, a man must now stand around making cocktail party chatter with the object of his lust, or seduce her with several expensive dinners.

Some men have tried to circumvent this problem by flirting in what they imagine to be a politically correct manner. For instance, one woman related how she dated a guy who kept telling her that he was very attracted to her "but not just sexually." Unfortunately, well intentioned though it may be, such flirting doesn't exactly send a woman's hormones coursing. "It would have been better if he'd just said, 'Man, you're some attractive dame!' " she moaned. "He goes by the book and takes all the spontaneity out of it!"

Why Won't Women Flirt Anymore?

With some notable exceptions (i.e. the sort of woman one man described as "the kind who'd come after you with an ax") women aren't taking the lead in flirting either. First, most women realize that many men still find the notion of a sexually aggressive woman distasteful. Second, despite all of their feminist rhetoric, many women are still waiting for Prince Charming to show up at their doors and sweep them off their feet.

"I'm very uncomfortable in the role of initiator," one woman said. "I guess I do want a man who chases me. I want some mystery, pursuit, romance. I don't want to have to do all the work. I don't want to have to talk them into it."

Not only are women stymied as to how to beam the messages, they're having a tough time deciphering the signals coming back. "I just don't understand this whole dance anymore," another woman said. "Partly it's because you ask what rules exist and none do. I try to figure out the signs: is he interested? Not interested? I wish I knew how to flirt, but I come across as way too self-sufficient, out of fear and vulnerability. And I don't get it when they're flirting with me. Usually I just stand there and pray for a miracle!"

Women are in such a depressed state over the signaling stand-off that Cynthia Heimel commented in the December 1989 *Playboy* that her new rule was "never believe that a person is interested until you feel his tongue down your throat."

Who Has to Make the First Flirting Move?

Clearly, if anything's going to get going, *somebody* has to make a move. And most of the current psychological research on courtship suggests that, in the early stages of the game at least, the ball is in the female court.

What the behavioral scientists have discovered is that while men *appear* to be the sexual aggressors (or did when they were still confident enough to go for it), they are in fact responding to subtle signals that women, the clever darlings, are sending out. Women draw men to them through flirtatious behavior: glint of eye, seductive posture, tone of voice, pressure of touch—the same gestures referred to as "display" in the animal kingdom.

In various studies she's done since 1978, Webster University psychologist Monica Moore has examined courtship behaviors. In one study, she covertly observed two hundred women for a hundred hours in singles' bars, in order to isolate and evaluate successful solicitation behaviors. What she found was that signaling was by far the most important factor in attracting a mate; a high-signaling but not so great-looking woman was much more likely to draw a man than was a low-signaling but more attractive woman. What's more, Moore has also found that certain solicitation behaviors are incredibly effective.

Predictably, men warm to a laugh, a smile or a touch. But when a woman carelessly executes a hair flip, head toss, skirt hike or lip lick, the needle goes right off the attraction-meter and the guys are off and running. Thus a woman's role in the initial signaling stages of courtship is both subtle and seminal: "The initial stages of courtship seem to be her call," Moore reported in Toronto at the 1989 meeting of The Society for the Scientific Study of Sex. "Men become more involved in the later, more overt stages: asking for the date, making the move for the first kiss, suggesting going to bed. In fact, men and women seem to have divided it up."

What Are the Flirting Do's and Don'ts from the Male Perspective?
Most men would dearly love to get a friendly come-on from a woman. "I live in the hottest part of town for single people," one man complained, "and I'm always checked out by women on the street, but they never follow through. I'd sure be happy if one of them started a conversation with me. Women complain that men don't feast on them with their eyes anymore; yet you do, and you get an icy stare back."

The only female flirting that turns men off—and it does so almost universally—is flirting that lacks a certain grace. As one man put it, "If she grabbed my crotch, that would be a drag." What men respond to is the woman who flatters, compliments and sweet-talks them without being phony, who knows how to be coy without being coquettish, who seduces by appreciation, not aggression. They're goners, they claim, if a woman understands those subtleties, for in them lie the mystery and allure of feminine otherness. "I love a woman to make a move, and as long as it's done with a sense of humor and a little soul glinting through the eyes, I'd welcome it," one man said. "All power to someone else who'll take the lead, because I'm not very good at it. I think it's outmoded crap that the man has to lead."

Another man recalled fondly a woman he'd met who knew a thing or two about the fine art of flirting. "Within an hour of meeting we were flirting like mad. She was instigating it, for sure, but I found it utterly charming. We had a mock fight in a subway station, and she touched me and the touching was pregnant with meaning. As she left, she sort of turned over her shoulder and asked in this curious, little-girl voice, 'Do men like anal sex?' God, it was erotic! It was the perfect combination of innocence and sleaze. There was a hint of more to come."

What Are the Flirting Do's and Don'ts from the Female Perspective?
Like men, women warm to seduction by appreciation. Courtship, they say, is a dance, not a duel—a subtlety they feel may be lost on many men, who tend to equate seduction with blood sports. Just as women love a lover with a gentle touch, so too do they cherish a gentle approach. An appreciative look scores big with women; a lurch, a paw or a leer does not.

"It's done with the mind," one woman said, "and it comes from within. The guys who are the great flirts—and there are very few of them left—are the guys who truly like women. They're subtle and sexy because they leave as much unspoken as spoken. The unspoken part is the sexiest because it's delicious to imagine the romantic possibilities. And even if there aren't going to be romantic possibilities—because maybe the guy's married or otherwise involved—it doesn't matter because in the best possible way he's conveying the message that he finds you desirable. A great flirt—available or not—always leaves a woman feeling good about herself. He knows how to compliment her on her charms without making her feel as if she's a piece of meat. He looks her in the eye, listens to what she's saying, jokes and spars with her in a delightful, engaging way, and the air just crackles! And so the flirting becomes a pas de deux.

"You go away from an encounter with a great flirt with the feeling that you have this magic power to turn the head of a smart, sexy guy. You go away from an encounter with a bad flirt—the type who's long on overkill and short on subtlety—feeling sleazy and invaded."

The guy who never fails to turn them off, women enthusiastically agree, is the type who comes on gangbusters with phony lines he's used on every other woman he's ever tried to maneuver into the sack. Any woman over the age of twenty-two can smell a line coming a mile away, which perhaps explains why increasing numbers of middle-aged males are looking for dates at the local high schools.

"I can't stand if a guy's an operator," one woman said. "I find it funny that they're so stupid—all that forced suave and debonair stuff. They tend to try to make you think they can't live without you. But all you're thinking is, this guy has lived without me for thirty-five years. How come now, all of a sudden, he can't live without me?"

Women reserve their supreme contempt, however, for the man who flirts outrageously until a woman takes him at his word and flirts back, at which point he gets nervous and backs off, leaving her feeling as if she's just been stood up.

"I went to a baseball game with a bunch of girlfriends," one woman said, "and this guy in front of us flirted with me all through the game. It was just friendly kibitzing, but after the game I bumped into him on the street and he made some joking comment like 'Hey, I think you're following me.' I assured him, playfully, that I wasn't and went on my way.

"Then, a few minutes later, I was standing on the street corner waiting for the traffic light to change when he came up behind me and said, in a teasing voice, '*You* again?'

"So finally the penny dropped and I figured that maybe this guy wanted to start something. He was cute and friendly and charming and so I smiled and said, 'Well...*it must be fate!*'

"All of a sudden he got nervous and started stammering that his wife wouldn't like it very much if she found him there talking to me.

"I was furious. What the hell did his wife have to do with this? I'm having a friendly little flirtation with a guy on the street—a guy who *came on to me* all night—and he can't hack it because he's not controlling it anymore! I guess he got scared, figured I was Glenn Close in *Fatal Attraction* or something.

"We could both have gone home feeling uplifted by what was a harmless, joking flirtation, but instead, by approaching and withdrawing, he made me angry, and I retaliated. I got very sarcastic and I told him his wife didn't have to worry.

" 'Oh no?' he asked me. 'Why?'

" 'Because I have a rule,' I said. 'I never ask a man to leave his wife on the first chance encounter on a street corner.' "

What Was a Date Like in the Good Old Days?

Once you've negotiated all the complications surrounding meeting and flirting, you have to test the limits of your budding attraction—usually by dating. This is unfortunate, because for most of the people I talked to dating is the modern-day equivalent of being stretched on the rack or having your fingernails pulled out. A date is now so clouded with ambiguities, people are unsure how to approach the experience, and how to behave in the middle of it. Since the dating ritual appears to have suffered some serious setbacks in recent years, a brief historical perspective is in order.

First there was the looking-forward part. This was the dreamy, highly charged state of anticipation, and it was an unspeakably pleasurable stage of any first-class date. She got the call on Wednesday night, let's say, and the two of them bantered playfully on the telephone for a while, and they both turned up the charm dials something fierce and then he asked her if she wanted to get together on Saturday, for dinner maybe, and she said sure, she'd love to, and then he said he'd speak to her later in the week to pin down the arrangements, and they said goodbye and hung up the telephone and that gave them exactly seventy-two hours to fantasize.

Of course, somewhere in those seventy-two hours she had to figure out what she was going to wear, and she had to set aside a few of those hours to try on fourteen outfits so she would get it right. Because if a date was nothing else, it was an occasion. Still, there's no question that out of those seventy-two hours a goodly portion was preserved for pure, unadulterated fantasy.

Mind you, the girl didn't have to make the call in the old days, so she didn't have to go through the excruciating possibility of getting shot down. That was the man's job. On the other hand, she *did* have to go through the torture of waiting. Lots of times she booked off weekends and camped out by the telephone waiting for that call, and it never came.

Anyway, eventually Saturday rolled around and he came to pick her up. This is an important point: *he* always picked her up and *he* always drove. These were absolute, carved-in-stone certainties. Another certainty was that this was a date. She didn't have to spend hours on the phone with her girlfriends, picking apart the entrails of his invitation, trying to decipher some sign from the gods (as women often do with the vague invites they now receive) that this man was indeed asking her out on a date. She knew back then. She was going on a date, a date was an overture of courtship and, by accepting his invitation, she was also accepting its hidden romantic agenda. She was agreeing to experiment, however tentatively, with the possibilities of attraction, romance, lust, love, intimacy and attachment.

At any rate, he picked her up and if he had any grace at all he told her that she looked lovely, and if she had any charm at all she told him that he looked great too, and he opened the car door for her and she sensed a kind of towering, knightly presence about him and he caught an intoxicating whiff of her perfume and somehow the two of them got through those first few awkward minutes when they were trying to get the conversation into gear, and they made it to the restaurant, skating on the shiny promise of it all.

He knew what to do when they got there. He was courteous to the maître d' and he knew which wine to order and he told some witty stories (and so did she), and he also knew something about the art of conversation. He listened as much as he spoke and he held her gaze when she talked and he *always* laughed at her jokes. Not loud guffaws or anything. Just delighted, amused chuckles, enough to let her know that he found her bewitching.

That gave her the courage to flirt and he flirted back and at some point during dinner, or maybe when they got up to leave, he took her arm, just for a moment, and she didn't pull away because she'd been waiting for him to do that all evening, and when he did every nerve ending in her body started to fry. By this point neither he nor she had any doubts about how this date was proceeding, because it was obvious to both of them that it was going swimmingly.

She invited him in for a drink, of course. And maybe he stole up soundlessly behind her and made his move to kiss her when she was getting the drinks. Or maybe he was so shy that he waited until the last instant, while the two of them were lingering at the door, because for about an hour he'd been pretending to listen to her droll stories but he wasn't listening at all, he was doing the mental calculations, figuring out whether she was *really* holding his gaze just a little longer than was polite, whether she had *really* been telegraphing the subtle signals he thought she was telegraphing or whether he was just imagining them. Now they were at the door and this was his last chance, and because it was now or never, he went for it.

It was a sweet, lingering kiss, and when it was over she smiled at him and told him she'd been waiting for him to do that all night. And then they laughed and held each other for a moment, and he told her what a good time he'd had and she told him likewise, and he said he'd call her tomorrow and she had no doubt that he would, because it was once possible for a woman to take a man at his word about such things—a long time ago.

What Is a Date Like Now?
My telephone rings one night. It's a friend calling. She's in a bar, waiting to meet her date. It's two minutes past eight. He hasn't shown yet and she's right over the edge.

I try to calm her down. "Shut up for a minute," I say. "He'll show. When was he supposed to show?"

"At eight o'clock," she wails.

"Christ," I say, "give the guy a break. Even the parking garages give you three minutes' grace."

"Oh Gawd," she moans. "I hate dating. I can't bear the thought of all those stilted, boring, awful questions. I just want to get married and have children. Why do I have to go through this?"

═══════════════

If one were looking for a metaphor for the sexual discombobulation of the times, one would have to look no farther than the convention of the date. Dating, unfortunately, has turned from a mutually pleasurable ritual into an arduous chore. "Dating has been the rudest adjustment," said one woman just sprung from a long-term relationship. "It's like childbirth. You forget how awful it is until the next time.

"I think a formal date is the absolute worst way to meet someone," she went on. "It's so planned, so *faux*. The connotations and the ritual mean more than the event actually is. You can't assume any comfort level. You're stranded there across a table for three horrible hours, in heels that are killing you, telling someone you hardly know about your life.

"I'd much prefer something informal—tea in the afternoon, visiting a gallery together or staying in to watch a video. A date should just be a comfortable way to get to know someone, and under different circumstances it would be. But call it a date and rigor mortis sets in. We can't seem to relax with it. We start attaching all this *significance* to it. Two of my dearest male friends recently got divorced and we go out together for support. I keep telling them, you're going to have to date eventually, guys. You can't keep hanging around with me. But they're sick at the thought too."

Part of the problem—a huge part—is that dating is no longer dating. It's strategizing, plotting, second-guessing. What's more, many people are not altogether sure that what they're doing *is* dating—and those who are sure are tentative about admitting it. "People don't want to say they're dating anymore," one woman observed, "because it's like saying too much. It's too much of a commitment. So people say, 'Maybe we'll get together...maybe we'll go to a movie...maybe we'll have sex...but no, we're not committed in any way. We're not dating!' Once you lapse into the convention of the date and assume the roles, then you get nervous."

Furthermore, because the ritual has become imbued with so many uncertainties, a significant segment of the populace seems to have retreated to bed—alone—with a debilitating case of dating fatigue.

First, there is the complexity of all the overwhelming questions. On the philosophical level, you have to grapple with the following: what, exactly, "Let's have lunch" means; at what point a "date" actually begins; what the appropriate time lag is before you should call back for a second date; when "dating" stops and "seeing each other" begins; when "seeing each other" stops and "going together" begins; when "going together" stops and "involvement" begins; when "involvement" stops and you can actually admit to yourself, the other person and the general public that you like each other. It's a snake-pit.

One man in his late twenties was so confused about all this rigmarole that he said dating had become a "living hell."

"We need to standardize these things," he went on. "If we all knew that we'd sleep together on the third date, we could relax on the first two. If we could figure out the timing of pursuit.... Some women don't *want* to be pursued anymore. And how much do you reveal on the first date? I think I blew a date because I revealed too much. I think I got into stuff a little too much and she freaked out. And do I call after a date? When do I call? Also, there's a big difference, if you call, between a woman saying, 'Let's have lunch' and her saying, 'Let's go see a Saturday night movie.' A movie Saturday night is a date. Lunch, or a movie Sunday night, is a friendly encounter. Because these standard signposts are gone, there's all this second-guessing, and people are so damn wary. I suppose there are some codes and rituals evolving, but I sure don't know what they are."

On the purely practical level there's heavy-duty confusion about who is supposed to do the inviting and paying and the executing of the first kiss, about whether it's still all right to go all the way on the first date, and so on.

"There's this whole new thing about who drives on a date," one woman said. "It's getting to the point where you can't get a guy to pick you up anymore. When the Bay Bridge was down in San Francisco, after the 1989 earthquake, I'd get dropped off at a subway station somewhere in a bad neighborhood and I'd be thinking, could you just drive me two more blocks? Dare I ask? All this independence and worrying about true equality makes a date not feel like a date sometimes, and that's sad."

Dating fatigue is especially pronounced among those in their late thirties and forties, who are usually single again and struggling to learn the new ground rules after a long time sitting on the bench, or who have been unattached their whole lives and have been dating, by this point, upwards of twenty years. As Cathy Smith (convicted in the 1982 drug-overdose death of comedian John Belushi) told *Mirabella* in August 1989, "Dating is more stressful than prison." And one man in his mid-thirties who had been on more go-nowhere dates than he cared to remember was so burned out that he said he'd prefer to forget about dating altogether, send out a promotional video of himself and just say, "Call me if you're interested."

Although most people I met are catatonically depressed about dating, they are also mature enough to recognize that, as one man put it, "Dating is sort of like democracy: it's a flawed system, but the best one we've got." Nevertheless, they are almost unanimous in their desire for some basic dating and mating rules. What follows is a survey of dating codes as they seem to stand at the moment.

Who Is Supposed to Ask for the Date?

Of all the stratagems in the game of chess known as the contemporary date, none is as daunting as the first call. The problem is that nobody knows who's supposed to make it. Women are terrified that, if they take the lead, they'll be perceived as desperate or pushy, and men are terrified that, if *they* do, they'll be rejected; so the first call winds up getting short-circuited by the usual foolproof combination of cowardice, second-guessing and self-loathing.

Let me share with you the words of a litigation lawyer who spends her days in gladiatorial combat, but who would rather face the Supreme Court than ask a man out. "We already walk around like vulnerable creatures, thinking our legs aren't long enough, our thighs are too big," she says. "To have to put ourselves on the line and admit we find someone attractive is horrifying. I know men do it all the time, but they must get used to rejection, don't they?"

Since you ask, no—they don't. Almost every single man I interviewed said that the time has come to spread some of the dreaded rejection around. Most admitted to getting very nervous calling a girl for a date, even today, and said they would not only be delighted if a woman asked them out, they'd be relieved and flattered. "At least, if a woman calls, you know she wants to spend some time with you," one man said. "The other way, you have to guess. You call and she's busy—maybe legitimately busy—but you start thinking, 'Oh God, does this woman really want to go out with me?' If she asks you, it's pretty clear."

While a call from a woman, especially one they're not enthralled with, may catch them a little off guard—they are, after all, less schooled than women at knowing how to say no gracefully—most men say they'd respect her, at the very least, for trying. After all, who knows better than they do how awful it is to get the kiss-off? (Although women always believe otherwise, men claim it happens to them more than it bears thinking about.) They also say—surprise, surprise—that rejection isn't any easier to take at forty than it was at fifteen. "You wanna know what the biggest fear is?" asked one 44-year-old radio producer. "It's that you'll announce yourself on the telephone and she'll say, '*Who?*' Oh Gawd, that's the worst."

Often it's not so much what the woman says as the way in which she says it. Tone, men say, is all. "People get so stuck," one man said. "They forget to use their imaginations. I call a woman up and she says, 'Look, I can't see you. I have to work. I'm too busy.' All she would have to add is, 'But boy, am I going to make it up to you on Thursday.' Just by turning it around, you can do so much. It's amazing how rare that is."

Much as some women wish that guys would go back to making all the calls, I have it on the best authority that this isn't in the cards. If women insist on calling themselves *moderne*, they are going to have to start acting *moderne*. The reality is that some guys will simply never call, not necessarily because they don't want to, but because they just won't make a move until they get a clear signal. Unfortunately, many women no longer know how to send a clear signal—and many men are no longer able to recognize a clear signal unless it mud-wrestles them to the ground. So good old-fashioned inertia takes over and they crawl into bed to watch "Arsenio" instead.

Some women who simply can't bear the thought of over-the-telephone rejection are asking men out by dropping them notes—a gentler alternative, since it gives the guy a chance to reflect on how he wants to respond. Some women are even faxing letters of intent. In fact, in the age of high tech, the possibilities of flirting by fax, floppy or voice mail are limited only by one's imagination.

Generally speaking, men have accepted this who-makes-the-first-call role reversal with grace and equanimity; the only type who annoys them (as it always has women) is the pushy sort who won't take the hint that they're just not interested, and persists in trying to nail down a date in 2001.

It's the women who are having the most trouble adjusting on this point—and who can blame them? They had no idea, really, when they said they could do anything that men always had, how daunting asking someone out could be. So they play games with themselves to make the fear go away. They tell themselves that while men may *say* they want a woman to call, they're lying. That excuse lets them fudge their invitation to make it sound like something other than, well, you know, a date. They just happen to have tickets to the theater, they say, as if theater tickets magically show up in a woman's purse. They believe they're sparing the poor guy's feelings but what they're really doing is dissembling because fudging things is so much easier than admitting the truth. The fact is, by pretending they're not romantically interested, they can maintain their dignity if the guy says no.

Guys are hip to this tactic, however. They know what's going on. Or they're pretty sure. They never admit that they know, though, because that too would involve being honest, and being honest seems to fly in the face of every diversionary dating maneuver.

So the contemporary reality is that two people are out on a date, but no one will admit that a date is what they're out on. The woman may be sitting there secretly waiting for the man to make a move, to get some sexual energy cooking, because that's the guy's job, no? And the guy may be secretly interested in jumping her, but how can he make a move if he's not sure (or supposed to know) that this is a romantic encounter?

And so, because he's no longer sure what role he's expected to play, he plays it safe and doesn't play; he acts like a eunuch. And because no sophisticated woman wants to be perceived as overly aggressive, she doesn't make a move either. Consequently, all possibility of sex and romance gets lost in the ozone, and two people go home with dashed hopes. Then they spend the rest of the night trying to guess what was going on in the other person's mind and attempting to figure out a name for the puzzling social encounter they have just had.

Who Plans the Date?

Planning the date always used to be the man's job. It's not supposed to be his responsibility anymore, but according to many men it often still is. This is another duty, however, that most men would happily share. Since one gentleman summed this issue up succinctly, I'll let him give you the goods: "It's still largely incumbent on men to be the social generators of a date. If they've had a helluva long week, anything—even choosing a restaurant—is more pressure. Any help in that department would be gratefully appreciated."

Women say okay, fair enough, but they want guys to know why they tend to be reticent about suggesting plans. Sometimes they're not sure what kind of date the guy has in mind, and since guys are so nervous these days, they figure it's safer not to assume anything, let the guy lead, and take their cues from him. If the woman suggests dinner at her favorite restaurant, for instance, and the guy is only thinking drinks after work, then what if the guy backs off even before the date has begun?

Since trying to guess what's in the other person's mind is the surest way to have a nervous breakdown, I vote for open negotiation of this contract with both parties bargaining in good faith.

What's the Smartest Way to Approach a Date?

Men have it all over women in this department. They are far more sanguine about dating, far more comfortable with the idea of a date for a good time's sake (providing they know it *is* a date), and they have something valuable to teach the modern woman, I think, about the ritual. Rather than treating every date as a quest for The One, they view a date as an experiment in meeting someone new. And they recognize that some experiments are going to fail. Of course, men have more time on their hands, biologically speaking, to find The One, so they can relax, try to have a decent time and not set themselves up for repeated disappointment. What also keeps their spirits up through a so-so date, many confessed, is horniness. They're cheerful about tolerating more than they ordinarily would in the hopes of getting laid.

Where Do You Go on a First Date?

Whereas once a first date was often like a Busby Berkeley production—an expensive dinner Saturday night at an elegant restaurant—such is no longer the case. And that's because a fancy Saturday night dinner has "date" written all over it. Also, if the date turns out to be rank, Saturday night offers less of an out. One woman told *New York* magazine in 1987, "I spent twenty-five evenings with one guy before I even considered spending a Saturday with him. I mean, what are you going to say if the evening stinks? 'I have to get up early and go to Mass'?"

Most people I met said they'd much prefer an informal setting for a first date, because a first date is horrific enough and a formal setting just makes both participants *more* nervous. However, few people actually confess to their prospective dates that an informal get-together is what appeals to them most.

One man, for instance, told me that his idea of the perfect first date was inviting a woman over to his place, making some spaghetti and watching a video. When I told him that many of the women I met would kill for a casual, comfortable evening such as the one he'd just described, he was surprised.

"I'd never ask a woman I didn't know very well over to do that," he said. "I imagine she'd think I was cheap for not taking her out to dinner. And my television is in the bedroom so I think she'd feel I was trying to put the make on her."

What we have here is a common problem in the nineties: making gross leaps of logic based on sensitive and well-meaning (but faulty and confounding) assumptions about the other person's expectations. Suffering in silence is apparently far more satisfying than just being straightforward. I hate to keep harping on this theme, but has anybody considered blowing the roof off all this anxiety and just telling the truth? I know it's a dirty job, but *somebody's* got to do it.

What about Dating and Sexual Politics in the Kitchen?
Like almost every exchange between the sexes, culinary invitations are riddled with sexual politics. In fact, the simple kindness of offering a member of the opposite sex a home-cooked meal is so laced with subtext that it's dangerous for a man to ask a woman to

whip up an omelet (or for a woman to offer) without both parties first assessing the strategic imperatives.

Some men are nervous about requesting a culinary favor because they've found that many women lack the time or inclination to boil an egg. They're also afraid of encountering a knee-jerk feminist who thinks a request for a boiled egg represents a deeply misogynistic desire to enslave them. Oh sure, their thinking goes, today he wants a boiled egg, tomorrow he'll expect me to beat his boxer shorts on a rock.

Dare I say this sounds suspiciously like overreacting?

On the other hand, men must take some responsibility here too. First, a guy will whine that it wouldn't be so terrible, once in a while, for a woman to offer a man a humble repast. Then he'll meet a woman who takes him at his word, and he'll get the heebie-jeebies. Let's say she masters risotto or fusses with a stuffed leg of lamb. Oh no, he'll start thinking, she's got something up her sleeve. Her nesting hormones are in overdrive, she's acting like my "wifey" and she'll want something in return—like a relationship. Some men admit they start sinking so deeply into this pit of speculation that they can't even get the dinner down.

Of course, when the man is the one serving the dinner, a woman may fear he's got a hidden agenda too. She knows that any guy who hasn't been living under a rock is aware that, when a woman meets a man who can stickhandle a whisk, she'll go weak at the knees.

The only way for both sexes to unravel this tangle of suspicions is to lighten up and proffer and accept generous culinary gestures, because they're all too rare in the modern world. Then to clean up the kitchen—together—afterwards. I mean, bottom line, you're getting a free meal and perhaps a pleasant evening out of the deal, aren't you?

What about Sexual Politics on a Date?
Many women today feel it's their moral responsibility to berate a man mercilessly when he accidentally behaves in the way he was raised to behave. These are the women whose mission in life is to convert every man to politically correct purity. These are the women who really piss men off.

Here's a common scenario: a man and a woman go to a movie. He pays for the tickets, because he was taught that paying for the tickets is the gentlemanly thing to do. She assumes, however, that he's a sexist pig, and lectures him about the fact that she's an independent, self-supporting woman, capable, thank you very much, of paying for her own movie ticket.

This blah, blah, blah bores him. (The truth is, it bored me just hearing about it second hand.) First, he's heard this tiresome rap before; second, he's preoccupied trying to figure out why he's getting blasted for doing what he thought was the gentlemanly thing to do.

"I was out on a first date with a woman," one man said, "and a couple of times I referred to my secretary as 'my girl.' That word in that context really irritated her. But she didn't go for my balls. She sort of reached over, gently grabbed my arm and said, 'I've gotta tell you something...just humor me for a minute. I can tell you're not the sort of man who would ever treat anybody unkindly. I know that about you already. But that word really bugs me.'

"I knew I was being censured, but she did it in such a kind way, and it was so honest of her—especially on a first date—that I was quite amused. And so I asked her what I should say. And she said, sort of offhandedly, 'Well, "secretary" would be better than "girl," don't you think? How about saying secretary?'

"So for the rest of the night, every time I wanted to use the word 'girl' in any context, I sent her up and said 'secretary' instead. I told her, for instance—referring to my daughters—that I had two 'secretaries' who were six and eight years old. But when she realized I was teasing her she didn't get all uptight about it. She just laughed and was a good sport. So we got over what could have been an uncomfortable exchange around sexual politics, with tact and a sense of humor on her part and respect for her feelings and irreverence on mine.

"I think she handled the whole thing quite gracefully. She had something she felt was important to say and she said it, but she made her point in a nice way. She didn't wag her finger at me, the way so many women do, or give me an Attitude and say, 'Listen, pal, I've got something to tell ya...so try and *get* this, okay?'

"The other smart thing she did was let me strut a little, and a woman who knows how to do that is a woman who understands men. By accepting my teasing good-naturedly, she allowed me to vent any shame or anger I was feeling for having been censured. I got a couple of zingers in and that restored the feeling that I was back in charge. That way I could maintain my dignity.

"If you want to talk in terms of who 'won' that round, in fact she did, because she got me to change my behavior. Now whenever I'm apt to use 'girl' when referring to my secretary, I catch myself, because I remember being corrected so nicely on that date. By letting me crack a joke and pretend that I'd 'won,' however, she was magnanimous in victory, and that made all the difference."

What's Bad Form on a First Date?

Since so much second-guessing precedes the first bona fide date, by the time it actually happens there are two pretty paranoid people sucking back the Beaujolais. Which is why, if either party loads the first meeting with anything even remotely unnerving, it's going to get ugly. Cartoonist Lynda Barry observes that, if you're female, it's probably best not to put in too much time worrying about The Relationship before the first date. I'd add that if a woman is looking for a baby stud, it's probably unwise for her to make her date wonder if she's got a sperm-sample vial in her purse. "They get that *look* in their eyes," one man said, "that sizing-you-up look that seems to be asking, are you Daddy?"

Asking terrifyingly private questions on the first date, assuming an intimacy you haven't yet established or sitting there with a miserable look on your face all night is extremely bad form. One woman reported that a guy once told her that she'd be a decent-looking woman if she did something about the way she dressed. She excused herself from the table, hailed a cab and landed, a sobbing heap, on her girlfriend's doorstep. And a man recalled a hellish evening where his escort complained interminably about the table situation and service. "She made a huge fuss with the maître d', was officious and pompous with the waiter and whined to me all night. I couldn't wait to get out of there."

Coming on too strong sexually or performing a set piece about the slug who was your ex is also *verboten*. One man said that his date bad-mouthed her ex-husband so viciously through the entire meal, all he could think of was that she'd chew him up and spit him out next.

If you're out for the first time, do try and choose a venue with some privacy so you can get to know the person you're out with. One woman said she suffered through a dreadful first date with a guy who thought he was a hail-fellow-well-met and kept chatting up the diners at the adjacent tables. Not only did they find him insufferable, so did she. Another woman said a guy took her to his favorite Chinese restaurant on their first (and last) date. "It was a noisy, crowded hole-in-the-wall," she said, "and we had to share a table with other patrons. When you know someone a bit better, that's fine, but there we were trying to get through all that awkward first-date conversation, and the other people at the table were privy to all of it. It was excruciating!"

Finally, those who ogle comely specimens of the opposite sex, before either party feels comfortable in the other person's company, deserve to have their eyes gouged out with a salad fork. (Ogling is such a fun pastime for both sexes, however, that it's certainly permissible at a less vulnerable stage in the relationship.)

What Do Women Hate on a Date?

Numero uno on a woman's hate list is the dreaded egomaniac. The average woman will sit there smiling sweetly but fuming silently through a self-serving male monologue, to the point where she's repressing so much hostility that it travels up her spine and she feels as if the top of her head is going to blow off.

What women find irresistible in a man is an ability to listen and to feed back what he's heard. But to expect such grace in the art of conversation from certain men may be unrealistic. Psychologists have been busily documenting what they call the "gender communication gap," and the news from the academic front is this: there are still strong cultural expectations on women to function as repositories of tact, to speak more politely than men and to be especially careful to say "please" and "thank you"—while men get to say whatever they feel like saying. Consequently, women toil at conversation, asking far more questions than men, partly to stoke the conversation but also to stroke the male ego.

In their own defense, men argue that they're not aware they're hogging the conversation; they blather on because they're nervous. In attempting to impress a woman, to appear fascinating or devastatingly well informed—and to avoid those long, deadly silences—a guy's first impulse may be to shift into motor-mouth speed.

Another big turnoff for women is men who feel so panic-stricken about "commitment" that they think they must state their position unequivocally on the first date. This predictable little spiel fills women with so much bile, they feel like running to the ladies' room, where they can vent their hostility by shouting obscenities at the vanity mirror. One woman reported that she spent an enjoyable afternoon at the beach with a first date and then invited him home for late afternoon tea. This gesture of domesticity was more than he could handle. "I don't want a commitment, you know," he blurted out, as she set the tea tray before him. "I don't recall asking you for one," she replied, her voice oozing with contempt. The first date, needless to say, was the last.

What Do Men Hate on a Date?

The biggest drag for a guy in a casual dating situation is the woman who gives him the third degree. This woman is a very focused sort of woman who doesn't like to waste time. She believes she has a right to know her options right off the top, and because she's a problem-solver, she decides to find out what they are by interrogating a man about his long-term intentions. This she does, well before he has a clue what they're going to be.

One woman who'd dated a guy only three times began to read him selected passages from *Smart Women, Foolish Choices* on the telephone, singling him out as The Perpetual Adolescent and demanding to know where the "relationship" was "going." "Has it ever occurred to you," he asked sarcastically, "that maybe I don't want to commit to *you*?" As a seduction tactic, especially in the early days of courtship, this approach ranks on about the same level as the technique of the man who talks about himself all evening and then expects a goodnight blowjob.

Men can smell female desperation, and it makes them extremely uncomfortable. What female desperation signals to a man is that the woman across the table is interested not so much in him as in what he represents: the possibility of a man on her arm, a husband, a meal ticket or a pair of sperm-producing testicles. Such an attitude is not likely to give a man a stiffie. There are many good reasons why a woman might want to rethink her need to grill a man about commitment, but that's as good a one as any.

Who Picks Up the Check?

On the first date, anyway, most men still prefer to pay, and most women still want them to. (If the woman did the asking, she agrees that it's her tab and may insist on paying it, but views as gentleman-ly any guy who offers to split it.)

After the first date it gets murkier, because people have developed their own arcane systems of rules which they neglect to reveal to the other person. Many women now feel strongly that they should pay their own way. Others feel that if the guy makes more money, he should pay for the more expensive outings—period. After all, they argue, women absorb tons of hidden expenses in the dating situation: keeping bottles of scotch in the house, buying swordfish steaks to offer a home-cooked meal, throwing together gourmet picnics, dropping a fortune on garter belts. And most women still don't make half of what men do. So they feel splitting the tab down the middle, or picking it up every second time, is not exactly fair play.

One woman summed this argument up brutally in a He-Who-Has-the-Penis-Shall-Pay decree: "If I'm dating a guy who can afford to take me to dinner, I have no qualms about spending his money. If he can barely make ends meet, I'll split it. But there are just some things in life that men do and some that women do. I'm sorry but that's the way it is. *We* have to carry the baby and menstruate every month. If they can afford it, *they* can pay for the goddamn meal."

Women may be surprised to learn that many men still prefer to pay for the first several dates or more—not because they're controlling, macho louts but because they were, as one man put it, "raised to observe the niceties...and that's one of them. If a woman wants to go Dutch, she's going to have to instigate it, but it will make me nervous if she offers too soon. It removes a certain amount of romance that I, for one—and I suspect a lot of guys— might not want removed."

What it all comes down to is this: since you may have no way of knowing whether you're out with someone who has a highly evolved political position on the subject, you have to make up the rules as you go along. And the only way to do that is to ask.

One final word: If a woman is sharing the cost of the date, she deserves some say in the plans, so she doesn't get stuck with half of an exorbitant bill she may not be able to afford. And if a man gets saddled with a closet Cinderella who expects him to pay the whole shot every time, he deserves better.

How Do You Turn Down a Date?

One woman did say she had never turned down a date in her life, simply because "it takes such courage" for a man to ask a woman out. However, moral rectitude such as this is not only exceedingly rare, it comes with a martyr's price: "As a result," she said with a sigh, "I've gone out with some truly sick people." The overwhelming consensus among ordinary mortals seems to be that you lie. In dating, as in life, there are good lies and bad lies. This is a good lie.

The underlying assumption here is that it's tacky to humiliate the caller. Since you can't really tell people you think they're repulsive, the quickest, most painless way for both parties is to say you're going out with someone else. Offering an excuse with an open door, like "I'm really busy for the next few weeks...," simply prolongs the agony, as it's a cue for the caller to try—and be rejected—again. As one man observed, "Sure, women have to deal with rejection, but it's all so internal: Does he like me? Will he call? Guys' rejections are so external. I mean, how many times can her mother be in the hospital? How many wisdom teeth can she have left in her head, for Chrissakes?"

How Do You Survive a Blind Date?

"I don't have many rules in life," one woman told me, "but refusing to go on blind dates is one of them. I would rather die a lonely old maid." Despite the general dread of blind dates in the populace at large, they have become an increasingly popular option in these difficult-to-meet-the-opposite-sex days. You can write them off as hopeless acts of desperation, but that does limit your chances.

Several veterans of the blind date (male and female) have developed an idiosyncratic set of rules for embarking on one, born of hard experience:

1) *Do not necessarily assume your friends will fix you up with the man or woman of your dreams.*

"It's downright alarming to find out how your friends perceive you," one man told me. This means it's advisable to do some background work on blind dates, and not commit yourself without cross-checking references with two independent sources. Otherwise, you may set yourself up for an awkward evening with a horrible mismatch, an experience one man described as akin to "picking nettles with your bare hands." A few months into 1990, for instance, one man heard a pitch about a single woman who was "attractive, interesting and fun." Tired of being fixed up with women who were mentally limited, he pressed the matchmaker for more vital details. "Yeah," he asked, "but is she bright?" "Well, she's no intellectual," the friend replied, "but she's bright enough." "Let me put it this way," the date-weary skeptic sighed. "Would she know that Nelson Mandela has just been released?"

2) *On a cold call, do get the person's name right.*

"Hello, Joan...?" one guy bellowed into his speaker phone. When the callee responded coolly that her name was Joanne, the caller, rather than apologize, blustered on. "Oh well...Joan...Joanne...close enough." She wanted to stab him through the heart, and she hadn't even met him yet.

3) *Apply principles of time management and keep the date casual, casual, casual.*

If you're in a particularly reckless mood, you can agree to a full-fledged dinner on a blind date. A more prudent tactic, however, is to meet for a drink in a bar near a theater showing a movie you're dying to see. If the date is proceeding swimmingly, drinks can turn into dinner and the time will sail by. However, if two Nubians are required to carry the conversation, you can casually suggest catching a flick so the night isn't a total write-off.

Late-afternoon dates, by the way, are another option. If things don't look promising (which both parties usually sense in the first fifteen minutes), a couple of hours in the company of a person who is nice (but not for you) are certainly tolerable. If that person is *not nice* (and not for you) two hours can seem like an eternity, but at least you can use the credible excuse of later plans once you've put in your time. And since almost everybody I met prefers a casual first date, baseball games (or other sporting events) are highly popular; you get to talk, but (unlike a dinner date) you don't have to kill yourself feigning fascination with your date's every word—you're legitimately allowed breaks to watch the game.

4) *Keep your sense of humor on a blind date that involves the company of others.*

The situation is already fraught with enough perils and pressures. If you subject yourself to the microscopic and prurient interest of friends, they may help to quell your terror, but they may also elbow you every five minutes to see how it's going.

5) *Arrive with your own transportation, or the means to pay for it in an emergency.*

One woman's escort excused himself to the washroom in the middle of a date and never returned, leaving her not only humiliated but stuck with the check. Penniless and paralyzed with embarrassment, she sat miserably at the table. Finally she burst into tears and admitted what had happened to the maître d'; that honorable gentleman restored her faith in men by cancelling the bill and putting her in a cab at his expense.

Who's Supposed to Plant the First Kiss?

Sooner or later, if a date is indeed a date, sex is going to rear its sweaty little head and stare the couple unswervingly in the eyes. Of course, it's been in the air all along. "Sex just hangs over a date so heavily," one woman observed. "You're both wondering about the big question, only you're dancing around it. You're supposed to act as if you're overcome by the moment—as if, the moment he makes his move to kiss you, that's the first time the thought of sex has entered your head. But you've been thinking about it all night. And so has he."

The possibility of sex makes its first unequivocal stand at the moment of the first kiss. But even that moment has become politically loaded. If women are supposed to share all the other dating duties these days, who's to say that they shouldn't be lurching across the couch at their escorts too?

One embarrassed man confessed that the one and only time a woman made the move to kiss him first, he was so shocked he reared back in horror. It wasn't that he didn't want a kiss, he said, or even that he objected to her executing it; it was just a surprising new experience, and it threw him. If it threw him, it doesn't even bear thinking about how his poor date must have felt, having screwed up her courage to seize the moment only to have it blow up in her face.

One brave (and now undoubtedly broken-spirited) woman notwithstanding, most women are still nowhere near the point of being able to execute the first kiss. They know that in theory they are perfectly within their rights to do so; in practice, however, it's usually out of the question, because they were raised to defer to men in this situation (just as men were raised to accommodate them). Also, the moment of the first kiss is so embedded in the female archetypal imagination as the moment when a gallant prince claims his prize that the breathtakingly dull equality of reversing the gesture strips it of its eroticism.

Should a Man Say He'll Call If He Doesn't Intend To?

No no no, say women en masse, voices raised in an exasperated chorus. What for men is a flip remark tossed off at evening's end is for women the cruel fraud of a fiend from hell. Let's kill the beast, they cry. Wring his neck. This drives us *craaaazy*! Not to mention it wreaks havoc in our lives. We know we're supposed to be above this sort of thing by now, but we're not. We wait by the phone, jump every time it rings, rearrange our days in expectation of The Call. We stare at the phone, take it off the hook when we take a shower, wonder if there's trouble on the line, hear the taunting dial tone, then smash the receiver down lest Himself is, at that very instant, hitting the final digit. *Rrring*. Stay calm now, let it ring at least twice. *Rrring*. Answer nonchalantly. But it's only a girlfriend wanting to know, "Has he called?" Women know that when a man says he'll call he could be lying, and that when he says, "I'll talk to you," he's lying for sure. But they wish men would just say, "Thanks, had a lovely evening." That lie they can take; all they want to know is whether he's on or off the list.

Men admit that saying "I'll call" is the coward's way out, but they feel a need to fill the dead air at the end of a date. Lacking a more gracious exit line, they rely on this fail-safe ruse. That way they spare the woman's feelings, right? They don't get any points deducted, they avoid a "scene" and they still get to look like gentlemen. In the male lexicon, "I'll call" is a good lie, equivalent to the popular female lie "I'm seeing someone else."

Saying "I'll call" serves another, more subtle male purpose as well: maintaining a certain amount of ambiguity. "You tend to want to leave things vague," said one man, "because otherwise, it becomes an obligation. You start feeling the pressure to call, and then the guilt sets in, and once that happens, forget it. The other thing going on here, too, is that when that exchange is made, you're both at a high. Maybe you just want to pay a compliment to the woman and so you say, 'Hey, let's talk again,' or whatever. You *intend* to follow through when you say it. You really do. But the moment passes and the next day comes, and fear takes over. I would say that most men who come on strong and then don't call do so because in the cold light of morning they think they imagined the woman's interest. And I think many men are even more sensitive than women about the possibility of rejection. So fear of rejection is probably the number-one reason for not calling back; fear of not feeling the same way if you do call back is number two. That's why, if a man does make the call, the tonality of a woman's voice is very important. Some voices are very sexy on the phone, and reverie is part of this game. You want to imagine the goddess."

Really? say women. We thought you did it because you were swine, and now it turns out that you're scared and vulnerable just like us. Who knew? Still, the fact remains that if you tell a woman that you'll call, she'll wait for that call. So if a man has said he'll phone, then the gracious thing for him to do is to keep his word. If he's not planning to, then a simple thank you will suffice.

Is It Advisable to Tell Someone That You Like Them?

I know this is going to sound bizarre, but if you actually like someone, and are maybe even toying with the idea of loving them, it's probably a good idea to say so; conversely, if you'd prefer to take a hike, it's probably a good idea to say why. "Tell the truth?" I hear you ask. "My, what a novel idea!"

Perhaps so, but making the other person guess what you're feeling (i.e. playing it cool) is really a dumb-ass thing to do—and that way lies madness.

Women are loath to admit that they like a guy because, in their experience, it makes guys freak out. One woman insisted that five guys broke dates with her when she told them she liked them.

If this does indeed happen, as it no doubt does, the woman may wish to ask herself a simple question: why on earth would she be interested in a man who can't stand to be told that he's liked?

For the guy who dares to admit that he's stuck on a woman, there are many rewards. One man who'd had a first date called her the next day to say what fun he'd had, and how much he'd been thinking about her. "I nearly fainted," she said. "It's so unusual for a man to do that. I had a great time too and I was praying he'd call, but I didn't want to let myself count on a call because you never know. You can go out and you can think you're both having a great time and then the guy never calls back. He was so forthright about his feelings, though, and he made me feel so appreciated, that his honesty gave me the courage to do something I'd never have done if he'd played it cool. He started talking about his week and he said he had to fly to Chicago the following weekend on business. Completely spontaneously—the words just popped out, really—I asked him if he wanted some company.

"He said in this little kid's voice, 'You mean, you'd come *with* me?' and I started to laugh because he sounded genuinely excited. There was absolutely no bullshit going on.

"I've never done anything like that in my life—invited myself along on a weekend with a guy. You don't do that sort of thing these days—most men would think you were pushy and run the other way so fast. But I think the important point in all this is that I *never* would have done it unless I felt absolutely certain that my offer was going to be well received. And I did feel certain, because he made no secret of how he felt about me! We had a great weekend, we've been together for nine months and we're very much in love. We're sort of like an old married couple already, and I mean that in the best possible way. He's always been very open about his feelings—partly because it's his nature, but also because I encourage him to be—even when he knows some of those feelings may be threatening for me to hear. And I'm always allowed to be very open about mine. We've never gone through any of that game-playing stuff where you have to hold your cards close to your vest. Other than the fact that we're extremely compatible, I would have to say that's the main reason that we've been able to come so far so fast."

What about the Transitional Relationship?

To the man or woman who has just been burned, the transitional relationship is a welcome elixir. It's the first real relationship you experience after your heart has been chopped up in little pieces by the Cuisinart of love. The transitional relationship is a trial run, where you actually dare to expose yourself to a soupçon of emotional danger.

Unfortunately it's rare that two people want a transitional relationship at the same time. Usually what happens is that one person has already done the suffering-and-rebirth number, while the other person is just going through it and is therefore needy, defenseless and into some serious self-flagellation. Usually, the already healed person (A) expends a great deal of energy nurturing the recently bludgeoned person (B) back to a state of emotional equanimity, in the hopes that when B gets better, the two of them will live happily ever after. What happens, however, is that B feels perky again, drops ten pounds, dumps A and sets off in search of a little adventure.

The thing to remember about the transitional relationship is that it has a limited shelf life. Once it has served its purpose for the transisher, it ends, and the nurturer gets handed walking papers.

How Do You End a Relationship?
Since breaking up is so hard to do, in *Healing Visualizations: Creating Health Through Imagery*, Gerald Epstein, M.D., suggests you try a visualization exercise to end a relationship and get on with your life. What you're supposed to do is close your eyes, breathe in and out three times and imagine yourself on a beach. The person you're trying to dump is lying there and you're carrying golden ropes with lead weights at the end. With these, you truss up your "friend," put him or her in a large rowboat nearby and row out to the Mariana Trench off the Philippines, one of the deepest spots in the world. Then you're supposed to stand up in the boat, lift your "friend's" trussed-up body and toss it overboard, knowing that you're ridding yourself of that person's hold over you. Next you watch the body disappear as it sinks and forms a small whirlpool, so you're secure in the knowledge that it won't ever resurface. After it's been swallowed up by the deep blue sea, you sit down in the boat and row back to shore with a new feeling about yourself, stow the oars, beach the boat and saunter home alone.

I can't comment on the advisability of Dr. Epstein's method, since I didn't meet anybody who'd tried it. I can however recommend therapy with a decent shrink so you can figure out why you're wasting your time with somebody who's making you so miserable. I met lots of people who'd found the courage to leave a lousy relationship by seeking therapy, and I also met some who'd found the courage by making sure they had someone else to hook up with before they checked out. I vote for the former solution, since the latter can get pretty messy, and because the experts say you're asking for trouble if you begin a new relationship before you figure out why the last one screwed up so badly.

What Are the Ethics of Dumping Someone?

Writing about the ethics of dumping someone is a tricky matter because, basically, there are none. Getting dumped is painful, demoralizing and awful. There's no chipper way to give someone the heave-ho, especially if you're unloading them for someone else with better tits, a fuller head of hair or a summer place by the ocean. All you can do is leave the dumpee with some semblance of dignity by making the break a clean one and allowing that person a reasonable length of time to have deeply satisfying revenge fantasies, in which you die a lonely, pathetic soul who realized too late that you blew the best thing that ever happened in your pitiful little life. Once this necessary healing period has passed, you can call, suggest having drinks and attempt to build, from the remains of a love affair, a warm and lasting friendship.

There are two ways to deal with the emotional burnout that comes from having had one too many dead-end love affairs. One is to give up, stay home, pull the duvet over your head, never go out, and play with yourself for the rest of your life. The other is to take a few calculated emotional risks with a new person, keep your eyes and ears open and stay tuned to what's going on. If that person proves to be unworthy of your love, then chalk it up to experience, dump him or her and move on. Falling in love involves risk, openness, trust and hope. Sorry, kids, but even in middle age there's no other way to do it.

What Is the Role of the Bimbo or Boy-Toy?

Sometimes a beaten, broke, busted, beleaguered person—often but by no means exclusively of the male persuasion—requires a longer period of healing before he can risk vulnerability and even think of getting serious. He goes through a transitional period, as opposed to a transitional relationship, and during this period he will fuck anything that moves, particularly anything younger, firmer of flesh and dimmer of mind. This period can last anywhere from several months to several years, depending on the man and his mental state.

Not all men go through a bimbo phase (many, in fact, are bemused by those who do), and most men who do go through it get through it. The bimbo phase does come highly recommended by some men, however, as a charming and necessary interlude. After the trauma of a breakup, an "eye candy" girl (as men lovingly call her) may be just what the doctor ordered, even for the most intelligent, sophisticated man. At such times, a man doesn't want any more aggravation. He needs to feel virile and manly, and bimbos are experts, it seems, at making him feel just that.

One man wryly told a columnist for *Chicago* magazine that bimbos were appealing because there was no pressure of accountability with them. "Sometimes they believe everything you tell them," he said, "unlike these *moderne* women who feel they have the right to ask a follow-up question or two." "It's like getting a new car every week," another man told me. "You can take her out, show her off, play with all the bells and whistles, but when she starts to act up you trade her in." Yet a third man told me that the envy factor is one of the bimbo's chief attractions. "You can't imagine the ego rush of walking into a room and watching every man's head turn," he said. "And the fact that she's in public with you trumpets the message that she's also probably sharing your bed. You can practically taste the envy."

Being a woman, I took a while to comprehend how such intelligent men managed to stave off boredom, hanging out, as they did, with women who were clearly no intellectual match for them. So I asked what they found to talk about with women whose charms were mostly physical. To a one, they stared at me as if I'd just asked the most idiotic question imaginable.

"You don't *talk*," they said.

Women have their own equivalent of the bimbo phase. When they need a little ego boost, they tend, like men, to shut off the more discriminating compartments of their brains and think with their nether regions only. (Generally speaking, men don't suspect that women are capable of thinking with their genitals, but they are. They're just more discreet about parading their playthings in public.) At such times women are inclined to lollygag about with brooding, Sean Penn–type boy-toys. Like Lady Chatterley's lover, these guys usually arrive and leave by the back door.

Women seem to get bored with their playmates faster than men do, and over the long term have more difficulty in putting up with the IQ of a plant just for the sex. A moment usually arrives at which even incredible sex is no longer enough to sustain the insubstantial liaison. This is the point one woman referred to as the "Down, Sybil" moment. (*Sybil* was a widely read book about a girl whose multiple personalities competed for dominance.) The "Down, Sybil" moment is the instant when illusions fall away and a woman's cool reasoning faculties reassert their mastery. Usually this happens when the boy-toy says or does something profoundly and jarringly indicative of the fact that he is an unsuitable mate. This incident precipitates a complete mental turnoff, and the woman can no longer delude herself into carrying on a relationship that she now realizes hasn't got a hope in hell of working.

For one woman who was dating a man eight years her junior, this moment came when he gazed longingly into her eyes and said, "Do you want to know what's the best thing about you?" Certain he was poised to wax lyrical about her charms, she gazed dreamily back at him and asked him, "What?".

"You saw Jimi Hendrix perform *live*," he answered.

"I know he thought he was giving me the supreme compliment," she told me, "but it just made me feel old, and that was the end. He might as well have said, 'Wow, tell me what it was like to be there on D-Day!' "

What about the Commitment Question and Ultimatums?

Eventually, in any relationship of substance, a man and woman may have to confront the fact that one wants more from the relationship than the other is prepared to give. This is the point at which the relationship either progresses to the next level (commitment) or ends in pain.

Over the centuries, women have believed that the best way to get a commitment from a man is to up the ante and jolt him a little. So, they invented The Ultimatum. The Ultimatum usually involves telling him, in a firm voice, that he has two choices: the first is to do what the woman wants; the second is to lose her altogether.

The Ultimatum, women often believe, will force a man to stop pussyfooting around and make up his mind. In fact, all an ultimatum will do is back him into a corner, where he'll feel powerless and his penis will feel puny. What the modern woman tends to forget is that there's already more than enough going down between men and women to make a man's penis shrivel. Faced with an ultimatum, the modern man really has only one option: he must regain a sense of power, a sense of manliness. The only way to do that is to refuse the woman what she wants. Consequently, it's a law of nature that a woman who gives a man an ultimatum is a woman who stands to lose big.

A far more mature way to encourage commitment—not to mention the possibility that he will come crawling back on his knees—is to send him sadly but sweetly on his way, wishing him luck in all his future endeavors. That has the advantage of leaving the door open. Maybe he'll come back and maybe he won't, but at least, if he chooses to come back, his pride won't be in the way.

"I'm dating a woman right now," one man said, "and she knows just how to handle me. I told her I didn't want to date her exclusively and she said, 'Go, do what you have to do.' She's giving me some time and room to decide whether I want to commit to her. I think that's called maturity."

5. Sexual Etiquette for the Nineties

LET'S SAY, FOR ARGUMENT'S SAKE, THAT GIRL MEETS BOY AND BOY MEETS girl. Let's also say that they manage to hack their way through the thicket of confusions surrounding dating and mating, and arrive at the sunny destination of the bedroom door. If one takes a strictly logistical approach, enjoying exemplary orgasms and sublime sex *should* be a cinch for them, because now there is more hard data around about the mechanics of the act than ever before. Kinsey, in the forties and fifties, was the first to illuminate the dark cave of human sexuality; by the sixties, Masters and Johnson were herding volunteers into the lab, and probing them in flagrante. By the late seventies, one researcher had managed, with the aid of computer technology, to document thirteen variables of the less ballyhooed male orgasm. Volunteers wore masks to collect expired air and humped away with ECG electrode wires and blood-pressure cuffs attached to their bodies. When they felt a Big One coming on, they pushed a button to signal its start. Post-coitally, they filled out questionnaires revealing, presumably, whether it had been good for them. Since that time, there has been a veritable explosion in sex research—or sexology, as the discipline is called—with the instrumentation growing more sophisticated, the knowledge more minutely detailed, by the minute.

In the fifties only two words were in common currency for sexual inadequacies—"frigidity" and "impotence." Since then the terminology has grown formidably complex, and there is now an infinite variety of jargon for things that can screw up. We can be PEs (premature ejaculators) or NPEs (non-premature ejaculators); we can suffer retarded ejaculation, retrograde ejaculation, post-partum vaginal apathy, inhibited sexual desire, anorgasmia, dysfunction, sexual addiction and so on. Thanks to the women's movement, female orgasms now come in deluxe models and neon-bright hues, and one has only to switch on Phil Donahue to get a fast-breaking news update on orgasm quality control. As well, because of AIDS, the craving for information about what is now safe in the bedroom has given previously *verboten* subjects a high profile: "On 'Donahue'," the talk show host was quoted in *Glamour* in 1988, "we're discussing body cavities and membranes and anal sex and vaginal lesions. We've discussed the consequences of a woman's swallowing her partner's semen. No way would we have brought that up five years ago. It's the kind of thing that makes a lot of people gag."

Once the province of stuffy medical textbooks, sex advice has gone public in a big way. Throughout the eighties, "Dr. Ruth" Westheimer fielded "anguished queries" and dispensed no-nonsense sex advice on talk radio, *Time* reported, to Debbie from Manitoba, whose low clitoral sensitivity was a matter of some concern; to Marvin of Hackensack, whose penis swivelled to the left; and to Elsi of Batavia, who couldn't achieve the Big O unless there was a chimp in the room.

In fact, by the mid-eighties Dr. Ruth (who evoked the cosy charm of a chicken–soup–toting Jewish grandma) was a North

American star. She had a book, *Dr. Ruth's Guide to Good Sex*, a hit nationwide radio call-in show which reached hundreds of thousands of listeners, and a cable TV program airing six nights a week.

According to *Time*, "You could spend a decade peering into the neighbors' bedroom windows and not get half the kick of a Westheimer show.... Who else would tackle the tough question of whether a devout Catholic like Bruce from Dubuque shows disrespect for his church by doing it dressed as a nun? These are the very issues they duck all the time on 'Face the Nation' and 'Meet the Press.'"

Dr. Ruth and her ilk are fighting the good fight: frank sex advice has never been more accessible. But the fact remains that men and women are still having immense difficulty getting it on.

Part of the problem is the form much of the information takes. Some of it comes in those scientifically valuable but ghastly clinical treatises that make your eyes glaze over—where you can look up things like uterine-elevation reaction, if you actually really care about such matters. Some of it comes in breezy, step-by-step how-to manuals implying that you can repair a complex sexual malady merely by treating the exercise as a merry task of togetherness—like wallpapering the baby's room. Also, because it's far easier to quantify orgasms than to measure the mysterious rhythms, shadings and flavors of love, precious little useful information exists to guide people on the psychic, spiritual or emotional side of sex—which many say is the area where they need most guidance right now.

Furthermore, this glut of technical advice has made the subject so massive, so intimidatingly complex, that the bedroom has become less a haven of respite than a pressure-cooker. Once all a woman had to do was lie back and think of England—and a man had only to pump away; suddenly the subject of sex is as big as the universe. So obsessed is everybody on getting the earth to move, they've forgotten how to relax and enjoy the scenery. Although the human race managed to muddle through for a couple of million years, scarcely giving a thought to how its genitals worked, people are now examining them with microscopic precision.

For instance, now that we have an official standard by which to measure orgasms, many people are developing troubling cases of orgasm angst. Are their orgasms, they fret, keeping up with the Joneses'? In Wendy Wasserstein's hit Broadway play, *The Heidi Chronicles*, one of the characters laments the burden of responsibility that such knowledge places on the women of her generation, who were raised functionally illiterate about the big O: "We grew up on fuckin' 'Father Knows Best,' " she moans. "You think Jane Wyatt demanded clitoral stimulation from Robert Young?"

Sex has moved so far so fast in the last ten years that even a story about a guy who likes to do it dressed as a nun seems tame. As the millennium hurtles toward its conclusion, the air is rife with a let's-take-sex-to-the-limit quality. The nagging question on the collective prurient mind is, how far can sex be pushed? How big, hard, long, deep, wide is it? Can you give or get more pleasure by putting a condom on a front-end loader?

You can now turn on the TV at any moment and see sitcom moms snickering about oral sex. You can see Madonna writhing in masturbatory ecstasy on stage; you can hear rap singers retching into microphones about sleazy sex. You can tune in late-night TV in New York and watch cooers and panters hustling gourmet-variety telephone sex. (Call 970-PISS, 970-BIG1.) You can buy porn where Everyman's sexual acrobatics are communal property: in one magazine a guy wrote in to say he'd figured out how to give himself a blowjob.

In New York and Los Angeles, kinky sex is the fashionable spectator sport. In Los Angeles' Club Fuck, for instance, you can watch a scantily clad woman moaning in ecstatic anguish while a man in leathers brandishing a riding crop pours molten candle wax on her belly. In New York's underground sex clubs, you can pay to see gangbangs, dirty-talking contests, fetish balls, striptahons and performances by the likes of Chi Chi, who can blow smoke rings out of her vagina.

For many men and women who don't necessarily frequent underground sex clubs but who like to think of themselves as in tune with the times, the knowledge of what some people are doing for sexual kicks raises disconcerting questions. If Rob Lowe is shooting videos of himself having it off with nubile young lovelies and *they* are using the camcorder only to record the kids leaving for camp, how boringly conventional does that make them? If it's true, as they've heard whispered, that now even accountants are peeing on each other to get off in bed, how sexually mundane—or even prudish—are they if they want to pee only in the toilet?

Indeed, the question I was most often asked during the writing of this book was "What's the weirdest thing you've found?" On one level that question is just healthy prurient interest; however, I often sensed that the question was more than mere curiosity. An evaluation of how weirdly people are behaving in bed depends a whole lot on your definition of "weird." That fact, however, seemed beside the point to almost everyone who asked. People crave some contemporary definition of "weird"—a standard, a norm, a comforting bell curve—to plot their own sexual proclivities against. Where, they wonder nervously, do *they* stand on the scale from bland sexual conventionality to kinky perversity?

It's been widely touted that one of the major reasons— if not *the* major reason—for the sexual nervousness of the day is AIDS; the boom in sex advice and the trend to push sex to the edge, however, have both played a critical role in promoting widespread sexual unease. Add to this scenario the ongoing problem that dating and mating rules are in a disquieting state of flux, and it's clear why—as huge a problem as AIDS is—the sexual angst is being propelled by a complex combination of factors, some of which are even more troubling to heterosexual men and women, in a day-to-day way, than AIDS.

In fact, the more people I spoke to, the clearer it became that, even by the end of 1991, AIDS was still largely an abstraction for most heterosexuals. (Basketball star Magic Johnson's announcement in November 1991 that he was retiring from the L.A. Lakers because he had contracted HIV was a stunning jolt to many heterosexuals who believed the disease was somebody else's problem; it remains to be seen, however, whether Johnson's courageous revelation and efforts to promote AIDS awareness will encourage more of them to engage in safe sex.)

People know about AIDS, of course, and they worry about what it can do to them. But they know about it in the same way that a teenager understands the lethal combination of drinking and driving, but still decides to take a risk.

On the other hand, the sexual tensions and contradictions people face wherever they turn are enormously confusing for them. At the same time as they are being goaded to test the limits of their sexuality, and encouraged to sample an exotic sexual buffet, they're being warned about the dangers of indulging, and abandoned to partake lacking clear rules of sexual etiquette with which to comfortably comport themselves.

AIDS isn't stopping the people I met from having sex. Often it isn't persuading them to have protected sex. And it's certainly not preventing them from falling in love. What AIDS *has* done— unquestionably—is complicated the already loaded exchanges they're having in, and on the way to, the bedroom. What follows is a survey of what's worrying people most in the bedroom these days, and the inventive solutions they're finding to cope.

What If My Partner or I Have Sores or Cooties Down There?
With predictions that approximately 33,000 new cases of sexually transmitted diseases (STDs) will arise in the United States *each day*, necessity has mothered some bizarre inventions. One perhaps overly cautious gentleman did resort to two condoms and a Band-Aid when his herpes was acting up, but that was an isolated event. Telling a prospective partner that you have something yucky down there is unquestionably the best policy, but this approach may lead to some dreadful situations, so it's best to approach the moment of truth with a sense of humor.

One woman who hadn't had sex in months reported that she was poised for a first roll in the hay with a guy she found exceedingly sexy when he declared that there was something he had to tell her. Since his tone was ominous, she feared he'd had his parts shot off in a war. Please God, she prayed, let him have a dick. As it turned out, it was just herpes. (In the light of what AIDS can do to you, herpes is now way down the list of life's worries.) To make sure the herpes was currently inactive, he got up and began inspecting his equipment from every conceivable angle, under the hall light. "I don't know how we ever managed to get it on after that," she giggled, "but we did."

By far the majority of people do sincerely appreciate up-front honesty about STDs, and react sensitively to the news. There is, however, the odd exception. As they were leaving the restaurant to go home together, one woman told her date that she had herpes. He excused himself politely, on the pretext of using the restaurant washroom, and bolted out the back exit. "I kept thinking how tasteful and up to date it was to announce it right up front like that," the gentleman later admitted, shamefacedly, "and I wish I'd been rational enough to go, 'No problem—that's fine, I'm sure if we take the right precautions....' But I dealt with it completely irrationally, and ran. This person observed every single positive rule of etiquette. It was all very proper—I was told in a dulcet-toned liberal fashion, in a sober moment, to give me a chance to back out. And back out I fucking did. I'm not big on sores, you see."

Since the gentleman above knows only too well that he acted like a slimeball, I'm not going to belabor the point. Suffice it to say that if someone is honest, brave, moral and courteous enough to tell you they have icky, oozing sores on their privates, the very least you can do is feel for them and whip out a condom—or say you'll be happy to settle for affection till the sores are gone.

Who Brings the Condoms?

While the prospect of becoming infected with an evil virus has spooked people, and more are buying condoms, there is still a casual attitude toward using them—and there's evidence of an increasingly lax attitude toward buying them, too. In 1987—the year AIDS paranoia peaked in the media—condom sales jumped astronomically. After that, sales grew at a modest 3 to 5 percent per year. (Magic Johnson's announcement, manufacturers predict, will probably kickstart sales again, but whether people will continue to take the issue seriously is anybody's guess.)

Women are usually the ones to bring up the subject, just as they have traditionally been the ones to worry about birth control. Since it's more likely that a woman will contract the AIDS virus from a man than vice versa, it's not surprising that women are taking the whole issue more seriously. In 1988, industry estimates indicated that women represented some 40 percent of the $200-million

American condom market. Gambling on the assumption that boys will be boys while girls will attend to the pragmatic details, manufacturers launched a full-frontal attack on the female market, producing whisper-thin condoms, rose–petal–embossed condoms, mint-flavored condoms and condoms in tasteful carrying cases. What's more, because oral sex devotees whined about the taste of latex, manufacturers developed condoms in as many flavors as Baskin-Robbins. Cinnamon, licorice and chocolate, market research indicates, are the preferred choices.

On the subject of who should carry the condoms, there is mixed opinion. "I always think the guy should bring the condom," said one man, whose sense of chivalry is clearly not dead. "Girls brought the diaphragm and the pill, didn't they? So guys bring the condom. It just seems to make sense. Protect your own organ." And some women fear that if they stockpile condoms, their partners will think they've been presumptuous about expecting to have sex. "Sure it's presumptuous," the same man went on, "but presumption in sexuality is flattering, don't you think? I mean, she brought one, it's so nice. I feel targeted."

However, timing is all. One woman on a first date at a swank restaurant chose the moment when the brandies were being brought to reach across the table and press two condoms into her date's hand. Not only did he find this gesture outrageously forward on a first meeting, the fact that she handed over *two* inspired performance anxiety.

Women are less than thrilled about making the trek to the drugstore. First, it annoys them that many men are still acting like pouty little boys about using condoms. Second, they figure some things should still be the man's job. Do they ask guys to buy the foam? But somebody has to do it, and so there they stand, perusing the bewildering array of options: lambskin, lubricated, nonlubri-cated, vibra-ribbed...*do they need this?*

Having managed the daunting task of getting the condoms home, some of them invite their girlfriends over to practice appli-cation techniques—and unfurl them on cucumbers! When faced with the specter of an actual blood-engorged member, however, these same women sometimes develop condom-amnesia, and the rubber languishes in the night-table drawer. If they do muster the courage to have The Talk, often it's after the fact; having The Talk beforehand, the thinking goes, will ruin the mood.

"No, I don't practice safe sex," one woman said. "I absolutely hate condoms and sometimes I think I'd rather not bother. The two men I've slept with in the last year tell me it's been a year since they've slept with anybody, and I believe them. I always rationalize it to myself afterwards, and I feel guilty and I definitely think about it, but I don't follow through.

"I think about contacts I've had, for instance. In 1985 I slept with a guy in a rock band from New York. I mean, come on, that's not a particularly conservative lifestyle! And I slept with a guy I met at a film festival, who'd had several affairs. A good gay friend of mine tested HIV positive a few years ago, so AIDS has even affected my life. It's not as if it's beyond my ken.

"I've brought up the question of condoms several times, but if I do raise the issue, I'm likely to raise it after we've made love, not before. I say, 'Don't you think we should be practicing safe sex?' And the reaction I get is usually a look that suggests *I* have something to hide. The implication is, *I* haven't been anywhere to worry about. Where have *you* been?

"We've all bought into this idea of being swept away on a tide of passion. It's taboo to interrupt sex with mundane concerns. You're supposed to be overwhelmed. So you just switch off the rational part of you. I play games with myself—okay, so this time I'm being bad, but next time I'll be good. When I was in university I did a paper on teenage pregnancy and there are very similar behavior patterns. Teenagers don't use birth control because they don't want to spoil the idea of romance. If they plan ahead, then they feel guilty because they're acknowledging that they're going to have sex. So they don't. Then they can tell themselves it 'just happened.' "

The perverse irony of this logic is that both parties may actually be *waiting* for the other person to produce the condom, and might be relieved to have the issue dealt with. Another irony is that each party has been strategizing like mad to get to the bedroom in the first place, has had to interrupt proceedings to go upstairs, take a pee, turn off the lights, get undressed, wrestle with a birth control contraption and/or spray the sperm-killer. Let's face it: sex is often logistics-heavy, and sometimes the logistics are going to intrude or break down—a situation which usually causes both parties to fall out of bed laughing, as happened when one guy lost his condom up his date and the two of them had to go on a "search and destroy mission" looking for it.

To be sure, no men or women told me they love using condoms, but the handful of people I met who are scrupulous about using them say they've adjusted comfortably, don't feel cheated in bed and don't understand what the big fuss is about. Women report that, if asked, most men are willing to go along with using one, although they sometimes whine. They say (and I quote), "Wearing a condom is like slapping down a perfectly cooked steak and then shooting your mouth full of Novocaine," or "Call me picky, but I happen to like the way a penis feels inside a vagina." One man said he won't use protection because "I can get it up in a condom but I just can't come." A few men declare that they hate condoms so much, if they have to use one, they'd rather just forget about sex.

In some cases those gentlemen get their wish, because more and more women are simply barring the door to them. If a guy whines, he's history. One 44-year-old San Francisco woman who said she could count on three fingers the men in her life who'd used condoms reported that she was poised to make love with one man when he informed her, at the last moment, that he had herpes. "I freaked," she said. "I said, 'Get your condom on right this minute!' " Under pressure, he complied.

However, women also report that some condom-toting males are perfecting a dazzling application technique. Women have always reserved an unspoken admiration for men who unhook bra clasps with finesse; now they are noticing other male talents. While he was passionately French kissing her, one woman reported, her lover did a deep backhanded retrieval from the night-table drawer and, stopping only momentarily to unwrap the package with his teeth, resumed kissing her while applying it, one-handed, to his stalwart erection. "I was utterly amazed," she said, a faraway look in her eyes. "And totally impressed."

To alleviate the awkwardness of this still-delicate subject, one woman suggests that people should keep a bowl of condoms on the coffee table and "be done with it." Another woman says that wisecracking with prospective lovers is the only way to go. "You bring the condoms," she quips, "and I'll bring the wine." And finally, one man has an ingenious solution if The Moment arrives but the condom has been forgotten: "He can say, 'Oh my God, darling, I've dropped my condom. Do you have yours? No? Well, maybe we can stretch your diaphragm then.' "

Is the One-Night Stand a Thing of the Past?

Not exactly, but this once venerable institution is no longer in vogue among a significant portion of the middle-aged populace. For them, the interest of sleeping with someone they're never going to see again has vanished. One man felt that, as long as one took the necessary precautions, "promiscuity" was "a charming act and quite novel, full of insights one rarely perceives any other way," but his view was atypical.

Is Casual Sex Finished?

All those articles you read in the eighties about AIDS sounding the death-knell of the sexual revolution and casual sex were grossly exaggerated. People are definitely less enthralled with the *idea* of casual sex than they were when it was invented in the sixties—and some are approaching it more cautiously—but they're not so disenchanted that they're willing to banish it from their sexual repertoires altogether. What's new about the "New Sexual Restraint" is the backburner anxiety about AIDS, the low-grade after-the-fact paranoia over having gone to bed without using a condom, and the skittishness about lovemaking because of the many new messy emotional complications surrounding sex.

For so long, for so many, casual sex was a dandy way to have an adventure, or merely an antidote to life's increasingly burdensome pressures. It didn't mean anything—it was just sex. And for a long time sex that was "just sex" had a certain charm and was valuable to a lot of people.

But many people have been astonished to discover, as they mature, that fast-food sex often turns out to give them a bellyache. "I think my generation—which grew up with casual sex—has outgrown it," one man told me. "We thought we could have sex without knowing the person well, but we've discovered that all we did was internalize the barriers. It's not possible to sleep around with people and think it means nothing. You just bury the problems with the other person."

It's a case of diminishing returns. Sometimes the thrills will carry people for a while, but often such relationships create more complication than clarity, more pressure than release, more emptiness than excitement. Consequently, many now reason that if they prudently hold off—then this time maybe, just maybe, love will last. They long for sex within the context of an intimate relationship, but they have no vocabulary for it. They just don't know how to go about it.

This discovery—that there's an emotional price to be paid for engaging sexually with another human being and that that price has grown higher and higher—is one of the most sobering lessons to have emerged from the sexual revolution. Still, it has been an arduous task for people to unlearn the spontaneity that so informed their liaisons in the past.

"Casual sex was a way to avoid intimate connection," one woman said. "You know, your hormones meshed and that was that. But casual sex wasn't what we thought it was, and one of the drawbacks of the sexual revolution is that we tended to sleep together too soon. It's hard not to when the hormones are raging, but you do now, and the guy doesn't call back.

"So now we have to go backwards, and it's hard. We have to learn how to really get to know someone before we sleep with them, when the energy and the pull to go to bed are there and we're used to acting on that pull instantaneously. We now know the price of that haste and so we hold back, but a part of us still misses it."

Is It Still All Right to Go All the Way on the First Date?
The shift in attitude about casual sex has definitely altered fashionable thinking on this point, too. Sex has become such a loaded gun that all too often sex on the first date turns out to be sex on the last date. And so, though you may want to partake on the first date, chances are that if you do (both men and women take note here), at best you'll encounter some resistance, and at worst you won't be respected in the morning. Instead, many men and women are becoming newly enthralled with discussing the merits of savoring a period of mystery, flirtation and pursuit—a delicious period their parents called courtship.

Opinion varies on exactly how long courtship without sex should last. I did hear lofty, theoretical suggestions of a few months, but most people admit they're caving in by the second or third date—a waiting period and triumph of restraint that's considered punishment enough. Women (who, by the way, were weaned on casual sex and can hardly believe they are talking this way) are opting to go a little more slowly. And they are quick to heap scorn on guys who figure they're entitled to it, if not by the first date, then certainly by the second. But they're equally critical of women who expect a man to come across right away. Men are also taking things more slowly than they once did, having left behind their urgency to bed the whole female population.

Having said that, I must report that if you're into sex but not into sex that night, it's advisable to give the other person a small clue that, one day before you die, you'd like to have sex with them. Otherwise a person may not automatically assume that you're just unsure and need a little time. If that person is female, she'll assume that either you find her ass too big and her tits too small, or you're just another fucked-up male who's afraid of intimacy. If that person is male, he'll assume that either you're making him play a high-school game of jumping through hoops before he can fuck you, or you're just another fucked-up female who can't have sex without the agenda of "commitment."

By the way, there are lots of sex experts out there going around telling people that they should never, never, never have sex on the first date. I don't subscribe to this view at all. Sometimes (okay, maybe rarely, but sometimes) for all the right reasons, sex on the first date is the most logical thing to do.

The only way to know if you should have sex on the first date is to be true to yourself. If you know you don't want to, you shouldn't, and if you know you want to, you should. Of course, lots of people fall into the slough of ambivalence: they sort of want to but they sort of don't.

You may choose to go ahead, feeling unsure, but you can't tell until afterwards whether you did the right thing, and afterwards may be too late. You'll know it was okay if there's a spring in your step in the morning and the other person is still smiling. You'll know it wasn't okay if you feel nauseated and the other person is bolting for the door. The choice is up to you.

What about a Little Sex without Commitment?

As we've seen, a man may feel ambivalent about sleeping with a particular woman, but if he still wants to get laid he may find a convenient way around his uncertainty: he may separate out the emotional part of sex from the sex part, and offer that woman what he thinks is a helluva deal: sex without commitment. Sometimes, that man will straightforwardly declare his intentions so the woman doesn't get the wrong idea (like thinking he's going to fall in love) or so she doesn't go and do anything stupid like fall in love with him.

One man who was clearly feeling jumpy about communicating

the wrong message waited until the moment after he got his blowjob to tell a woman that he didn't want "a relationship." Since he was being candid about his intentions, he may have truly believed he was dealing fairly with her, and sincerely expected that she would give him points for honesty. What this woman felt, however, was the urge to put out a contract on his life. When a man—an admirably honest man, but an admirably honest man with incredibly bad timing—informs a woman in whose mouth he has just come that his behavior in no way implies "relationship," what she will likely take from his frankness is this: I want to fuck you. I just don't want to know you.

Another woman met a guy at a party who asked, at the end of the evening, whether he could go home with her. She replied that she'd like to know him better first, gave him her business card and said she'd love for him to call. His response? "I don't want a relationship."

"I should have said, 'Are you on drugs?' she told me, furiously. "I should have said, 'If you don't want a relationship then go out, get a plastic fuck-doll and beat off into that!'"

Men, of course, have encouragement everywhere they look to separate sex from accountability. As Barbara Ehrenreich eloquently argued in The Hearts of Men, the American male's flight from commitment had been going on for a full ten years before the feminist revival of the sixties, and is celebrated at almost every level of the culture.

Certainly, some men themselves recognize the seductive pull to avoid commitment. "Freedom is so valuable in this culture," one single man in his thirties observed, "that to be alone seems more enticing. Men think, my income is disposable. I can do what I want. And since society denigrates women and children, a man walks around with this primal fear that he'll be turned into something that will hedge his bets, take away his opportunities. You know, guys are all still waiting to be asked out on a hunting trip some weekend that they're never going to be asked out on, but that, if they're married, they think they won't be able to go on."

Sometimes a man goes beyond declaring that he doesn't want "a relationship." Sometimes he feels compelled to deliver a speech. The most arrogant (albeit colorful) speech I heard on the sex-without-commitment theme was delivered by an advertising copy-writer in his late twenties.

"I tell women that I'm a Masai warrior," he said. "I tell them that there's a time in a man's life to roam and sow wild oats and suck the marrow out of life. When I'm an old man, I will settle down." The man who spoke these words acknowledged that he liked being in love but that falling in love didn't happen very often, so in between, he liked to "get laid like a bandit." He also liked to get laid the first night. When I asked him how the women he dated responded to this philosophical stance, he shot me an ironic glance. "They usually pull the rip-cord, do an ejecto trip and bail out." He sighed.

Men are by no means the only creatures who just want to get laid, however. Many women have become quite adept at compart-mentalizing their emotions, and some of them are behaving with equally brutal insensitivity when they want a no-strings-attached fuck. So many women are frankly vocal about their sexual hunger these days because they have trouble encountering men at all, and the ones they do encounter are often reluctant to hop in the sack. (Also, they believe they have the same right to express and act on their sexual needs as men do.) "It really pisses me off that men don't know that we can get just as horny as they can," one woman groaned. "Would you tell them that for me?"

How Are Women Who Just Want Sex Trying to Get Men into Bed These Days?

Women who want to hustle a guy upstairs don't usually signal their desires by sidling up to him and giving him an affectionate peck on the cheek. (That they're still terrified to do.) What they feel far more comfortable doing is arguing him into bed. So they wait for the guy to make a move, and when it's clear he's not going to, they confront him and try to talk him into it. One woman became so exasperated trying to talk her date into bed she finally just said, "Look, put out or get out." Another announced bluntly: "Listen, Jake, I'm tired, I'm drunk and I'm horny." These seduction techniques are not likely to put a man in a highly erotic mood, however, nor would women (they often forget) likely welcome such approaches themselves.

What a woman who operates thusly fails to take into account is that the man she's trying to strong-arm into the sack may have many legitimate reasons for feeling queasy about sex, and that often those reasons have nothing to do with her or her inalienable right to fuck. What he needs is some time and understanding to help him deal with his apprehensions.

"Sometimes you sense that a woman has an agenda attached to sex, so you pull back from her," one man said. "Or, if you're not sure about your feelings for her yet, sex can complicate those feelings so much, you pull back. But sometimes you don't want to go to bed with her because, much as you like her, you're just not sexually attracted to her. You're old enough to know that chemistry is important, but you're also old enough to know that sometimes chemistry develops when you get to know a person over time, and so you want to give yourself that time to see if anything changes."

Clearly, the "let's have sex but let's not pretend it *means* anything" approach isn't going down terrifically well with both women *and* men; the only way for both sexes to negotiate around this issue is to be straight with each other about what they're feeling, keeping in mind that a little tact, humor and a sense of timing will go a long way.

What Do You Do about the Sexual History Question?

This one has to be dealt with delicately, without extinguishing the possibility of romance; neurochemistry, however, often wreaks havoc with people's better judgment. When two people fall in love, a switch is thrown over at command central in the brain's pleasure center. The brain signals nerve endings to release chemicals and the brain's pleasure center goes bonkers.

These chemicals don't fool around; some, like endorphins, trigger euphoria, and all, in one way or another, alter mood. One is a painkiller stronger than morphine. Another is a chemical similar to speed. In fact, when the attraction-motor starts revving, the brain reacts much as it would if the person had snuffled up amphetamines—which could account, the biochemists say, for the exceptionally bad judgment both stimulant drug users and lovers sometimes show.

Naturally, with chemicals boogieing in your pleasure center, bringing up the matter of your partner's sexual history issue is tough. That's why all the experts advise you to have a cool-headed chat some time before the chemicals kick in. Because they only want the best for you, they make handy-dandy recommendations like casually dropping a reference to AIDS into the dinner conversation. "Gee, AIDS is a bitch, isn't it?" let's say, is supposed to be a conversation-starter, from which the two of you will then launch into a deeply meaningful dialogue about whether you've ever mainlined with a communal needle, sprouted genital warts, had diseases with polysyllabic Latin names, partaken with switch-hitters or thrashed around without latex.

The problem, however, with going the you-tell-me-yours, I'll-tell-you-mine route is that people will do or say anything to get laid. They'll lie shamelessly. In one University of California study published in *The New England Journal of Medicine* in 1990, of 422 single, sexually experienced college students, 34 percent of the men and 10 percent of the women admitted they had told a lie to maneuver their way into the sack. Even more said they'd lie if it would be to their advantage.

Three times as many men admitted to using deception as a seduction tactic than women. One in four males confessed he'd hide an ongoing sexual liaison from another prospective partner. But sexual dishonesty is hardly a male prerogative; 42 percent of the women said that, if a new partner asked, they'd low-ball their total number of former lovers, and 34 percent said they'd never admit to a one-night stand. (The males logged in at 47 percent and 43 percent, respectively.) Twenty percent of the men and 4 percent of the women said they'd lie about having been HIV-tested, and pretend that they'd received a favorable result. And the researchers point out that lying itself may be affecting their findings; it's entirely possible that people are even bigger liars than they admit to being.

Men and women aren't bad at lying to themselves, either. Many individuals I met have developed their own personal criteria for determining their AIDS risk, the logic of which is often a tad shaky. The rationalizations go like this: she's got nicely manicured nails—she's safe. He's got custom-made suits, he's okay. One woman I spoke to got out her pocket calculator and did the math. Let's see...this guy says he's been in a fifteen-year monogamous marriage, and he tells me he hardly slept around in his single days...he passes.

Heterosexual men are especially proficient at this loosey-goosey logic. To most of the men I interviewed, the idea that AIDS might have something to do with them is inconceivable. All too many, unfortunately, are bona fide card-carrying members of the Ostrich School of Reality. You can almost hear them hauling in another truckload of sand.

AIDS is a gay disease, they argue. Or a junkie's disease. "When my first heterosexual male friend drops dead from AIDS," one man told me, "then I'll worry." What's more, the idea that the enchanting, well-groomed woman whose bed they're sharing may have racked up as many notches as they have is laughable. "What are you going to say?" asked one man whose personal track record was, by his own admission, "spotty." "'I hear you're a killer in bed?'" And then he added, "I like to think that the women *I'm* sleeping with don't have a checkered history."

Men who subscribe to such theories should note that while women may tell their girlfriends every juicy morsel in graphic detail (they have total recall about their sexual misadventures, and their blabbing is far worse than men fear), they will rarely tell their lovers. That's because they're sure that, if they do, their lovers will be appalled—and given that so many men are still operating by a dastardly double standard, they probably would be.

But aside from small matters like the double standard and the ostrich-headed denial syndrome, there's another problem: how do you define exactly how pristine a sexual history has to be to guarantee a reasonable degree of safety?

According to researchers, the incubation period for AIDS is thought to be up to twelve years, so every time you have sex with a new partner, you're also having sexual contact with all his or her lovers for the past twelve or so years. Even if your partner *is* telling the truth about being sexually loyal now and monogamous or almost celibate up until now, it doesn't prove a thing. That faithful, trustworthy partner you're sleeping with may have been infected somewhere down the line. Sleeping with more people only increases the risk of picking up the virus. What's more, even if you and your bed-mate have passed an HIV test with flying colors, there's a slight risk that it may be inaccurate, and it's only valid until one or the other of you exchanges bodily fluids with somebody else. A false negative result is possible if you're tested within twelve weeks of contact, before the HIV antibodies have had a chance to develop; a false positive result is extremely rare, but can happen if you've had a gamma globulin shot prior to taking the test.

In San Francisco, having an HIV test is becoming as routine as working out or sticking to a low-fat diet. In one case, a newly divorced architect became racked with guilt because he'd failed to use a condom. He raised the matter on the next date, and both parties agreed to an HIV test. Off they trotted, in mid-date, to a public health clinic, waiting their turn in line behind the junkies. From there they proceeded to an elegant restaurant. "I guess you could call it a New Age date," he told me dryly, not quite believing that his life had come to this.

In fact, although hetero condom use is not nearly as widespread in San Francisco as one might assume, given the sizable gay population, a negative HIV test certificate is displacing a piece of jewellery as the favorite gift for a smitten man to bestow upon a woman. One man made an elaborate surprise of presenting his, like an engagement ring, over dinner. Such grand gestures, while well intentioned, don't usually sweep women off their feet.

One woman's date kissed her romantically, then raced to his desk drawer, where he proudly unfurled his sterling credentials. "I think I said something sarcastic like 'Hey, glad you passed,' or 'Why don't you frame it?' " said the woman in question. "I don't see anything wrong with having a test; in fact, I'd been thinking of having one myself. I just thought the way he brought it up was tacky." Some good did emerge from this disaster, for she decided to get tested as well. "And while I was there," she added, sighing, "I figured I might as well get my cholesterol tested too."

Naturally, some people who haven't been tested have become extremely demoralized doing all this risk-computation. Since the likelihood of transmitting HIV in urine and saliva is infinitesimal compared to the likelihood of transmitting it through sperm, vaginal fluids and blood, one responsible (albeit severely depressed) man worked out a personal strategy: "I figure genital sex without a condom is out. But, hey, no problem. The next time I'm ready to make love I'll just say, 'Listen, darling, it's no big deal. You can pee on me and I can pee on you.' Great, eh?"

In light of what is currently known about AIDS—and, more important, what isn't known—AIDS experts generally recommend that you assume that everyone you're sleeping with is infected. In other words, use a condom every time—and stop worrying.

The bottom line here is that two people can play the bedroom odds any way they see fit. But however they choose to interpret the data, they ought not to imagine that they're engaging in safe sex on the basis of bone-headed assumptions about their partner's sexual history. What they would be engaging in is a convenient little exercise in self-delusion.

The AIDS workers have a catchy little aphorism on this subject, and it's worth mentioning: "ESP doesn't work with HIV." I mean, would you sleep with yourself without using a condom?

Cunnilingus: What Do Women Want?

Not every woman likes receiving oral sex, but the ones who do like it a lot. In fact, such women tend to reserve their highest sexual kudos for the man who knows how to go down on them with flair. According to devotees, the guy who is really proficient in this area is a rare breed—and, sad to say, he's getting rarer. Fewer men, or so women claim, are willing to perform this gesture of affection nowadays. Undoubtedly, AIDS concern has to take part of the rap here. But some women postulate, rightly or wrongly, that AIDS is just an excuse for men to get out of doing something most of them were never too wild about in the first place.

In a bad-news era for sex, there are some sunny tidings for oral sex fans. Let's all raise our glasses in a toast to the AIDS researchers for this bit of news: out of the millions of people infected with AIDS worldwide, only a handful of people, researchers believe, are thought to have been infected through oral sex. Consequently, oral sex (when a man does a woman or she does him) is considered to be a minimal-risk to low-risk activity. Oral sex involves the same minimal risk with or without protection, and even if the guy comes in the woman's mouth; it only moves up to the low-risk category if the woman swallows. (Generally speaking, in terms of HIV transmission risks, AIDS experts classify all the things people do to each other in bed into three risk categories—minimal, low and high.)

Whether they love or hate oral sex, it's always a charged subject for women. Deep down, every woman fears that no man really wants to go down on her. Women live with their privates day in and day out, and despite all those maxi-pad TV ads with carefree lovelies skipping merrily through the woods like sprites, what with yeast infections, medium-to-heavy flows and the like, it can get pretty gamy down there. What's more, women have heard all those "fish" jokes men tell. The fear that a man will find the whole business disgusting beyond words is as palpable to most women as a man's fear about the size of his equipment.

Consequently, women abhor the finicky types, the guys who do it but then bolt for the washroom to gargle. They make a woman feel smelly, slimy and ugly, and—let's face it—self-loathing is not going to turn a woman into a wanton and willing bed-partner. "I hate guys who are squeamish about it, who dart their tongues in and out of you a few times as if they're sticking their tongues into a swamp full of snakes," said one woman. "Or the ones who go down on you as if they had nose plugs on. Oh, they're delightful. They might as well not bother."

A subspecies of the finicky type is the fellow who dutifully goes south if asked, but never spontaneously offers. It doesn't occur to this guy that it might be a thoughtful gesture on his part, now and then, to volunteer, particularly if his partner has been getting knee-burns for the last forty-five minutes taking care of him. Then there are the guys who whine about their jaws seizing up. And the ones who make a grand gesture of performing cunnilingus on the first encounter, then act as if the whole area has been quarantined and never go near it again.

Women notice these things—believe me, they notice. "It's like they have to prove they can do it," said one, "but they really can't stand it and they never want to do it again. So they get it out of the way right off the bat."

But there are those who perform the rite sublimely, and women speak of them in reverent tones. This is the man who, in one woman's words, "dives in there, can't get enough of the rolling around in the muck and makes you feel as if he's worshipping at the altar of your pussy." When a woman finds such a princely speci-men, she will forgive him almost anything.

One woman whose marriage broke up in 1986 had an inauspi-cious introduction to the world of contemporary sex when the first man she slept with after the break-up gave her VD. She sent him a letter saying, thanks a lot. But a few years later, when he blew into town, she slept with him again. When I wondered what would prompt her to go to bed a second time with a guy who had given her a dose, she looked at me sheepishly. "He gave the very best oral sex I've ever had in my life," she giggled. "This guy had a nose and a mustache that *worked*."

Blowjobs: What Do Men Want?

No doubt about it, men love blowjobs. In *The Hite Report on Male Sexuality*, in 1981, Shere Hite found that almost all of the more than 7,000 men she polled were positively effusive about fellatio and gave it two thumbs up. "If I could find the woman who would suck me off in the morning to wake me up," one respondent told her, "I would lay my life in the mud at her feet...."

Pepper Schwartz and Philip Blumstein also found, in *American Couples* (1983), that getting oral sex was pretty high on the list of men's favorite pastimes. "Heterosexual men who receive oral sex," wrote the authors, "are happier with their sex lives and with their relationships in general." What's more, several men I interviewed got all misty-eyed remembering the best blowjobs they'd ever received, even if they'd been performed twenty years earlier.

Men love getting blowjobs for good reason. First, they're an antidote for depression. "If I'm feeling down," one man told me, "give me a blowjob. Oral sex will cure most things." They love blowjobs because blowjobs make them feel like warriors and kings.

"If you've got your cock in a woman's mouth," said another, "you feel a tremendous sense of virility, but at the same time, you're completely vulnerable—I mean, she could bite your cock off if she wanted to! The combination of those two feelings—power and danger—is intensely exciting." Also, since many men can't comprehend what enjoyment a woman can possibly derive from performing one (forgetting that wonderful sex is as much about giving as about receiving), they figure the blowjob is 100 percent for them. What's more, a blowjob is the pause that refreshes: the man gets a much-needed break from worrying about whether the woman is going to get off.

Despite the passion with which they speak of blowjobs, men complain that they don't get blown nearly as often as they want. If one takes a long-term historical perspective, however, great strides have been made since the fifties. In fact, no men in recorded history have ever had it as good, in the blowjob realm, as the nineties man. In *Erotic Wars: What Happened to the Sexual Revolution?* Lillian Rubin reported that 90 percent of her female subjects were doing the deed—double the number in Kinsey's time. Although men have had their gripes with feminism, it seems to me that these statistics completely lay to rest the notion that the women's movement and the sexual revolution haven't been munificent to men.

Each man, naturally, has an idiosyncratic definition of the sublime blowjob, but there are some universals. "A good blowjob involves whatever it takes to get you off," one remarkably unpicky man said. "A bad blowjob takes too long to bring you off."

Most men have given the matter somewhat more thought. The woman who knows her way around what one man described as "that little rim around the head of the penis where every nerve ending in your body shorts out" knows what she's doing. So does the woman who coaxes a penis to attention with soft, feathery touches and teasing licks. The woman who drags her teeth across the head of the penis does not. A great blowjob, one man observed, is like a ballet; a seamless performance involves a well-orchestrated blend of "lots of saliva-work, lots of tongue-work and lots of hand-work." And, just as a woman senses a man's sincere interest in her nether regions, so does a man know when a woman's heart isn't really in the job. Since the whole point about a blowjob is having all that loving attention focused on his dick, it brightens a man's spirits enormously to meet a woman who treats it with playful adoration when it's limp, with awe and reverence when it's ready for action, and who takes a break now and then to gaze up at him with smiling eyes. For the record, men give a lower rating to blowjobs that are all too obviously being performed out of a sense of duty.

On the swallowing issue, there is divided opinion. Some guys live for it; some don't. Some women gag at the thought; others quiver. The only way to find out whether swallowing is part of the deal is to ask—and if someone does ask, it's not on to stare, point or throw up, or this delicate moment is going to get ugly. Really ugly.

For instance, one woman decided to run the swallowing issue up the flagpole. She turned to her lover in bed and said, "I have this idea. Why don't we fuck another way? Before you come, you stop fucking, pull out and I'll give you a blowjob."

"*What?*" said her partner, utterly aghast. "You mean, like *come, in your mouth?*"

"Well," she asked, hoping against hope, "would you want that?"

"He seemed totally taken aback," she reported. "Partly astonished that I would suggest it, partly attracted to the idea and partly afraid of it at the same time, because the suggestion came from me.

He said, 'I've never met a woman who's suggested such a thing to me.' Let me tell you, invidious comparisons are not great in bed. I felt like a freak."

Is There Such a Thing as a Politically Correct Blowjob?

While having a woman on her knees is by no means a prerequisite for a splendiferous blowjob, for some men it's the penultimate erotic charge. That's because, with a woman on her knees, a man can imagine all kinds of nasty, lovely power associations. Sophisticated men know, of course, that they aren't supposed to be thinking such thoughts. They also know it would be politically suicidal for them to admit to enjoying any kind of power over a woman, let alone the intensely erotic phallic-power associations engendered by the sight of a kneeling woman catering enthusiastically to their needs. The bald truth is, though, many do. (For the same unmentionable reason, coming in a woman's mouth, doing her up the bum or doggie-style gives many men a glowy feeling too.)

This kneeling business, however, has sparked a passionate debate about whether there's such a thing as a politically correct blowjob, and it goes straight to the heart of one of the most controversial issues of sexual politics of our time. Some women agonize over whether they should agree to perform blowjobs in a kneeling position (or do that other submissive stuff lots of guys seem to love) because complying means assuming blatantly servile postures, and we all know how women feel on *that* subject. What drives women completely nutso on this volatile matter, however, is the fact that a fair number of them, though disinclined to admit it, get their *own* erotic buzz from performing the handmaiden role in these little fantasy-dramas too.

Meanwhile, some men who once got off playing the master role are finding they simply can't enjoy lording it over a woman in bed anymore, so riddled with guilt are they about getting a charge out of seeing a woman in a subservient position. What a mess!

While there is by no means a consensus, most civilized men acknowledge that this one is the woman's call (although they do make an impassioned plea for mercy). They will no doubt be encouraged to learn, then, that I did encounter female voices of moderation. Such women argue that there are now precious few places men can go, except in their fantasies, to be uncomplainingly serviced by women, and this (as men well know) is not going to change. Men have had to endure a lot of hits below the belt in the latter part of the twentieth century. If two consenting adults decide, in the privacy of their bedroom, that a master-slave role-play will nourish their souls *and* get them off, what's the big deal?

For those who just can't get past the kneeling problem, there is, in the nineties, the option of the politically correct blowjob: two supremely equal human beings get into the "69" position, shout "On your mark, get set, go..." and do each other in perfect unison. Alternately, she can straddle him and get her licks in from above. That way, she's in command, he still gets blown, and both parties can take pride in the fact that they're doing something to make the world a better place.

How Do You Let Your Partner Know You Want to Try the Back Door?

For those who feel the need for a change of pace in their sexual repertoire, anal sex is an intriguing detour. And there's evidence that anal sex is to the nineties what oral sex was to the seventies. According to Lillian Rubin in *Erotic Wars*, twenty years ago oral sex was just making a name for itself on the American sexual agenda; it was new, interesting and titillating because it was still largely considered to be naughty and unconventional. Now that oral sex has inched its way into standard practice, thrill-seekers are, more and more, trying the back door.

Rubin found that, although there are no reliable data on how many Americans are partaking of anal sex, most experts estimate that about 30 percent have at least given it a shot. She reports that a 1983 *Playboy* survey found that 61 percent of its readership had done the deed, and she also notes that 51 percent of *Self*'s readers were doing it in 1984, up 13 percent from the magazine's 1980 survey. In 1989, June Reinisch of the Kinsey Institute for Research in Sex, Gender and Reproduction told a reporter for *Science News* that "in a new study that we've done in middle-class college students in the Midwest, at least one out of four have (*sic*) already experienced anal intercourse, even though they became sexually active at the average age of 17 and are now...an average age of 22."

Rubin's own data revealed that over one-third of today's American college students have at least experimented with anal sex, while close to half of the older men and women she interviewed "have had some experience with it—an extraordinary increase in the years since the early 1970s, when it was almost unheard of among heterosexuals."

Male anal sex fans say that once you've tried it, it's hard to go back to old-fashioned humping. On a purely erotic level, anal sex offers everything these guys are looking for. First of all, they get to act like cavemen. What's more, if the woman has never tried anal sex before, they get to introduce her to its pleasures and "deflower" her. Feminism has pretty well robbed men of the chance to act like beasts around women, or to be the first to initiate them, and, truth to tell, they miss the feeling. Anal sex gives them permission to be downright savage, to throw their partner on the bed, "take" her from behind, and savor the indescribable erotic pleasure of sex that is exquisitely steamy and intimate, but at the same time, as one man put it, "cold, violent, and impersonal." They also say that the back door is tight, and men like tight. It's a funny little quirk of theirs.

Female anal sex fans (their numbers are fewer) agree, but for different reasons. They don't like to admit this much to men, especially in board meetings, but they get a charge out of being mastered in bed; a modest degree of pain or masochism lets these women push the erotic envelope, which is how they get their thrills. And anal sex allows them not only to submit, but to play at being "bad girls." Also, because most women don't go around offering anal sex to just anyone who shows up at the back door, they too consider it to be the ultimate intimacy.

Many women, however, say it hurts like hell, especially if the guy's got a big one. (K-Y jelly, female devotees respond, eases the discomfort of entry tremendously.) Women especially resent men who barge in and try to pretend that they were just so transported by ecstasy that they charged the wrong entrance. They liken these guys to the ones whose idea of polished sexual manners is to grab them by the hair and push their faces down into their laps when they want a blowjob.

Men who crave anal sex, then, are advised to ask the woman if she's game to try it. (Ordinarily, men and women welcome a partner who surprises them in bed, but under these circumstances that rule doesn't apply.) Renting *Last Tango in Paris* to watch the notorious butter scene together is one wily way to raise the topic. Alternatively, a man may gently introduce a digit or tongue into the general area and see how that flies first. (Good news for asslickers: anal tonguing is a minimal-risk activity.) This sort of foreplay is what one man called "laying the groundwork," and he advises men to lay it gradually, over time. If the woman seems to be enjoying the proceedings, then he can up the ante and—I can't underscore this enough—proceed gingerly.

Women who want to give anal sex a go needn't be shy about asking. They just have to pick their moment and whisper coyly that they wouldn't mind being partaken of from the rear one day. Said one woman who'd discovered the pleasures of this particular orifice and had some experience in coaxing men to enjoy it too, "You don't have to get into bed and announce, 'Stick your cock up my arse.' You can start by leading him gently, asking him to touch or tongue you in the general area. When he sees it's turning you on, he'll get the picture."

One final sobering word here: no amount of mealy-mouthed rationalization can change the fact that anal sex is the most dangerous activity you can practice in bed in terms of AIDS-risk. If you have anal sex, use a condom or two (and stick to K-Y jelly—Vaseline's not recommended with latex). If you don't use condoms, you're playing Russian roulette.

What's the Latest on the Female Orgasm?

So much ink has been spilled on the subject of the female orgasm since the sixties, it's no wonder guys sometimes feel that their orgasms are supporting actors in the sexual drama. Indeed, although the male orgasm has been studied, it's never really been in the media spotlight to the same degree as the woman's. But here Nature must take some of the responsibility. Not only did the God of Orgasms bequeath most guys the ability to come with predictable regularity, this munificent deity also gave them the tools to locate their orgasms about a million years ago. Women have had to embark on a quest to find theirs, which, for some reason, tend to be nomadic.

Writing in *Time* in 1986, journalist John Leo observed that the perennially restless "Great Traveling (female) Orgasm" moved around more than "Elizabeth Taylor, the QE2 and the wandering albatross." In the old days, said Leo, it used to hang out in the vagina. Then it moved to the clitoris, where it remained stationary for a decade. Now, "under the majestic scepter of science, not to mention the cattle prod of sexual politics, the Big O is thrashing about once again... and now seems headed for the brain and back to the vagina. ...ardent males will soon be advised to rub everything once...one never knows where tomorrow's sexual climaxes will be located."

Leo then offered a brief history of the peregrination. Freud started all this toing and froing by declaring that a truly "mature" woman should be satisfied, thank you very much, with orgasms born of penile thrusting. When Freud had an opinion it carried a bit of weight, so in his time, and for some time after, vaginal orgasms were in and clitoral orgasms were out. These were dark days for a clitorally centered woman. If she was so bold as to suggest that her clitoris needed some attention now and then, she was made to feel like a juvenile.

When the feminists came along, penis-vagina sex became passé. We don't need men to help us come anymore, cried the feminists. We will march through the streets with our multispeed vibrators and spread the word that we can do it to Our Bodies, Ourselves. During this period pro-vagina forces suffered debilitating losses, and any woman who was fool enough to claim that she had an orgasm thanks to a penis, and actually enjoyed it, became a pariah to be cast ignominiously aside and to walk the streets branded with a scarlet O. During this period, an orgasm was less a physiological event than a political statement. Wrote Leo, "For all we know, women who used to fake vaginal orgasms for their hubbies began to fake clitoral ones for the women's movement."

As if all this weren't confusing enough, the eighties saw a resurgence of interest in the G spot. German gynecologist Ernst Gräfenberg was credited with discovering the G spot in the 1940s, and, fittingly, it's named in his honor. He spent many years working on hired prostitutes and cut-up cadavers, until one day he came upon what he claimed was an identifiable erogenous zone on the anterior wall of the vagina.

In the late seventies psychologist Alice Ladas, nurse Beverly Whipple and minister/sexologist John Perry conducted interviews to validate Gräfenberg's work. Their book, *The G Spot*, claimed that 100 percent of their four hundred female volunteers could locate their G spot, and were thrilled to have made its acquaintance. If properly massaged by a thrusting male member, the authors said, the G spot would blow up to the size of a half-dollar and become a wellspring of untold female pleasure. Moreover, sometimes, during G spot orgasm, women would even release a semen-like fluid through their urethras.

Although both Kinsey in 1953 and Masters and Johnson in 1966 had discredited such a thing, *The G Spot* had a lot of women getting out their Itty Bitty Book Lights for a while. The theory enjoyed a brief moment in the G spotlight again during the "post-feminist" late eighties because here, at last, was an argument for reinstating the prominence of the good old penis.

All this voluminous and often conflicting information has served mainly to create a state of orgasm overload. Women are spending more time being obsessed with their orgasms than actually having them, and somehow they've gotten men obsessed with them too. Consequently, the subject of the wandering female orgasm is murkier than ever in people's minds. One man confessed that, despite all the hype about the Big O, "what a guy knows about a woman's orgasm he could put in his bellybutton."

However, thanks to Kinsey and many protégés, there are some well-documented facts about the female orgasm. They bear reviewing for a moment.

1) For most women, orgasms take place in a context of intimacy and trust and are likeliest to occur in a regular, stable relationship. In one 1975 *Redbook* survey of 100,000 readers, a striking 77 percent of respondents said they'd never had an orgasm during a one-night stand.

2) The average length of time it takes for a woman to reach orgasm is anywhere from ten to thirty minutes, although thirty to forty-five minutes is not unusual, and it can take up to an hour. (To a man who is trying to do the gentlemanly thing and wait until a woman is taken care of before he lets go, forty-five minutes to an hour can seem like an eternity. One man insisted that it took both his ex-wives two weeks to get there.) And most of the prominent researchers have found that the majority of women, anywhere from 50 to 75 percent, depend on clitoral stimulation from something other than a penis. Only a small percentage can get off from the friction of intercourse. Despite this evidence, the idea that all a guy has to do is hump away till the cows come home persists, not only in men's minds, but in many women's.

3) Most current sex studies show that between 5 and 10 percent of women never have an orgasm. The ability of a woman to have an orgasm (or the ease with which she can have one) depends on her state of mind, health, energy and age. It also depends on her ability to conjure up (if that's her thing) a fantasy with a cast of tawny-muscled, ankle-chained sex slaves, on whether she's distracted worrying about a big meeting tomorrow, and probably on whether the moon is in Jupiter, not to mention about ten gazillion other factors which may have nothing—I repeat, nothing—to do with the technique of the man making love to her. As one woman put it, "My orgasm has very little to do with whether the guy is a skilled lover. Whether I have an orgasm depends on my mood. Am I preoccupied? Am I wound up? If I am, I'm not going to come. You can forget it."

4) Many women report that they don't have to have an orgasm to have great sex. For them, great sex is about more than having an orgasm—like a feeling of reciprocity and love, for instance. "For me, an orgasm is not necessarily a reliable barometer of whether I'm enjoying the experience," one woman in her early thirties said. "It's a fairly recent thing for me even to be able to come with a man. And yet I didn't feel cheated before. I always enjoyed sex."

5) If they don't fall asleep (which women report that many men do), men tend to come back to earth much faster than do women during the rosy afterglow period—what Masters and Johnson called the "resolution phase" of an orgasm. This perverse, wired-in biological difference explains why women, who are still twenty thousand leagues under, get annoyed with men who turn on the TV right afterwards, and why men who do are completely baffled as to why women are making such a big deal about this. One guy whose resolution phase was clearly short-lived turned to his partner immediately after he'd come and casually inquired as to where he could get some nice end tables. A poorly timed query such as this, however, will not only give a woman the bends, it will make her feel as if her lover remained on dry land through the whole encounter.

6) Another one of God's cruel little jokes is that men achieve their orgasmic peak somewhere in their late teens (as any male who spent his adolescence locked in the washroom knows); after that, they're basically riding the crest of the wave. Women, however, don't usually hit their stride until they're into their thirties. Although guys do get a testosterone rush in their teens, the main reason women are slower to come into their own is because it usually takes them a while to get rid of all the nice-girls-don't-like-it propaganda that's been shoved down their throats.

7) As the hit movie *When Harry Met Sally...* so hilariously demonstrated, most women have, at one time or another, faked orgasm. This they do for a variety of reasons. Since often neither partner realizes that it's unusual for a woman to be able to come by thrusting alone, she may fake one because she feels embarrassed that it's taking so long, or inadequate if it's just not going to happen, or anxious that the guy will find her a washout in bed if she doesn't scream and wake the neighbors. Sometimes she fakes one to protect what she imagines to be the fragile male ego, and sometimes because the sex is so pathetic that she just wants to get it over with. One woman recalled that she faked one, in her teens, to avoid brain damage. Thrusting madly away in the back seat of a car, her lover failed to notice that her head kept smashing against the armrest.

8) The female orgasm typically lasts from six to ten seconds, although the rolling, mega-intense ones can go on for fifteen. However, if off-the-Richter-scale intensity were all that mattered to a woman, she could stay home and play with herself; many women claim they have more intense orgasms by masturbating than they do during sex.

Since women started making so much noise about equal rights for orgasms, men have unquestionably made tremendous leaps in acknowledging this trend—a civilized advance women graciously acknowledge. However, some guys seem to find the female orgasm so endearing that they've started to fuss over it unduly. Not only are many now waiting patiently for a woman to come before they'd even *consider* getting their rocks off, in a generous gesture toward equality, they've also taken on the female orgasm as *their* responsibility. "I blame myself if she doesn't come," one lawyer told me. "I must not be doing something right. I tackle the problem like a brief. It's the flip side of male performance anxiety."

Because men have been encouraged to believe that bringing a woman to orgasm is a noble endeavor, a man's honor is now as much at stake in the dynamic as a woman's pleasure. Understandably, a man may think a woman's orgasm is his achievement, but it's not. Her orgasm is a physiological event, and often a temperamental one. No man can "give" a woman an orgasm—he can facilitate one, certainly, by lubing the engine, or tinkering away in the right places until it turns over. But if the battery is on the fritz on that occasion, all the tinkering in the world won't get the engine purring.

As one woman pointed out, her eyes bugging out in mimicry of the sheer concentration required to bring an orgasm off, "It's not like it's so bloody easy to have one, you know." The point is, maybe it's going to happen and maybe it's not—which is why, when a guy gets all wrapped up in a woman's Big O, his single-minded obsessiveness can make her edgy.

Since women were the ones who put all this heat on men to pay attention to their orgasms, they know it sounds terribly ungrateful to start carping that men are now paying too much attention. So they don't. That's why I'm going to have to be the messenger here.

Women *hate* to be asked if they've come. They hate it more than not coming. More to the point, if a guy asks *during* the proceedings, it's an almost airtight guarantee that a woman won't. That's why she gets annoyed at the guy who clocks her orgasm, grilling her every five minutes about whether she's come yet, as if he's her coach for the Orgasm Olympics and she's going for Gold.

Men never believe any of this, however, because for a man having an orgasm is kindergarten stuff. Men can have an orgasm with their eyes closed and one hand behind their backs. (In fact, many do.) And for them, sex without orgasm is not nearly as much fun as sex that ends with a big come. Furthermore, many a man is sure that if he doesn't come, he'll get what one guy called DSP— Deadly Sperm Buildup—which will not only paralyze him from the waist down, but cause his penis to fall off. And he makes the fatal error of assuming that what's bad for him is also bad for her.

There are other reasons why men feel cheated if women don't come. "I think a man wants you to come," one woman suggested, "not only because it makes him feel like a skilled lover, but because you're getting to see him in a totally vulnerable state when he comes, and he wants you to become just as vulnerable. It's an exchange, and it's understandable that he would want you to submit to that overpowering loss of control too. If I'm going to be that naked in front of you, he thinks, then I want you to be that naked in front of me. And I understand that. Also, I think men always think they're enjoying sex more than you are, which isn't true. You know, they think they're more sexually motivated, more horny, all that propaganda. But they're not, they just think they are."

Some independent women have found a thoroughly modern way around the did-you-come-yet? problem by taking matters into their own hands. Since nobody has had more practice at making them come than they have, they simply play with themselves during the proceedings, or they let the guy go first, and then play with themselves afterwards. This is called teamwork.

Many positive benefits flow to the woman who is woman enough to take care of herself during sex, and the man who is man enough to let her. He gets off, she gets off and a good time is had by all. Since the pressure's off, both of them can stop worrying, relax and abandon themselves to some first-rate, filthy fantasies. This way lies ecstasy.

Why Are Men Faking Orgasms?

Since these are strange times indeed, it should come as no surprise that men are faking orgasms too. The sex mavens claim that when a man comes he only gives up, on average, about one teaspoon of fluid; since the woman is a little gooey herself, for a man to fake an orgasm is really quite simple. As long as he makes the necessary sound effects and then dutifully asks for the Kleenex, with a little sleight of hand he can pull a faker off.

Sometimes men fake orgasms because they can go on and on but just can't come. This is called retarded ejaculation and psychologists say it may have something to do with a man's pathological fear of letting go. A cock that never comes may be a novelty for a woman for a while, but sooner or later the novelty wears off. The guy knows this, so he fakes it. Sometimes a man's come, which should be traveling down his urethra, backs up into his bladder; the man feels as if he's had an orgasm, but he has nothing to show for it, which makes him feel glum.

Some men withhold their orgasms as a tactical maneuver, although they may be doing so quite unconsciously. One woman claimed that her lover would be all set to come inside her, when he'd gaze into her eyes and say that he really didn't know if he wanted to be so involved in the relationship. While he decided, she became morose.

It must be noted that faking orgasms is still largely a female ploy. The overwhelming majority of men I interviewed said they'd never faked an orgasm. In fact, one man was so incredulous at the suggestion that men were actually doing this sort of thing, he stared at me in wonder. It's with his wise words that I leave this subject: "Who the fuck has time to fake an orgasm?"

Does Size Matter?

No man wants a small dick. In a perfect world, all men would own what psychologist Bernie Zilbergeld, in *Male Sexuality*, calls a "fantasyland" model, one that's two feet long, as hard as steel and can go all night. "In fantasyland," says Zilbergeld, "penises come in only three sizes—large, gigantic and so big you can barely get them through the door." What's more, in literature, fantasyland dicks are forever behaving peculiarly, "pulsating," "throbbing" and generally leaping about. In the more prosaic real world, penises are available (talking ballpark figures) in less Brobdingnagian forms: average length when at ease just under four inches; average length when saluting about six inches; average diameter at the base one and a half inches. Even then, nature has a way of evening the score, since a dick that's punier when flaccid hardens up by making a heftier percentage increase than its brawnier cousin.

But ballpark averages impress men more in the ballpark than in the bedroom. In almost every major current sex study, men admit to being obsessed with the size of their penises. Shere Hite found over and over again that they wished to be more stunningly endowed; one man wanted a woman to gasp when she laid eyes on the sucker. Many of her respondents knew, to within a quarter of an inch, how big their equipment was, both limp and waving in the breeze, having taken a tape measure to it. One had even snapped Polaroids. Their cocks were either "sinister," "not good-looking enough," or "shrunk" or "shrivelled" to a "short stub." One man consoled himself by checking his dimensions only in the mirror, arguing that a penis always looks larger on other men because of the "foreshortening" caused by the angle of self-perusal. Only the occasional respondent actually liked his dick for its esthetic qualities—one so much that he claimed he was going to have it bronzed when he died. (Sorry, Hite never does report its dimensions.)

Sexologists are always trying to reassure men by telling them that size couldn't be less important to a woman. The vagina is a remarkably versatile, flexible instrument, they intone. It adjusts to any fit. And, they go on, length is unimportant because only the outer one-third of the vagina has pleasurable nerve endings anyway. In fact, length can even be a liability, because a long penis can bump the cervix and give the woman a rough ride. Women, they add, are not aroused by the visual in the way men are; how many skin mags are marketed for women? *Ergo*, the sight of a long schlong won't do a thing for a woman. Couldn't interest her less. When all is said and done, women just don't care about penis size, so grow up and deal with this already.

Men listen dutifully to this rational argument, nod sagely and think it's the biggest bunch of crap they've ever heard. C'mon, they're dying to know. Level with us. What do women *really* say to each other about men's dicks? Does size matter or what?

It's going to be hard to handle this one without wiping out half the human race, but I'll try. Does size matter? Yes and no. When the lovemaking is purely mechanical, size may make a difference. But here we must define our terms. Size, in the female vernacular, generally means "thickness"—length is a male preoccupation. During a sportfuck, size may matter, only because sportfucking tends to be a disassociative experience, and there's not much else to engage the mind. In sportfucking, if a penis takes on a life of its own in the woman's head, it's because it's the penis the woman is having a relationship with, not the person. When a woman feels kindly disposed toward the man involved, penis size is way down the list, paling by comparison with more metaphysical matters. Some of their best lovers, women say almost universally, have had small ones. And that's because, when sex is civilized, the experience is always about more than the sum of its parts.

What about Male Equipment Failure?

This debilitating little problem—to which any woman can attest—is a lot more prevalent than most men think. Even as you read this, an estimated 12 million North American men are failing to get it up. At the Kinsey Institute and Masters and Johnson clinic, failing to get it up is the number-one problem.

Equipment failure is probably the least funny moment in a man's life. A wave of panic washes over him. That's it, he thinks, I'm washed up. Hang it up. "At that moment," said one who'd been there (as most men had, at one time or another), "you're thinking, shit, I can't control the damn thing. I want it to work, it's never failed me in the past, but now it won't work. And so, with all due respect, how a woman feels at that precise instant is way down your list of priorities. You're not worrying about her or thinking about her or even sweating about what she's going to think about you. You can't even hear what she's saying, for Chrissakes! You're obsessed with *you*.

And your *dick*. Is this it? Is it over? Am I ever ever gonna get hard again?"

Perhaps it's best to begin with what a woman should never do at such a time. Laughing and pointing are ill advised, as is sobbing or getting angry and shouting at it. What a woman must especially avoid, says Cynthia Heimel in *Sex Tips for Girls*, is getting "rattled" or "impatient"; nor should she keep "kneading the penis as if one were preparing dinner rolls." Making reassuring noises and telling a partner there's more to sex than penetration is probably the best tactic, especially as it happens to be the truth. No man, of course, will believe this, but it's the best a woman can offer. Some guys even say they'd appreciate being drawn into a discussion about it, having had some of their most illuminating discussions around sex at those moments. Others prefer that a woman just say, "Listen, it's no big deal," and change the subject.

Just as a woman's Big O gets moody from time to time, a man's honorable member can betray him at the crucial moment for many reasons: maybe the problem is in his head and not in his penis at all, maybe he's ambivalent about being there, maybe he's flipped out from stress, maybe he's worrying about the kids barging in or maybe he's got a few cash-flow problems. Indeed, in the way in which men and women react to life's economic vicissitudes, they couldn't be more unalike. "Their checkbooks don't balance," said one woman who'd conducted an uncontrolled study of such matters, "and they can't get it up; our checkbooks don't balance, and we want to fuck our brains out."

For men who suffer from chronic impotence, however, the problem, about 75 percent of the time, is not in their heads at all; it's physiological, and it's a miserable plight. If a man is not too mortified to seek help, he will go to almost any lengths to have it fixed, including trying vacuum devices, penile splints, or drug injections which, through the miracle of modern medicine, can give him, at the outside, a two-hour hard-on. Like most miracle drugs, however, they do have a down side. Sometimes what goes up won't come down, and the hard-on, like an Energizer battery, keeps on going. To a woman this may sound like a tolerable side-effect, but it's not. A prolonged hard-on not only makes a guy feel as if he's going to have to put a leash on his dick and walk it around the block, it may also start to ruin the lines in his snappy Italian suits. In such cases, he can check in at a 24-hour emergency clinic for an antidote.

Whether impotence is first-night, occasional or chronic, it's an agonizing experience for a man; a woman of substance will always remember that.

Who Makes the Post-Coital Call?

If a man puts his penis into a woman's vagina (or any other orifice, for that matter) he must call her the next day. Not to call, or to acknowledge in some civilized manner that he has spent the evening this way, is the most cowardly, rude and hurtful breach of modern sexual etiquette known to humankind. Unless there is an absolutely airtight understanding on *both* parts that what is going on is a one-night stand, he must call, even if he never intends to see her again.

This is a stunning revelation to many males; indeed, even though they've been a guest in a woman's bed, an appreciative call often doesn't occur to the same men who would think it exceptionally ungracious to neglect saying thanks after being someone's dinner guest. Whereas it used to be wham, bam, thank you ma'am, now some guys aren't even bothering with the thank you. This lapse in sexual civility has taken its toll on women, and has probably done more to set back the cause of harmonious relationships than just about anything else.

Let me tell you about what happened to Lily, because Lily's story is depressingly common. Lily meets a guy through a friend's personal ad. The guy doesn't make the cut with Lily's friend, so the friend gives him to Lily. He is, says Lily, "98 percent assets, 2 percent zing." Lily has always gone for 98 percent zing and 2 percent assets, but, she reasons, "where has that gotten me?" So she gives him a try. She dates him three or four times over a month, and, although she thinks he's a nice enough guy, she pretty much makes up her mind that she isn't going to sleep with him. "There's no zing, right?" But, as often happens in these situations, he presses her a little and one thing leads to another, and, says Lily, it seems right, so "finally I succumb." Now, this is where the story gets ugly, because the guy never calls again.

"You know," said Lily, "I thought to myself, well, maybe he died. Women tell themselves that...well, maybe he died. Because they just can't believe a guy would be such a snake as not to call. So I'm on the phone moaning about this to one of my male friends, and he says, 'Oh, Lily, I guess we guys have a lot to learn in this world.' And I say, 'Well, I've certainly learned something from this. You wanna know what I've learned? I've learned that if a guy wants to sleep with me again he's gonna have to crawl on his belly over crushed glass.'"

This story does have a coda. Not one to leave business unfinished, Lily gives herself a few weeks to cool off and then sends the man a note. The note says, "My curiosity has gotten the better of me. I consider myself to be a good judge of people. Did I make a mistake on you? You could at least have written me a note. Not to hear was really a shock, because I liked you."

Because I liked you. Therein lies the crux of the matter. When we are dealing with people we like, we tend to have certain base-level expectations of common decency. If you like someone and they're your friend, you expect to hear from them once in a while. If you like someone, and you're a girl, and the two of you sleep together, you expect to hear from him. (Guys would get this in a second if *they* had vaginas, but so far they don't—that's why I have to rattle on here.) Calling back is a way of touching base, of acknowledging in some small way, that putting a penis inside a vagina has some vague connection with the person whose vagina it is.

In the end, the guy did respond to Lily's letter. He left a message on her answering machine, but here's where the story gets really disheartening because now Lily won't return *his* call. "His message wasn't very encouraging," she said. "He said he was sorry I was upset, but since we hadn't made any 'commitment,' he didn't think he'd done anything wrong, and so I just figured, what's the point? He's never going to understand."

While I empathize with Lily's frustration, I don't think her refusal to call furthered the cause of accord between the sexes, and I suspect it set that cause back. It's a classic nineties scenario. The guy does something he thinks is normal. The woman gets furious because she doesn't agree. The woman corrects the guy on his "misdemeanor," at which point the guy often disappears because he prefers not to deal with a potentially messy situation. But this guy didn't disappear. He called back. Okay, so he called back defensively, but at least he responded and that took courage. By this point, however, the woman is over her mad-on, mucho fed up with guys who talk "no commitment" in lieu of having polished sexual manners, and decides it's not her job to patiently educate all men. So the guy goes away clueless about what he did wrong, and concludes not only that there's no way he can win, but also that all women are impossible.

Why, I hear some of you ask, must the man make the post-coital call? Why can't the woman call him? She can, of course, and in a perfect world she would. However, most women have not yet evolved to the point where they can make this call. They need to receive it. In sex, a woman lets a man in; afterwards, she often needs some gesture of resolution, some male-initiated validation of the fact that what transpired, whether it will take place again or not, deserves recognition.

Such a phone call may end in grief, for expectations and inter-pretations of what happened may be wildly out of whack. All that suggests, however, is that sex is a risky business. But sex has *always* been a risky business, and there's just no way of getting around that. Feelings get involved. It's precisely for that reason that a phone call—and a response to a phone call, however late it's made—is in order. Anything less is dishonorable.

What's the Latest on the Post-Coital Coma?

Every woman knows it's a truism that there are three things a man can do under any circumstances: one is watch the news, two is spend forty-five minutes taking a dump and three is fall asleep after sex. "Is there some biological reason why so many men fall asleep right after sex?" one woman plaintively asked. "Is there some scientific explanation that would make me feel better?" Sorry, guys, I know you're hoping to read this next section aloud to your mates, but there appears to be no scientific reason why a man should be more tired after having sex than a woman. Once, long ago, there was the vitalist physiology theory, which held that sperm nourished the brain and that when a man had an orgasm he was losing his vital fluid and brain power. (In other words, if the threat of warts and blindness didn't deter a guy from beating off, maybe the threat of retardation would.) That theory, of course, has been completely refuted.

Also unsubstantiated is the myth that a male orgasm triggers the release of a sleep-inducing hormone. Since I talked to a lot of men and women who seemed remarkably intelligent and articulate, and who admitted to doing a fair bit of wanking and to being perky as all-get-out afterward, I'd have to concur that this theory holds no water at all. Many sex educators and medical experts polled agree that, while some orgasms can have a sedating effect, this should be true for both partners. (A few picograms of endorphins—those lovely natural opiates—get released into both male and female bloodstreams during orgasm.)

Scientific evidence notwithstanding, men for the most part remain unmoved on this issue. Can't we just talk beforehand, they groan, and get the talking out of the way? Insisted one, "It's called the post-ejaculatory refractory period. It's a built-in time relapse system to get the old machine working again. It's like when the copier goes off because there's not enough toner. You just have to chill out for a while, or go to another office. You just have to accept it."

Many women, however—demanding harridans that they are—are reluctant to "just accept it." They want to lasso the elevating feelings they've just had and bask in them for a while; otherwise the experience seems too perfunctory. To be kept at arm's length before sex is alienating enough, but to be kept at arm's length right afterwards is downright insulting. For them, sex is a play in three acts. The guy who drops off right after the climactic scene, refusing to stay awake for the dénouement, is an uncouth oaf.

The extent to which this has become a sore spot for women was thrown into high relief in the eighties, when Ann Landers conducted a much-publicized poll. "Would you be content to be held close and treated tenderly, and forget about 'the act'?" she queried her readers. The survey drew a staggering 90,000 responses, 72 percent of which made it abundantly clear that the respondents would take a pass on the act if they could have a little tenderness. Forty percent of the disgruntled writers were under forty. "I'd expect that some women fifty to seventy," Landers told *Time*, "had had enough sex. But in this so-called enlightened age, with liberated womanhood—that's pretty startling.... Clearly, there's trouble in paradise."

What Do Women Love in Bed?

Well, no big surprises here. Women love a lover with a slow touch. First they love a titillating verbal seduction ("He has to fuck my head before he fucks me," one woman put it), and then they love a gradual physical seduction. What this means is that they love being undressed adoringly, and caressed from the top of their heads to the tips of their toes. On the other hand, sometimes they just love being bent over and plowed, so go figure.

What Do Women Hate in Bed?

The sexual brontosaurus is rare but not, alas, extinct. This is the guy whom every woman's studies course issued warnings against. Usually this man inspires reactions ranging from silent contempt to open vilification, and you can be sure his name goes out on the female tom-toms almost as soon as he's zipped himself up.

The brontosaurus's idea of lovemaking is to rip his partner's clothes off, hop on, do his business, grunt several times, then hop off. He rarely knows how to kiss, undress, fondle a woman or find her relevant parts. It's unlikely he'll perform oral sex, although he appears to have no objection to receiving it. Despite the fact that he's probably the lousiest lay the woman has ever encountered, he thinks of himself as a real swordsman, simply because he can get it up and keep it up.

The brontosaurus's approach is not to be confused with up-against-the-wall sex, for which a fair number of women have a distinct fondness. Sometimes the occasion simply demands dispensing with the preliminaries. What's objectionable is the man who leaves a woman with the distasteful feeling that he's merely been masturbating inside her.

If a woman meets this man, she owes it to him and to womankind in general to show him gently and tactfully what he might do to reform, to give him a chance to, and then, if he shows no willingness, to throw him unceremoniously out of her bed.

One other quirk deserves mention: talking about one's penis in the third person is risky. One man tenderly cupped his flaccid organ after a first sexual encounter and explained to his partner, "He's tired now." She thought he was deranged.

What Do Men Hate in Bed?

Men are either far less picky than women about what's unacceptable in the sack, or they have been, on the whole, luckier. In any event, the men I interviewed were not nearly as vocal in their complaints. There are several standard turnoffs, however, so here's a list of the top ten things a woman shouldn't do in bed:

1) Rattle off a list of ordained rules like a drill sergeant.
2) Lie there as if there's a flag over her head (aka The Necrophiliac Lay).
3) Insist that sex always be performed in a bed, at the same appointed hour of the day, or after the last dish has been put away.

4) Ask if it's in yet.

5) Say, "I'm not sure what's wrong, I always got off with my last lover."

6) Refuse to watch porn as a turn-on because it's "disgusting and perverted."

7) Wear her sexual politics like a badge.

8) Run to the washroom to make up before he wakes up in the morning.

9) Run to the washroom to clean up right afterward.

10) Fake an orgasm.

Why Do Men Love Sharing Fantasies with a Sex Buddy?

What many men want in a sex partner, but often have a hard time finding, is a sex buddy. A sex buddy is just like one of the guys except that she's got different parts, so men not only get to hang out with her and have fun, they get to sleep with her too.

The sex buddy understands guys and how guys think about sex. Because she can see sex through male eyes, she's a good sport about accommodating the male point of view. What this means is that she's adventurous—up for anything. She knows how to watch and enjoy porn. She understands the pleasures of quick and dirty sex. She doesn't flip out when a guy ogles women, because she's secure enough to understand that ogling women is something guys like to do. She doesn't press—every time—for an hour of foreplay before, an orgasm during, and a talk afterwards. Above all, she knows how to relate to a guy's politically incorrect fantasies without feeling the need to call the cops.

"You want a woman you can tell all your sexual fantasies to," one man said, "even if your fantasies involve lusting after other women or fucking a sixteen-year-old girl with gorgeous tits and a great ass. Even if your fantasies involve watching other guys fuck *her*.

"Sometimes you fantasize about The Hunt—anonymous, impersonal sexual encounters—because fantasies like that are an intense turn-on. I mean, if you want to get really straight about this, I'm talking about fantasies where the man is the king of the castle and the woman is there basically as a piece of ass so he can get off. You want a woman to understand that these are *fantasies* you're having, that sometimes you need to have them, and that they don't mean that you're a sexual reprobate or in the habit of abusing women.

"For instance, I find the *idea* of overpowering a woman sexually and taking her against her will extremely erotic. That's rape, and I would never dream of acting on that desire in reality because rape is vicious and horrible. There's a difference, though, between having an erotic desire and acting on it. A fantasy is a pretend story. You want a woman who can share your pretend story and relate to it—a woman who isn't going to get defensive and withdrawn and start chastising you for having it.

"In my experience, women usually want a leisurely, romantic sexual encounter. They want you to make slow, magnificent love to them, and sometimes that's a lovely thing to do. But it's not the only kind of sex that's erotic. I tend to associate that kind of lovemaking with phoniness, because I did it so often in a state of mental detachment. I was going through the motions, emotionally outside the experience, watching it. For me the best sex, the most erotic sex, is honest sex. A woman who knows how to let me be me in bed understands what honest sex means."

What Do Women Say about Sharing Fantasies with a Sex Buddy?
Although megastar Madonna has no trouble walking the fine line between girlish submissiveness and womanly sexual mastery (what's

a little S&M between friends?), for the average woman the balancing act is still tough. Even though a woman may *know* that a fantasy is just a fantasy, often it's difficult for her to abandon herself to a politically incorrect one.

"I'm going through hard times with my boyfriend right now," one woman told me. "I turn on the TV and everywhere I look I see news reports of little girls who have been sexually assaulted or mutilated. There was one just the other day about a six-year-old kid who was assaulted, murdered and stuffed in a boiler room. And on every TV program I see women being completely objectified. Then I go into the bedroom, where my boyfriend wants me to act out fantasies. I'm supposed to wear lingerie and be a little French maid and he's supposed to 'take' me. He's apologizing like mad, saying, 'I'm sorry, I'm a product of my culture. I can't help it. I get turned on seeing you like that.'

"And even though he's a loving man, and I understand the eroticism of such fantasies, I can't get into the games right now, because all those degrading images of women are in my head. I can't make those fantasies work where I'm the coy innocent little woman being overpowered by the masterful man. I keep getting flashes of that little kid being murdered."

Patience and mutual understanding are the only way around this dilemma. Fantasies are a pleasure to share in bed when two people can get off on them. If one partner tries to improvise a scene, however, and the other keeps fumbling because of static in the brain, better to bring the curtain down and try another improv. But criticizing someone for having a particular fantasy, or trying to exercise absolute veto power over a politically incorrect one, is an exercise in futility. One woman who regularly shared fantasies with her boyfriend related that one time he tried one out that really turned her off. "It was this gay thing," she said, "and I just couldn't get into it. All these men were doing various and sundry things to him and to each other, and I realized afterwards why the fantasy bothered me. It wasn't the gay aspect, because I'm aware of his homosexual fantasies, and I understand such fantasies because I have ones about making love to women. The problem was that in all the other fantasies we share, there's an element of female sexual power. Even if I'm not at the center of his sexual attention, I'm participating in the story in some way, or helping him to achieve erotic pleasure with another woman. In his gay fantasy, though, I was completely excluded. He was traveling in a world of male sexuality, and I felt disenfranchised, cut off from my sexual power. I was so alienated by the fantasy that I just went stone cold in bed.

"It was never a problem for us because I explained how I felt and he understood. Also because there are so many fantasies we invent that both of us can share. And I think one of the reasons we have such a great sex life is because we do share them. I'm very politically aware but I don't let myself fall into that trap of using outside standards to judge which fantasies are 'proper' for us and which fantasies aren't. I don't think there is such a thing as a 'proper' fantasy. A fantasy is an extremely personal thing, and it springs from some drive in you. You can argue all night about the politics that underlie the fantasies people have, but if you're in bed with a caring partner, and that partner respects your needs and desires, I don't see what good can come from arguing the sexual politics.

"What I do is listen to my own feelings and to his feelings. Those are the only standards that matter to me when we're making love."

What Kinds of Fantasies Are Men and Women Having?
You name it. I heard female fantasies that involved a woman

masturbating in a roomful of guys, being tenderly caressed by two adoring men, being the only woman on a plane hijacked by Iranian terrorists and being savagely "taken" by them in the cockpit, having her pussy licked by a German shepherd, seducing an uninitiated teenage boy who was hired to clean out the garage, servicing a hundred guys in a hotel room, all of them eating beer and pretzels and waiting for their turn in the "on deck circle."

And I heard male fantasies that involved a man bending a woman over a couch, spreading her legs and gazing at her asshole, several men coming on a woman's face, one man masturbating while a woman offered telephone sex to another man, having a woman dress like a hooker and offering her money for sexual favors, performing anal sex on a teenage girl by lifting up her private-school skirt and taking down her knickers, being "initiated" as a teenage boy by one of the ladies in his mother's bridge club.

I assure you that the men and women who are having these fantasies are solid citizens and contributing, productive members of society.

What about Threesomes?

Many people who grew up in the sixties, but didn't seize the opportunity when they had the chance to screw everything that moved, still dream of having a threesome. Threesomes can involve two men and a woman, or two women and a man. Some guys just can't stomach the notion of being in bed with another hairy guy, but would happily buy season's tickets to watch two women go at it. On the other hand, for some guys the idea of two women inspires performance anxiety.

For many women the prospect of two men is highly appealing because they figure they'll get to be the center of attention. One woman who did partake in such an arrangement wholeheartedly recommended it; she said that two pairs of hands were definitely better than one, not to mention two tongues, and two penises. She also said that men in on a threesome are grateful fellows, because they can't believe their good fortune. And because guys love to show off in front of each other, the result is a lot of ego-strutting—which can only work in the woman's favor. What's more, men in a threesome also tend to compete in chivalry. "When I said my knees were giving out because I was in the doggie position on the wooden bench in a sauna," the woman giggled, "they both leapt up and started stuffing towels under my knees to make sure I was comfortable and wasn't going to call it quits!"

One man who'd fantasized about having a threesome for years felt as if he'd died and gone to heaven when it finally happened. The most sublime moment transpired when he took a short break from going down on his lover, tilted his head upwards and saw her sucking another man's cock. He has gone to bed many a night since then with that heartwarming image dancing in his head.

In the interests of balanced reporting here I must point out that some who have engaged in this sexual rite of passage say it's not always everything it's cracked up to be. For one woman it turned out to be a huge disappointment: "There was a guy and another woman, and the problem was that she was more interested in me, and he got freaked out by that. We couldn't figure out who was supposed to do what to whom, and so everybody wound up unhappy."

Watching a partner make love to another person, maybe even another person of the same sex, is not everybody's idea of sexual nirvana, but people who don't think they're up to the challenge say that just imagining the permutations and combinations works wonders for their sex lives.

How Do You Let Your Partner Know What You Want?

These days many people are simply asking, tactfully and gradually, for what they want. Many others, however, are painfully shy about stating their needs in bed, assuming that if they have to ask, they'll be perceived as demanding. Both men and women report that it's best to save the kinky stuff until you've gotten to know a partner better, because if you announce "I love bestiality. Wanna have a go?" it's a little scary right off the top. For instance, one man confided that a woman once said, a little too hastily, "Do me, doggie style," and all he could picture was "two dogs fucking in the rain, and a pooper scooper." Also, there are still a fair number of women who aren't altogether clear about what they want in the sack, with the result that there are a fair number of bewildered men.

What especially turns men off—and this breed is quite common—is the woman who barks out orders. "Men don't like to be taught by a woman, particularly in bed," one man told me. "It goes back to all those finger-pointing female grade-school teachers we had." Also, men readily admit that they like to think they're already giving a woman what she wants.

While women react poorly as well to the partner who expects to be serviced on demand, they also report that too much shyness in bed is just as unsettling as too much aggressiveness. "Every lover has different desires," one woman said. "Sometimes you try something out that worked like a charm before, so you figure you'll try it again, but maybe it doesn't do a thing for another guy. Worse, maybe it even turns him off. That's why you need some indication of whether you're on the right track."

Both men and women are well advised to make a low-key request or, better still, turn up the volume on the "oooh babys" when a partner gets near the right spot.

When Is It Okay to Say, "I Love You"?
There's an aphorism circulating that a woman should never believe a man who says, "I love you," before sex, and a man should never believe a woman who says, "I love you," after sex. In the film *Parenthood*, for instance, Dianne Wiest counsels her teenage daughter, who's sobbing because her boyfriend has just dumped her.

"But he said he *loved* me," the distraught teenager moans.

"Yeah, well, men say that," Wiest observes dryly, "and then they come."

"I love you" is certainly a more loaded phrase than it used to be; however, this development has turned a lot of people into misers when it comes to using the phrase. The problem with never saying, "I love you," is that the other person is left wondering. Having to guess can make a person profoundly unpleasant company.

I know you can't hurry love, and if you say, "I love you," before or after coming you may not be thinking clearly, and if you say, "I love you," and you change your mind, the other person's hopes may get dashed, and the relationship may turn sour. I know all that. But I still think people are going right off the deep end of caution here. One woman has been dating a guy for two years, for instance, and he still hasn't been able to spit the words out.

Saying, "I love you," is such a personal matter that there aren't any rules for when you should take the leap. Except for the obvious one: when that's how you feel. The general consensus on this matter is that a man or woman should be allowed to say, 'I love you,' and have those words understood as an expression of feeling in the moment, and not necessarily a long-term commitment or promise to love the other person for eternity.

One woman did report that she was seeing a raw and recently separated man who just couldn't get the words out. And so, taking his cue from Woody Allen, for a couple of months he opted instead to say, "I l...l...lerve you." Hey, whatever works.

How Are Men and Women Coping with the Ménage à Moi?
For both sexes, extended periods of sexual famine have become a way of life in these hard-to-meet, hard-to-connect times. Dry spells for men and women who are desirable in many ways range anywhere from several months to several years. One woman said she sometimes thought she was a born-again virgin at forty, while another said she was dealing with celibacy but not very well, since she had a "roaring libido that's roaring more, not less, as I get older." Most people have celibacy thrust upon them, but some choose it because it has become a more attractive alternative than meaningless sex. One refugee from the sixties told me, "I'd rather deal with celibacy right now because it has more integrity." When he realized what he'd just said, he almost choked. "Who would've guessed twenty years ago"—he laughed—"that I'd come out with a comment like that?"

All this abstention has inspired dread and fear in both sexes: will I still know how? Will I come too fast? Will my parts ossify without a yearly maintenance check? One man who hadn't had sex in four years said he'd mentally rehearsed a thousand times what he would tell a woman, should he ever get the chance to go to bed with one again. "I figure I'm going to say that I've got good news and bad news," he said. "The good news is, I'm probably low-risk. The bad news is, I'm probably rusty."

If you're nervous about "the first time," admitting your fear to your partner is unquestionably the best policy—but make sure you add that you've been enduring enforced celibacy because you haven't had any opportunities—or any worth taking. If you're not absolutely clear on that point, the person beside you in bed may start making some false and dangerous assumptions out of incredulity that such an enchanting person as you can't get laid.

One man told me, for instance, that he'd been in bed with a woman who confided that she hadn't had sex in two and a half years. Because he didn't realize that there were many lovable women walking around who hadn't been laid in years, he assumed she was the sort of person who took sex very seriously, and who would never sleep with a man if it wasn't going to be for keeps. Since he liked and admired her but didn't think she was The One, he decided "not to lay a hand on her," thereby ensuring that she wouldn't have sex for two and a half years plus a day.

"There was this performance thing, too," he said. "I figure a woman who hasn't had sex in two and a half years is going to be voracious, and I had visions of being taken out of there on a stretcher by St. John Ambulance."

As I was saying, if you have the courage to confess, perhaps it's best to confess with a full explanation.

On a cheerier note, those who have returned from the jaws of this particular hell say that sex is a lot like riding a bike, and the knack comes back as soon as you hop on. In the meantime, the *ménage à moi* can be a spirit-booster to get you through a lonely time. Fortunately, self-abuse is getting great press these days.

According to John Money—a widely respected American sexologist and author of numerous acclaimed books, who has spent forty years in pioneering sex research at Johns Hopkins University—there's data to show that if you stop monkeys from engaging in sex play, they become "extremely abnormal." This means that when they reach puberty, they cringe and hide, chew the flesh off their arms, and can't even get into the proper position to go at it. Their "lovemaps" (the internal wiring that determines sexual propensities) have been "vandalized," and they don't know what the hell they're doing. So Money figures that monkeys have something to teach us: sex play is a necessary rehearsal stage in our preparation for the big show. Jacking (or jilling) off is a good thing.

This is highly encouraging news—to have self-abuse officially sanctioned—because, times being what they are, solo sex is about all many people have got. "Let's face it," said one man, his voice dripping with irony, "you don't have to worry about commitment. You're not exactly having a deeply committed relationship." Another man who was beating off twice a day wished he had other options, but tried to look on the bright side. "Masturbation," he said dryly, "is sex without aggravation."

People are supporting each other wherever they can, though. One recently separated woman in her mid-thirties received a deluxe vibrator as a birthday gift from one of her single female friends. When she protested that "it hasn't come to that yet," her friend—far more experienced in these matters—told her to put the vibrator in a drawer until she needed it. "I'd recommend a handy drawer," she added. "I wouldn't store it in the basement."

A year later, the same friend gave her a battery recharger. "I was so smug," said the birthday girl. "I'd just split and I thought, how bad can it be out there? Then I found out. I was going through a *fortune* in batteries."

On business trips, another woman straddled the hotel john's bidet and turned herself on by turning on the jet spray. The whirlpool bath jets, she confides, also provide yeoman service.

———

Many singles—especially those whose sex lives reach their apex in the bathroom as they're hunched over *Hustler* or the whirlpool's pulsating jets—dream of better days. Sometimes they dream of settling down. Married sex must be so *cosy*, they coo. So available. So free from all the stress.

Couples who've been together for a long stretch know that these are delusions. In fact, when I told one very married woman that I was writing a chapter about sex in marriage, she arched an eyebrow: "Sex in marriage?" she asked. "Isn't that an oxymoron?"

Not exactly, but it is a challenge. Read on.

6. Sex and the Long Haul

COUPLES TEND TO IMAGINE THAT SINGLES ARE TYING EACH OTHER TO bedposts every night, while singles imagine that couples are getting it regular with a sure thing. The truth is that, at one time or another, sex goes AWOL in most people's lives, whether they're single or coupled. And just as the reality of most singles' sex lives falls somewhat short of married couples' fantasies about them, the reverse is also true. Couples just have different obstacles.

Usually, in a long-term relationship, there's already a body in the bed. Couples don't have to go through all the angst of dating, wondering, "Does he (she) like me?", pretending to find the other person's boring stories fascinating, laughing heartily at dumb jokes. They're already fucking each other, so they don't have to lay on the charm. Also, they're well past that dreadful instructional stage, what one woman described as "You know...'Touch me here...there...no, higher...no lower,' and all that crap."

So, assuming that the person beside them in bed is somebody they still want to have sex with (a gargantuan assumption, no doubt, in some relationships), the problem is not so much how to get somebody into bed as how to stay excited about, find time to make love to, and keep from straying, the person who's already there.

Before peering into the marital bedroom, it's probably useful to pull back for a few moments and consider the odds of making it through with the same person over the long haul. The odds, as most are painfully aware, are sobering:

1) During the 1950s, most people believed in the notion of wedded bliss, but today far more are skeptical about the institution of marriage. According to a study published in the *Journal of Marriage & the Family* in 1988, U.S. national survey data showed a "rather steady decline" between 1972 and 1986 in the positive relationship between marriage and reported happiness. The authors attributed this decline to two main factors: at the same time as never-married-males were reporting more contentment with the single life than their predecessors, married women were reporting less contentment with the wedded state than theirs. "Marriage," wrote the authors, is "no longer viewed as the sure road to happiness, as it was in the 50s.... This change calls for a reassessment of the belief, widely held by family social scientists, that the institution of marriage in this country is as strong and viable as ever."

2) Martha Farnsworth Riche, director of policy studies at the Population Reference Bureau in Washington, wrote in *American Demographics* magazine in 1988 that Americans (and, with some minor statistical variances, North Americans) are living in a "post-marital" society. They are spending far less of their adult lives married. Although many people still crave the constancy and continuity of a good marriage, they no longer know how to stay married. They are staying unattached longer, divorcing sooner, remarrying later and less frequently. There are more singles, more weddingless cohabitations, more births out of wedlock and more female-headed families than ever before. People no longer regard marriage as the only way to love, nor, increasingly, do they regard it as the only way to parent. In fact, the unequivocal evidence is that marriage has become less relevant to them than ever before.

3) First-time marriage rates have dropped to record lows since the sixties, and the median age for those entering first marriages has risen to record highs.

4) Many young people are postponing marriage for so long that an unprecedented number will never marry at all.

5) One in four middle-aged Americans is unmarried. By the late eighties, according to the U.S. Census Bureau, 2.4 million U.S. households consisted of unmarried couples, and one-third of them were raising children.

6) Although the media predict that marriage and "family values" will be back "in" throughout the nineties, divorce has by no means gone out of style. Demographic forecasts predict that between 50 and 60 percent of all marriages will end, and 20 to 25 percent of them will fracture within about four years.

7) Contrary to popular opinion, people who cohabit before marriage are *likelier* than their more traditional counterparts to divorce.

8) Once burned, apparently, twice shy. Remarriage rates for the divorced have taken a sharper nosedive since 1970 than even first-marriage rates.

9) Love is not necessarily lovelier the second time around; a second marriage is even *less* likely to work out than a first. (The odds of getting it right do improve, however, on the third go-round.)

10) Demographic forecasts predict that by the year 2000, the number of households headed by a single adult will equal the number of households headed by married couples. For the first time in history, marriage is becoming an alternative lifestyle!

In the face of such lousy odds, the question men and women who are contemplating a long-term commitment should be asking themselves, then, is not "Is this the person I want to spend my life with?" but "Is this the person I want my kids to be spending alternate weekends with?"

Of course, people don't ask themselves a question like that when they're in a swoon, because the notion that marriage is a happily-ever-after commitment for life continues to fuel an extraordinary number of romantic fantasies. In love's brighter moments, people think they'll beat the odds, and unquestionably some do. But you have a chance of outsmarting the statistics only if you plant your feet on *terra firma* for a moment and consider some serious questions. Is there an intelligent way to stay coupled in the nineties? Is there a way to make love last? And is there a way to enjoy great sex in a long-term relationship and make that last too?

It cheers me immeasurably to report that, yes, there is. The people who have satisfying, enduring long-term relationships say so. They also say that you're kidding yourself if you think it's going to come easy.

There are three fundamentals on which everyone who has managed to preserve a vital and rewarding relationship agrees.

First, maintaining a kinetic relationship in these stressful times—and keeping a sex life from lapsing into a coma—can be achieved only through the one thing our parents lectured us about when we were too young and cocky to listen: bloody hard work.

Second, the person sharing your bed and your life had better be your best friend because, when the lust settles, only a best friend will get you through.

And third, you can forget about sustaining the same kind of passion you had when you first met, because if you tried to do that, you'd be dead.

The thing to keep in mind about sex over the long haul—a foreign concept in this fantasy-driven, sex-obsessed, stay-young-forever, what-about-Me? culture—is that it's not going to be like sex in an affair. "There's not the same mystery or discovery," one woman told me. "There's not the same passion or lust as there is with a new lover. I think we're so conditioned to think that rush you get with a new lover is what love is, that when we don't feel it, we feel cheated. But I think something has gone terribly wrong in our culture when we equate that rush with love. It's totally divorced from intimacy.

"I mean, let's face it, a lot of us are coming from a background where we tended to fuck people we hadn't yet broken bread with. What we don't have much experience with is intimacy. You've got to develop intimacy in a relationship, and you can get another kind of rush from that. Developing intimacy—that's the trick."

It's a lovely thought and I heartily endorse it, but over the marathon of a marriage, the sexual blahs can hit, or the burdens of being a grownup can slow a person down, or one partner can get the hots for another person half his/her age and/or IQ, and jog off in another direction entirely. When hard times (or soft, for that matter) occur, couples can get just as distressed about their sex lives as anyone else. What follow are the questions most couples with relationships of significant duration (ten years or more) eventually confront in the bedroom.

What Happens When the Passion Goes?

Okay, so everyone agrees that if you kept having the kind of sex you had when you first met, by now you'd be a charred fuse. You know what they're talking about: upside-down and sideways sex, up-until-four-in-the-morning sex, where you did it and you did it again and you fell asleep in each other's arms and you awakened and had another go.

Sure you had to be at work in the morning, but you were younger then and your recovery rate was quicker and you could manage on two hours' sleep, and sex like this was worth making sacrifices for.

Depending on whom you believe, the passion is going to settle down somewhere between the second and third year. At the beginning it's the honeymoon phase, the infatuation phase, the courtship phase, the do-it-in-the-road phase. Whatever you call it, it's definitely the most active phase.

"If you kept up the passion you had at the beginning of the relationship," one man who's been with the same woman for a dozen years put it, "you couldn't function. I mean, if I fucked like that now, I'd explode. It'd be nice to get that rocket charge, and I don't know if I'll ever get it again, but there are other things that have replaced it, and they are by no means a consolation prize. You still have moments or periods of great sexual ecstasy in a marriage, but you don't get the pinnacle every time, and the fact is, you don't need the pinnacle every time."

To a one, couples who are content say that although sex was boffo at the beginning, now they're going for quality and not quantity. And for many the quality of sex has improved over time. That's because there's a comfort-level and intimacy informing every encounter, which only time can deepen. In the relationships worth writing about, the passion doesn't vanish—it just changes.

As one man observed, "I think it's important to realize that it's going to be cyclical. It's not that sexual boredom sets in—the passion is definitely still there—but a certain rhythm enters that you can anticipate and like—a certain familiarity and comfort that need to kick in. There are so many moods in sex, and if you're sensitive to where the other person is, it can feel good and different and new all the time. Sometimes it's tender, sometimes it's about deep love and connection, sometimes it's about aggression and sensuality, and sometimes it's just plain old-fashioned lust. It's exciting to acknowledge lust sometimes. We go into the bathroom when the kids are milling about the house and I just throw it in and we have a quickie.

"You know, I looked at her yesterday and asked myself, if I had to do it over again, would I, and I would. I still find her extremely attractive and a turn-on. She takes care of herself. She hasn't gained a hundred pounds since we met, and neither have I. That consistency is very important. And of course all the other basics are there—the love, warmth, humor, respect and acceptance. I can't stress enough how important the acceptance is.

"I think a healthy sex life over the long term just means that you have two willing partners, both of whom can initiate or beg off, depending on their mood, and they can do that knowing the other partner won't feel rejected. The mechanism of it all is the feeling—the fit—and a sensitivity to the other person."

What Do You Do When the Desire to Sleep with Someone Else Hits?
"You know how old you have to be before you stop wanting to fuck strangers?" writes Nora Ephron in *Heartburn*. "Dead, that's how old. It doesn't stop. It doesn't go away. You put all this energy into suppressing it and telling yourself it's worth it because of what you get in exchange, and then one day someone brushes up against you and you're fourteen years old again and all you want to do is go to a drive-in movie and fuck her brains out in the back seat. But you don't do it because you're not going to be that kind of person, so you go home, and there's your wife, and she wears socks to bed."

At some point in a marriage—even the strongest marriage—one person or the other is going to get restless and have at least a twinge of a thought about sleeping with someone else. For some people, this desire occurs about six times a minute. For others, it occurs around age forty. The thing to keep in mind is that nobody gets into bed with the same person every night for a period of years and listens to them pass wind without at least imagining a more alluring alternative.

One recently married man in his mid-thirties related a story about a conversation he'd had with a close male friend. "This guy has been happily married with a couple of kids for a number of years," he said. "One day I was telling him about how I was having a drink with this young, attractive woman who'd called me up to get some advice about getting into television, and how she came on to me and offered me a threesome with one of her girlfriends. And my friend is salivating listening to this story, and a few days later he calls and asks me if I've been thinking about it a lot. I told everybody I knew about it when it happened, but I hadn't really given it much thought after that, and I told him so. "Yeah," he said. "Well, I'm glad you're so well adjusted, because I've been obsessed with it!"

The social scientists have been mulling over this restless feeling and have come up with a benchmark of four years—four years into a relationship and a man or woman is apt to start getting antsy and casting sidelong glances at the kid in the convenience store.

Dr. Helen Fisher, anthropologist and author of *The Sex Contract: The Evolution of Human Behavior*, figures that the four-year itch is pre-programed, coded right into our genes. It rears its head in the form of a fidgety, insistent, some might say prehistoric urge to make love or fall in love with someone different. She also believes that the divorce statistics reflect this restless tendency.

Dr. Fisher says she examined divorce statistics from fifty-eight nations, regions and cultures, from urban societies to rural, from bankers to tribal hunters. With remarkable consistency, like a duck in a shooting gallery, number four popped up as the vulnerable year in a relationship, the year when divorce was likeliest to happen.

The interesting thing, then, is not the restless feeling, because most people, sooner or later, get that. What's far more fascinating and instructive is the question of what separates the people who choose to stifle that feeling from the people who choose to act on it. (Of whom more in the next chapter.)

Some of you who have acted on The Urge, or are busily making plans to, won't like what I'm going to say next. You're going to think that my attitude is incredibly passé and boring and that nobody who is truly hip actually subscribes to it anymore. But don't blame me: I'm just the messenger.

The fact is, in the top-drawer relationships, nobody has a loosey-goosey attitude about sexual fidelity. *Nobody*. In those unions, the notion of fidelity is a given. That's not to say that both partners aren't intensely aware of the constant threats to monogamy—they are indeed. And that's not to say that some of them don't have vulnerable moments or close calls. It's just that they don't go around saying things like, "Well, we'll see what happens..." or "There's no way of knowing if I'm going to be faithful down the road...."

For such people there *is* a way of resisting temptation, because the pledge of loyalty is serious and non-negotiable and it affords them inner resolve. They don't leave their options open or give themselves permission to be unfaithful down the line by rationalizing that, what the hell, everyone's doing it and fidelity is an outmoded concept and they may as well gather rosebuds while they still can. In other words, they don't kid themselves with all that moral relativity crap.

Believe me, these people are not any less horny than anybody else. Or any more straight. Or any less tempted. They want a kick at the can too. What stops them, however, is not so much the sex part as the lying part. They tend to subscribe to the quaint notion that a solid, enriching relationship is based on certain fundamentals, and that trust and honesty are two of the biggies. They figure that once they start lying to their mates, they've tarnished something absolutely rudimentary about what holds them together. They also know that if they start lying, they'll have to live with the lie, that lie will poison something worth cherishing, and they'll never be able to restore it.

Mind you, that still leaves them with the nagging problem of what to do with the desire to sleep with someone else. And that desire is more or less pressing, depending on the person, the state of his or her mind, and his or her relationship.

Some people take their fantasies right into the bedroom, working them out by cooking up a story about all the filthy things they want to do to their fantasy-fuck, and sharing those desires with their mates in the throes of passion. That way everyone gets off and the "infidelity" becomes a family affair.

One couple experiencing the sexual doldrums decided to go a step further and, by mutual agreement, actually have extramarital affairs. Then they came home and whispered all the details of their adventures to each other in the sack. This modus operandi is not to everyone's tastes, I'll admit, but it worked for them. And the reason it worked, according to the husband, is that the marriage was solid and nobody was having affairs on the sly. There was no lying involved. In fact, most people who've lived through the discovery of a mate's affair say that the most painful part of the experience (and the most damaging to the relationship) is not the sexual betrayal (although men do seem to feel the sexual deception more acutely than women do), but the breach of trust. The real agony is having to confront the truth that they're living with a deceitful person whom they thought they knew intimately but didn't really know.

The people who don't play around first and ask questions later have a great deal to say about why they don't; anyone who's wrestling with the problem of staying monogamous in a long-term relationship may find their words interesting. Here's one representative comment from my interviews:

"Yes, I want to sleep with other men. I've been interested and I've had opportunities, but I haven't been tempted. I figure it's better to pay a therapist to work out our problems now, than to have an affair and pay a lawyer to divide our property later. The fact is, even though we're in an off-period with sex right now, sex is more exciting for me if it's with someone I'm comfortable with."

Here's another:

"I lust after other women all the time, but I share my fantasies with my wife and she gets into them with me. If I'm walking down the street with her and I see a woman with great tits or something, I make a crack, and she always smiles and says, "You like those, honey?" Because I can express those desires and have them accepted without making her feel threatened, I work them through that way. That's why I don't follow my penis around and get led astray. I think that what my lusting after other women means to my wife is that I'm not dead yet. She knows she's living with a man who's still alive.

"I don't have affairs because, even during times of difficulty, I know that it would be very hard to get all the other things that we have together. I'm old enough to know that it's easy to fall in lust, but it's a hell of a lot harder to fall in love. That's why I don't put at risk what I have."

And another:

"I have no doubt that my wife could find a better lover than I am—certainly a more interesting one! I consider the fact that she chooses not to sleep with another man a tremendous compliment to me. You can go crazy desiring other women and sometimes I do, but I always come back to that compliment my wife is paying me and our marriage by being loyal, and I see the wisdom of repaying it."

If You're a Partner in a Dual-Career Couple, Will You Ever Have Sex Again?

Dual-career couples (especially those with kids) will be relieved to learn that, even in the most stellar relationships, months can go by without any action. This is because almost everything in the contemporary dual-career couple's life mitigates against doing it. (This demographic group has garnered its own snappy acronym—DINS—which stands for double income, no sex.)

For most two-career couples, the twin burdens of work and family responsibilities create such a motherlode of stress that sex just isn't a high priority. This used to be called the Barrister Syndrome ("I can't get it up, I have to be in court in the morning") and it was almost exclusively a male malady. In a survey done for *Coping with His Success: A Survival Guide for Wives*, a book published in 1984, Frances Bremer and Emily Vogl noted that 67 percent of the women married to very successful men reported unsatisfactory sex lives. But, as so often happens today, where men have gone, women are following. One female CEO told a columnist from *Mademoiselle* that her "Kegel muscles had atrophied" from lack of use. Despite a sex life that had plummeted to ground zero, she and her mate laughed about their "pathetic" sex life, "as all 'dual career' couples do...."

One lawyer in her mid-thirties who had watched her sex life go first and her marriage disintegrate second said, "I've had lots of conversations with professional women like me and they all say their sex lives have gone to rat-shit. You're aggressive all day in what is still largely a man's world and you haven't got anything left over at the end of the day. Even getting together is a big problem. You get home late, and by the time you eat dinner it's 8:30 p.m. and you have two minutes to relax because you have a big closing. And that's when you're lucky enough to arrive home by 8:30."

What we have here, then, is not so much a sexual problem as a lifestyle problem. For, even if you part company with Freud on the penis-envy and vaginal-orgasm issues, you have to admit that he did have a point about love and work being the two essential driving forces in life. But the demands of our work lives are so exhausting that we have little spunk remaining to invest in our love lives.

"I think lifestyle change is the only answer," one man told me, echoing the sentiments of many men and women. "We have to make choices about how we want to live our lives. I work as a television producer on a high-profile public affairs show. Last year I was overseeing several major stories and I was flying out of town constantly, for days or weeks on end. I was flipped out all the time.

"I don't relax anymore. I don't work out anymore. It's work, work, work, all the time. I've let the physical, sensual side of my being go, and when you do that your sex drive just shrivels up and dies. And then you start fearing your own performance and so you avoid sex. Or you just get it over with.

"I mean, those morning sessions my wife and I have! You do it and then check your watch and leap out of bed and say, 'I'm outta here. Give me the granola bar and orange juice and I'm gone. History.'

"My wife gets me out of town periodically for a relaxing weekend. She's adamant about it, and I'm glad she is. I've got to be relaxed to have sex, and I'm never relaxed. And you can't cultivate intimacy on the run, either. Sometimes when she comes home, after she's been away on business, it takes me a while to realize there's this other person there, I'm so preoccupied.

"I'm so competitive with the other guys on the show, too. They've read some book so I have to read it, and go them one better and read another. But I read three books and I'm so burned out trying to stay ahead that I can't get a hard-on."

In the face of such stresses, many couples try to keep in touch in other ways, just to reassure each other that they're not completely washed up. This means that he grabs her boobs in the kitchen while they're throwing together what passes for dinner during the week, and she grabs his crotch playfully while he's shaving—the contemporary couple's way of reaffirming that, yes, I'm still interested, yes, you still turn me on, and even though you haven't seen my genitals in several months, one day you really will fuck me again.

Another factor is the role the nightly news plays in the marital bedroom. Give a man the option of watching the late news or having sex with his mate, and he'll almost always choose the former. In fact, in 1982, when the Canadian national news moved from its traditional eleven p.m. time-slot to ten o'clock, the CBC switchboard in Ottawa received a grateful call from a woman who'd been married sixteen years. Her sex life had dwindled during that time, she reported, because her husband always watched the news while she fell asleep. Since the time-switch, however, life was better.

The most giant obstacle inhibiting a passable sex life, though, is the kids. In 1988, *Parenting* magazine published results of a survey about the state of their readers' sex lives after the birth of a baby and found that "many parents go into a sexual hiatus that lasts for at least a year." The respondents cited fatigue and lack of desire as the major sex-killers: 22 percent of them were managing to get it on only once a month or less, 33 percent between once a week and twice a month.

"When kids enter the picture," one woman told me, "fatigue is a big factor. The demands of kids, coupled with all the other pressures in life, don't exactly turn you into a sex kitten. And when they get older, privacy is a big factor. You feel the way you used to feel trying to do it at other people's cottages."

Dumping the kids with the grandparents and doing some creative financing to find the money for a dirty weekend is a superb solution here. Kids hang around for eighteen years or so, and these days, the cost of living being what it is, some of them are refusing to leave home altogether. Unless you're a Tibetan monk, eighteen years can be a punishing interlude without sex.

You Hardly Ever Want It—Are You Dysfunctional? Should You Get Professional Help?

It's probably not a bad idea. But take heart; if you have to have a sexual dysfunction, the hip one to have right now is Inhibited Sexual Desire. The phrase Inhibited Sexual Desire (known affectionately in the sex field as ISD and officially as hypoactive sexual desire) was first coined in 1977, by Dr. Harold Lief, professor of psychiatry at the University of Pennsylvania School of Medicine. What ISD means is that a person just doesn't have the yen to do it. We're not talking about occasionally temperamental equipment, or not being in the mood. We're talking about *complete absence of erotic interest*, "neither thinking, caring, fantasizing, nor having the remotest concern about anything to do with sex or things sexual at all," as Maggie Scarf puts it in *Intimate Partners*. According to Dr. Lief you have to have "two or fewer desired sexual experiences a month" to qualify as an ISD sufferer. The key word here is "desired." Even if you're not having sex, as long as the thought of sex doesn't make you sick, and you're hoping to get it on, or you're playing with yourself now and then, you're okay. The ISD sufferer may be too stressed out, too anxious, too bored, too threatened or too depressed. Maybe sex used to be fun for that person, maybe it was never fun, but it's certainly not fun now. Whatever the reasons, the mere idea of messing around—even with oneself—hardly ever occurs.

Most of the luminaries in the field of sex therapy say that ISD affects about 20 percent of the population. (The problem, experts say, has likely always existed to some degree, but greater social sanction to seek treatment for it has brought ISD out of the bedroom into therapists' offices. What *is* new about ISD is that in the fifties it was perceived largely as the woman's problem and lumped in with what was called "frigidity"; in the spirit of the times, it has become an equal opportunity dysfunction.)

ISD commonly hits married and cohabiting couples in their thirties and forties. Because its causes can be biological, psychiatric or rooted in the dynamics of a relationship, there's not one treatment for it. The best thing to do is to get yourself into therapy and let the professionals figure out what's going on.

What's the National Frequency Average, and Should You Be Worried If You're Flunking Out?

Let's say you can scratch ISD from your list of things to fret about, but you're still concerned about frequency. Is there such a thing as "normal" frequency?

It's foolhardy to talk numbers without putting them into context. Yes, study after study indicates that the U.S. "national average" for married and cohabiting couples is two to three times a week, that frequency tends to beget frequency, and that there is generally a strong correlation between a contented sex life and reported overall satisfaction with the marriage.

However, line all the sex experts up against the wall and each and every one of them will chant that a frequency standard means nothing. Not to worry, they'll say, in that commonsensical way of theirs, frequency normally goes up and down in any marriage (textbook statistics: from three times a week in the first year of marriage to once a week after ten years—a phenomenon sometimes referred to as the "Saturday night syndrome"). They'll also say that when people talk frequency they're usually talking only about missionary-position-with-the-lights-out sex. But that's an impoverished view, insist the experts, because "sex" can be defined in many, many ways.

Still, here we have a bit of a Catch-22. It seems a little unfair for them to unearth the data that set the frequency standard in the first place, and then beg off any responsibility when people start measuring themselves by that standard. And let me tell you, some people get very uncomfortable when they hear these statistics. Sometimes they don't even have to know the official numbers—they just find out how much somebody else is doing it, and they feel inadequate.

For instance, one 43-year-old woman in a dual-career marriage with a couple of young kids reported that her 65-year-old mother confided in her one day that she hadn't been doing it as much since her husband's prostate operation.

"How often are you having sex now?" her daughter asked.

"Only a few times a week," the mother told her.

"A few times a week?!!" she replied, trying to act nonchalant. "Well...how often were you having it before?"

"Five or six times a week," her mother answered, thoroughly depressing her daughter, whose sex life wasn't close to being in the same league.

What keeps couples going through the dry spells is that they pay scrupulous attention to connecting—physically or otherwise—on a daily basis. "I can't imagine not wanting to touch him, even if I don't want to have sex with him," one woman said. "I can't imagine not being entwined in his arms when we sleep. I can't imagine going without the day-to-day physicality, the hugs, the kisses, the emotional intimacy. That best-friend/buddy stuff rarely falters. The absolute consistency of that is what's comforting."

What's worth keeping in mind about frequency is this: if elsewhere in the relationship things are cruising along fairly respectably, it's best not to make too big a deal of it.

Stress Makes You Horny But Turns Your Partner Off. What's a Couple to Do?

I heard a lot of grousing on this theme from men and women alike. It's the old problem—what happens when an irresistible force meets an immovable object?—and many couples are confounded by it. Many, but not all:

"He says, 'I need sex twice a day,' but I say, 'Well, I only need it twice a month,' and he goes nuts. So I say, 'Well, I guess we're going to have to find a compromise somehow.' So we talk and we come to an accommodation. I say I can live with twice a week. He's not thrilled, but he says he guesses he can live with twice a week too. So then I suggest we schedule it, you know—plan when we're going to do it. Because at least that way I figure I can get into the mood. The stresses, the pressures of day-to-day life, don't seem to affect him the same way as they do me when it comes to sex; he's usually up for it. In fact, when the stress gets really bad, that's when he seems to need it the most. But sex is the last thing I feel like then.

"So he goes nuts again. 'Plan it?' he says. 'Aw c'mon. That's so contrived.' But I say, 'Just try it,' and so, grudgingly, he agrees. Well, you know what? It works. We don't get into those situations where he presses and I resist and we both wind up feeling lousy. I know tonight's the night and I find myself thinking about it during the day, looking forward to it. I dress up a little, fix my hair. We feed the kids first, get them to bed, and then we spend some time with each other, maybe just talk for a while, or rent a movie. It's kind of like a date, and it gives me a charge. And, much to his surprise, he likes it better too, because he knows it's a sure thing. There's not going to be an argument. He's going to get lucky."

I have to admit that this solution sounded contrived to me when I first heard it, too. I thought, well, this is what it's come to:

sex by appointment. Regimen is the one thing two-career couples understand, so if their sex lives are out of whack, regimen will set things right. But although I was skeptical and judgmental at first, I started hearing similar testimonials from others, and I got sold on the idea of regimen when all else fails.

In a world with more equilibrium there would be no need for appointment-book sex, because sex would be one aspect of a balanced life; you wouldn't have to clear time for it. But if you find that sex is being pushed off your schedule by other commitments, I'd strongly recommend getting out your appointment books and penciling each other in. Scratch that—maybe you'd better use indelible ink.

If You Want to Punish Your Mate, What's the Most Perverse Way You Can Do It?

Withholding sex is one of the most popular ploys for torturing a mate. Usually the person doing the withholding is extremely pissed off about something but would never dream of coming right out and saying what's bugging them (thereby clearing the air and getting on with life). It's so much more effective and satisfying to push a mate's vulnerability buttons, punish them and watch them squirm. You could call it a depraved version of foreplay.

Withholding sex is also a wonderful tactic to use in a relationship if you're feeling a little bored and you want to make your mate feel lousy, unattractive and past it sexually. And it's useful as a distancing mechanism, or a fail-safe tactic for stirring up a little hostility and provoking a go-nowhere cycle of blame and recriminations.

For centuries, withholding sex was the woman's job. Men didn't go around withholding sex as a weapon because "proper" women weren't supposed to want sex in the first place; a man couldn't very well punish a woman who was supposed to view sex as a loathesome duty by denying her his penis—she'd think she was getting a lucky break. No—withholding sex as a power maneuver was the wife's trump card—it gave her a lovely bit of leverage in the unequal alliance called marriage. But as marriage evolved into a more equal partnership, husbands (just like their single male counterparts) saw the wisdom in employing this stratagem too.

Massachusetts psychologist Dr. Peter Wish told *The Washington Post* in 1989 that in the sixties "husbands dragged their wives in [for sex counseling]. Now it's the opposite. Women are no longer willing to settle, and men are under more pressure to perform." And in *Is There Sex after Marriage?* Dr. Lief tells author Carol Botwin that he saw this reversal time and again among his patients. The number of wives complaining about husbands who won't come across is "striking."

Just as the long-overdue unleashing of the female libido has turned upside down every dynamic between the sexes, so too has it rocked the connubial throne. Now men have all kinds of dandy new reasons for getting into the punishing/withholding game. Now they are committing to women who not only have sexual "pasts," but sexual pasts they remember with fondness, due to the often passionate intensity of here-today, gone-tomorrow couplings. Even a "progressive" man may become a tad uncomfortable with a sexually literate woman, regardless of how delightful he found her at first. Over the longer haul of the relationship he may come to see her as a sexually demanding harpy, or he may feel she's secretly comparing him to previous lovers. Furthermore, he may still want to be the teacher, or may think, consciously or not, that sex is primarily for him.

But the classic I-want-it/I-won't-give-it-to-you conflict always requires two partners, and although it may seem to be the man who's holding back, the woman is undoubtedly playing her part too. Perhaps she's demanding sex on her terms every time, or insisting on perfect equality during every sexual encounter, believing she has not only the innate right but the political responsibility to show him what to do, when and how to do it. Her coming on like General Schwarzkopf instructing the troops may lead him to respond by shutting down altogether, as only men can do, by not getting a hard-on.

Such men don't get a hard-on because they can't. Women rarely understand this; women get angry because they think the men are purposely withholding their hard-ons just to punish them, or they bridle at the insulting implication that they're not sexy enough to turn their men on. Punishment may indeed be the goal, but it's somewhat counterproductive to blame the man for it—he's doing it unconsciously; when he looks across the pillow, what he sees is a distorted image of a nagging, finger-pointing shrew. Also, a woman who believes she's going to arouse a man by folding her arms, glancing contemptuously at his shrunken wee-wee and saying, "So, are you gonna get hard and do me tonight or what?" is a woman who has a lot to learn.

When a man is in bed with a woman he views as aggressively demanding, all he can think of is that he's got to protect his *cojones*. How can he feel like a man with a woman who's always demanding a performance—and a flawless one at that? And so sexual politics wreak havoc with his erection. What his limp condition may really be saying to his mate is "Listen, honey, go ahead. You can have your independence and your sexual equality and your career and your disposable income, but you can't have my cock. *Nyah nyah nyah.* I still own you, baby"

Of course, two can play at this game; often the woman will

counterattack by closing her legs when her mate decides that he wants it. Ain't love grand?

The only way out of this trap is recognition on the woman's part that penises don't usually get hard—or people amorous—when they're being insulted, and awareness on the man's part that gamesmanship may score points in business negotiations, but is the surest road to misery in the bedroom. Sex is supposed to be an expression of affection. When the groundwork for affection has been laid—by acknowledging what's really going on—there's greater likelihood that both partners will get laid as well.

How Do You Cope with the "Not Now, Honey" Moment?
Even among couples whose sex lives are proceeding swimmingly, one moment that crops up a lot in the bedroom is the Not Now, Honey moment. It often happens when one person—sometimes the man, sometimes the woman—makes a subtle sexual overture to a partner, like telling her (if it's the man) that he needs to fuck something. What he hopes is that she'll be sporting enough to come across.

At this point one of three things will happen. Once in a while both parties will actually be into having sex at the same moment, and the two of them will eventually fall asleep blissfully. Sometimes maybe the woman won't be interested in sex right then, so she'll adopt an apologetic tone and say gently that she just isn't in the mood and is that okay, honey? At other times, however, she'll turn to him with a look of abject disgust and ask him in a shrill voice how he can possibly *think* about doing it now when she's not feeling the *least* bit horny. After all, he knows she's got PMS, he knows she was up at six in the morning and he knows they haven't resolved the fight they were having about his boorish family at dinner time.

Then the two of them will launch into the Right Time discussion, and he won't have a clue what she's talking about and she won't have a clue what he's talking about, because men simply don't see why women always have to wait until the Right Time to have sex, and women simply don't see how men can think about having sex at what, to them, is obviously and appallingly the Wrong Time.

I want to stress that I doubt this centuries-old debate will ever be resolved. It's largely the fault of the God and Goddess of Relationships, who must have shared an extremely sick sense of humor, because they decreed that men and women would bring such infuriatingly different needs to sex. Although there are clearly exceptions to this rule, women usually need to feel relaxed before they can fuck, while men need to fuck before they can feel relaxed. For such men, sex is like a workout.

Women tend to view men as especially crude beasts when they want to do it after a fight. They get really put off by the guy who wants to have sex instead of making up, because such behavior only confirms their view of men in general, which is that men are hopelessly obtuse about emotional issues and seem to think, in their naivety, that they can just ignore what's really going on and that fucking will solve everything, while of course women know through their highly evolved moral and psychological superiority that only talking endlessly about the relationship will solve everything. So it's a law of nature that no woman on the planet can even think about having sex until a fight has been resolved.

For men, however, making a sexual overture after a fight is the most natural thing in the world to do. The reason is that men are far more romantic about sex than they let on, or than women believe them to be. A man who wants to have sex after a fight, even if the fight isn't resolved, is hardly ever thinking what the woman thinks he's thinking. If he's a romantic, he's thinking that sex will allow him to stop sweating the small stuff, to reconnect with his mate and reaffirm something exquisite in their lives. Once they've reconnected, maybe the issue won't seem like such a big deal anymore, or maybe they'll feel affectionate enough to resolve it more easily. His logic works as follows: if he fucks, he gets to come. And what works better than coming to make him feel relaxed, unwound and perkier about life in general? He then figures—and this is why his trusty sidekick, male logic, gets him nowhere on this issue—that the same result will be true for a woman.

To a man, then, waiting for the Right Time is sort of like waiting for the moment when the Cubs win the World Series. It feels as if that moment is never going to come—and, sadly, neither is he. This, needless to say, irritates him.

Some couples do find that fighting and then fornicating is a great first step toward resolving conflicts. Instead of getting angry, yelling at each other and saying things they're inevitably going to regret later, they try a little violent sex and work out their anger with a good fuck. After they've cooled off and had a chance to sleep on the problem, *then* they talk. "I hate not being able to resolve arguments with my husband," one woman said, "but I hate even more the feeling of going to bed upset when we haven't made up. I think we're drawn to sex at those times because, underneath the angry feelings, there's a chemistry or connection between us and we're both longing to find our way back to it. That chemistry pulls us toward each other when we're off balance—it's a kind of sanctuary at the center of our relationship—and the sex reminds us that we're still connected on a deeper level, even though words have failed us and we're taking cheap shots at each other."

Is It Politically Acceptable to Say, "This One's for You, Honey"?
Not only is it impossible, it's inadvisable for a woman to try to have

politically correct sex at all times. Sometimes she may not be in the mood at all when the man beside her in bed just wants to get his rocks off. If she is feminist in her inclinations, she may think it's incumbent upon her to view his request as swinish, and may say, "Forget it, you slavering pig, I'm not here just to be a vehicle for your pleasure. I'm a person too, you know."

A far more mature way of dealing with this moment is to say, "Well, what the hell, honey, I love you, so this one's for you." If she can't get these words out without choking, she can qualify her response, after the deed is done, by uttering softly in his ear that he owes her one.

Is Anyone Faking Orgasms in This Bedroom?

You'd think one of the big perks of a long-term relationship would be that a woman could finally put behind her the need to fake orgasms. Such, alas, is not the case. Men may be chagrined to learn that many of their mates are still faking it, but perhaps it will cheer them to learn that, although most of the women don't feel good about doing it, they're faking for the most generous reasons. No matter how much they reassure their mates that it's okay for a woman if she doesn't come all the time, their partners still feel disappointed. So the women fake it out of respect for tender male feelings.

"As far as I'm concerned," one woman said, "it's just good manners. When I'm feeling quite orgasmic, I tell him that it didn't happen tonight but it will tomorrow. But when I don't feel sexual or confident about my sexuality, I can't imagine when it's going to happen again, so I fake it to make him feel better."

Any man who wishes to banish fakers from his bedroom, then, must learn not to take the matter personally, and not to get a morose look on his face if his partner doesn't come.

How Do You Keep Sex Interesting?

There are no rules on this one, because what's "interesting" to some is conventional beyond words to others. If I tell you, for instance, that some couples revitalize their sex lives by lighting candles in the bedroom and taking baths together, some of you are going to think that's baby stuff. If I tell you that some couples watch porn regularly, or make their own dirty movies, or make dirty movies with other couples and watch them together, some of you are going to say that's disgusting while others will say, "Yeah, tried that...what else have you got?" And if I tell you that some couples try quickies on the kitchen floor, or peeing on each other, or having group sex, or getting it on with a Labrador retriever, or that some couples get off just by fantasizing and talking dirty about all those possibilities, some of you are going to be titillated as hell and some of you are going to vomit.

Okay, so I'm exaggerating a bit. I didn't meet anyone who admitted to getting it on with a Labrador. (That's not to say they're not out there, of course.) But I did meet people who had tried, or contemplated, just about everything else.

Let's start with the basics. It should come as no surprise to learn that a lot of women complain that their mates aren't nearly romantic enough when it comes to sex. They want a leisurely encounter, but all too often the men think, as one woman put it, that "you should screw for ten minutes, come and that's it." The women eventually figure out that, if they want to kickstart their sex lives, they're going to have to seize the initiative. For some, this means investing in ropes and chains. For others, it means investing in garter belts and peek-a-boo underwear. (One woman who regularly stocked up at the lingerie counter reasoned that she couldn't afford to surprise her man with a new bustline or tush, but sexy undergarments were within her budget.)

Most men admitted to me that they were lousy about paying attention to romantic details, and they do appear to be lagging behind women in that area. However, when the sex gets routine, they're more than willing to go out in a snowstorm to track down some good porn.

"I have to remind my husband about the romance," one woman said. "Sometimes I'm sarcastic. I make cracks. He does something and I say, 'Ooooh...that was romantic!!' When I feel needy I want more than just sex with him. I want to get away for the weekend.

"Women must trust their instincts about romance, I think. Sometimes I'll light candles when we make love, and he'll say, 'What the hell are you lighting candles for?' and I'll say, 'Oh, shut up. I'm lighting candles because candles work.' And he just laughs. Or sometimes he asks, 'What's that?' and I say, 'Just shut up and listen. It's love oil. You buy it in one of those places it's embarrassing to be seen in. But it gets hot when you blow on it. And it works too.'"

One of the best ways couples have found to inject a sexual thrill into long-term relationships is to treat the encounter as an affair. Here's my favorite success story. He had always dreamed of a nooner. For his fortieth birthday, she asked his secretary to clear his afternoon and she picked him up at the office at twelve. Then she drove him to a tacky motel, where she unpacked a little "whore's kit" of bubble bath, a couple of joints, and various jellies, unguents and motorized devices. After an extended bubble bath *à deux*, they leapt on the waterbed and prepared to indulge, at which point he turned to her with a leering look and murmured sweetly, "Okay, honey, let's put whitecaps on this sucker!"

The message here is that the element of surprise goes a long way, and if the sex is getting boring, you've got to shake things up a little. The degree to which you shake things up depends on how mired your sex life is in tedium, what you *both* need to give it some cheap thrills, the limits of your imagination, and your partner's tolerance, stamina and receptivity to visionary thinking.

What Role Can Porn Play in a Couple's Sex Life?

The video revolution has been a blessing for many couples confronting the problem of flagging desire, because it has taken X-rated movies out of the sleazy downtown porn emporiums, where women rarely ventured, and into the home.

During the eighties, the industry realized that by cleaning up its act a bit, and by pedaling some good raunch with a little class (not to mention clean sheets), it could now draw women, who would use the movies as a turn-on before making love with their mates.

By 1987, *Time* was reporting that "women account[ed] for perhaps 40 percent of the estimated 100 million rentals of X-rated videotapes [in the United States] each year." This new female audience began to make its voice heard, pressing for some writing and direction tailored a little more to their tastes.

In conventional male-oriented porn films, there's usually some heavy-duty humping and a stunning ejaculation or two fairly early on, or the movie is thought to drag. But women prefer the build-up of romantic tension and are more turned on by the mood—unlike men, whose brains are wired to get cranked up by visual imagery. (This is a fact that any woman who has seen a man slink into the bathroom with *Penthouse* furled beneath his arm, or has been in bed with a gentleman who obsessively fixates on her pussy, will surely realize. One woman I talked to was totally nonplussed when her lover sheepishly requested to snap a Polaroid of hers.)

"The new couples tapes," reported *Time*, "have at least a vague story line, an interesting location and far more foreplay than films

aimed primarily at male audiences.... Impatient males watching
the new tapes for couples must put up with five or ten minutes of
character and plot development before the clothes finally come
off." What's more, in this new porn the sex scenes flow not only
from male desire, but from female passion or need as well, and
women are often the initiators.

I met many couples for whom the pleasures of watching porn
together—whether it was the new porn or the more traditional
variety—often created a lovely little oasis in their humdrum sex
lives. "My wife and I sometimes have arguments about which parts
of the tape to fast-forward," one man said, laughing. "She loves
watching women go at it, but those scenes don't do a thing for me."
And then he added jokingly, "I guess, as with everything else in
marriage, you've got to compromise. We both have to be in the
mood to watch porn, but if we are it always gets us going. I heartily
recommend it."

I also met some people, by far the majority of them women, for
whom porn is a problem, because pornography is viewed by many
feminists as a Bad Thing.

Some leading feminists have lobbied to clamp down on the
lucrative industry and get rid of the stuff altogether, because they
believe it perpetuates degrading and sometimes violent attitudes
toward women. Others have supported the burgeoning new fe-
male-oriented porn, and what certain feminists such as Gloria
Steinem distinguish from porn entirely—"erotica."

The social scientists have also gotten in on the act and they've
complicated matters further, because they can't provide any con-
clusive evidence about whether porn spawns deviant sexual behavior
or not; some studies have claimed a strong correlation, while others
have found not even a dubious link. Meanwhile, accusations and
counter-accusations of personal bias, flawed methodology and gross-

ly misleading conclusions have flown between the two groups like rotten apples.

This public debate has created a great deal of confusion for women. If they find themselves getting turned on by politically incorrect porn—which many of them do—they believe they're traitors to the cause. And so the ghost of political correctness has entered the bedroom once again.

One of the most credible voices I heard on the subject of pornography was that of sexologist John Money. He argues that pornography is not "contagious" and will not make anyone do anything he or she is not already programmed to do. In other words, if you're not already a sexual degenerate, watching porn isn't likely to turn you into one, because people's "lovemaps" (the internal coding that determines personal turn-ons) are pretty much set in childhood.

John Money attributes much pathological sexual behavior to societal attitudes which encourage the separation of lust from love. He sees America as an above-the-belt and below-the-belt culture: steamy, alluring but naughty below-the-belt impulses are denied and punished, while poetically pure above-the-belt impulses are enshrined. He has crusaded tirelessly against "anti-sexual" policies in the culture, and on the subject of pornography he is adamant. "We don't believe in demon-possession theories," he told *Psychology Today* in 1988. "We've given up the mid-18th-century idea that you degenerate yourself by losing your vital fluids. So now we're absolutely certain that we know what causes all this weird sexual behavior: pornography. The only kind of pornography you can like is that which corresponds to your own lovemap. An example I give in lectures is that I could shut you up in a room for five hours of coprophilia movies and there's no chance you'd eat shit sandwiches for breakfast in the morning."

Sex over the long haul may be different from sex in the first blush of love, it may be difficult and dreary now and then and sometimes it may even disappear. But with a little perseverance, patience and creative thinking, anything's possible. That's why, although a lot of sophisticated people sometimes snicker about what happens to their sex lives over time, maybe it's useful for them to remember that marriage is sort of like baseball. Theoretically you *could* hit a homer every turn at bat, but not bloody likely. It's a long season.

7. Dangerous Liaisons

HERE ARE A FEW THINGS TO KEEP IN MIND ABOUT MARITAL INFIDELITY in the nineties: there are a lot of married people fooling around out there. It used to be that married men did most of the fooling around and married women did most of the suffering. Married women are fooling around far more frequently these days, so married people are now suffering equally.

There are also a lot of single women who've gotten the hang of doing it guiltlessly with married men, and a lot of single men who are doing it enthusiastically with married women.

Very few of these people appear to be using condoms.

On one of my research trips for this book, I sat on a plane beside a man in his mid-forties who traveled often on business. To pass the time we struck up a conversation; I soon learned that he was a senior executive with a large media organization, on his second marriage and family. From what I could gather, he was successful in his career and happily content in his marriage.

He was attractive, engaging, intelligent and witty, and in short order the two of us established a rapport that was on some level kinetically sexual. When he discovered I was writing a book on contemporary sexual relationships, he visibly brightened. "So what have you found?" he asked.

I made some observations, he listened and then he casually turned the conversation around to the subject of extramarital sex. AIDS is having a huge impact, he insisted, on married men who fool around. He subscribed to this theory because he knew several men who'd occasionally strayed in the past but, with lethal viruses floating around, were now nervous about cheating. Although he didn't come right out and say it, I sensed that he too shared this anxiety.

I told him that, despite what he was hearing in conversation, AIDS appeared to be having little impact on the number of extra-marital affairs; furthermore, like many singles, unfaithful spouses had not exactly cornered the market on condoms either. He was skeptical, but mulled this information over for a few moments and then, quite subtly, crossed a line.

He'd just found out, he said, that he was going to be free in Toronto for a day before flying to New York. Since Toronto was my home, did I have any ideas as to how he might kill some time? It was the kind of question any woman over the age of eighteen has learned to recognize as an invitation; she has also learned to decide in a split second whether she wants to accept it, or to gracefully decline.

The invitation was flattering and the possibility of a brief adventure enticing, so I weighed the pros and cons. I wasn't involved with anyone at the time, and certainly found him attractive. The downside was that he would be here today and gone tomorrow. At one point in my life such a consideration would hardly have mattered, but at that instant it tipped the balance. I told him he might want to check out the art gallery or museum.

I tell this story not because there's anything exceptional in the fact that a married man hit on a woman sitting beside him on an airplane—it happens all the time—but because it contains in microcosm a lot that is both old and up-to-the-minute about an illicit encounter, or at least the possibility of one: the person who made the first move was apparently happily married, yet willing to seize the day; he could seize it with a woman who was his equal and who was, at the very least, as interested in and available for an encounter as he was; he was skittish about the risks but went for it anyway; despite the mutual attraction and equal balance of power between us, *he* initiated the proceedings; I was a single woman who seriously entertained the invitation of a married man on pragmatic grounds alone—unattached men don't exactly fall out of the trees; I passed up the chance, not out of moral rectitude, but because I concluded that there would simply not be enough in the encounter for me.

———————————————

What Are Women Doing in the Extramarital Affairs of the Nineties? The Affair has undergone a sea-change since the sixties, and—like almost all transitions since that time—it has altered most dramatically for women. That women have made great strides toward equality in their conduct in extramarital affairs is evident in many current studies, surveys, anecdotal accounts and therapeutic observations. But none of those sources reveals the degree to which The Affair has "progressed" for women as compellingly as the article "Betrayed" which appeared in *Esquire* in June 1990.

Lisa Grunwald wrote the article because she wanted to do a piece about adultery, updating the words Iago speaks to Othello when he warns him to think twice about Desdemona: "Look to thy wife; observe her well." She sought her subject through the personals. Her ad ran for only one week, but after seventy calls she stopped counting. The twenty-first caller was "Susan."

Susan was in her mid-thirties, articulate, sophisticated and willing to tell all. She said she had gone to an Ivy League college, would only describe her profession as doctor, lawyer or banker, "had been married for ten years and lived with her husband and daughter on the Upper West Side of Manhattan." For the last eight years, she'd been having serial affairs. A frequent business traveler, she engaged in out-of-town flings several times annually. Her husband knew nothing about her affairs and she saw no reason why he should; they had a wonderful sex life and a terrific marriage.

Over the course of several weeks, Grunwald conducted numerous telephone interviews with Susan. What emerged was a profile of an unabashedly contemporary woman enjoying unabashedly contemporary affairs:

> There had been only one time, she said, when she'd had a close call—the one time that she'd had an affair in familiar surroundings. It had taken place on Cape Cod...when her husband had been away and she had gone to their summer home alone. She had spent an afternoon with a neighbor whom she'd been seeing. They had necked on the beach...then made love in the outdoor shower. They had come back to the porch, and he had put on his clothes and left.
>
> He had been gone for what seemed like a minute...when she heard a car pull up in the driveway and figured that he had forgotten something.
>
> "Well, it's the husband," she said. "So they literally could have hit each other with their cars. That was a miracle. The awkward part about it for me now is my husband comes in and announces that he's incredibly horny. He grabs me by the hand, takes me into the

bedroom, and he wants to make love. And he gets undressed. Now what do I do? This guy has just come inside me. I go into the bathroom. My husband comes in with me. I start to feel paranoid—I'm thinking, *He's not letting me out of his sight*. But we get into bed, and he's kissing me and, as happens from time to time, he wants to go down on me. And I just think, *God, what am I going to do?* Because I just know that he's going to taste something, he's going to see something. On the other hand, I don't want to say no because I don't want to do anything that wouldn't be natural. And I'm thinking I should tell him.

"But he goes down on me, and I'm lying there and...you know, he's not saying anything, and at one point he does pop up his head and says, 'Gee, you're really wet.' And I say, 'Well, you know, you've been away.' And I guess I realized that he didn't know, and it was okay. I was still incredibly nervous. God, I felt really bad that he's down there doing that, and some other guy's semen is there.

"At some point I just pulled him up and said, 'I want you inside me.' It's one of the only times I can ever remember faking an orgasm. But afterward, an interesting thing happened. I began to find it exciting.

"I still think about it a lot. And sometimes when I think about it, I get excited. There he was. I can't tell you how many times I've been by myself taking a bath or something and just started laughing."

My, my. In developing a certain comfort-level with deceit, the nineties woman has come a long way, baby.

Susan can compartmentalize, rationalize and guiltlessly enjoy her illicit liaisons, exactly as many men have always done. She doesn't fall in love with her lovers, nor does she intend to become emotionally involved—the affairs are strictly physical. And if her husband never finds out, she reasons, how can he possibly be hurt?

Susan emulates traditional male behavior in other ways, too: in order to avoid discovery, she operates with Machiavellian duplicity. She owns two diaphragms, so her husband will never notice one missing. She doesn't pack fancy lingerie, but because wearing it with new lovers is a pleasure, she buys, wears and discards camisoles and panties in other cities. She never uses her real name, reveals where she works or lets anyone see her wallet. She calls her husband at the usual time, from wherever she happens to be. If she will be spending the night away, she asks the hotel desk to hold all calls. If she phones home from a man's apartment, she uses her corporate credit card. Finally, like many men, she furiously upholds a double standard.

"I don't think what I do is particularly moral," she says. "But the bottom line is, I've seen or known my husband's male friends who routinely have these casual flings, and other than that, they're very loving and wonderful husbands and good fathers. The bottom line is, I find it tremendously exciting to be with somebody new. You know, that moment when we're both getting undressed for the first time—that's indescribable.

"...I'd kill [my husband] if he had an affair: I guess I do feel the way men say they feel. I know there's nothing emotional when I have an affair, and it doesn't mean I love my husband any less, and if he were to have an affair, I wouldn't know what that meant."

As Susan's story unfolds, Grunwald stresses to her subject that eventually the two of them will have to meet so that Grunwald can be sure her story is not a hoax or an elaborate fantasy. She promises to guard Susan's anonymity, but at some point she has to learn Susan's true name and see her apartment or the journals she admits to keeping about her affairs. (She has kept them for years, she says, to record such things as whether men are moaners or grunters when they come, how different lovers taste and so on.) Susan accepts these terms, but is coy about where and when such a meeting will transpire.

Then the story takes a curious turn. Although she has always been scrupulous about calling the reporter as promised, one day Susan simply stops calling. Grunwald tries exhaustively to track her down, but to no avail.

In the final pages of the article, Grunwald wrestles with the nagging question of whether Susan's story is authentic. "Even after all the fruitless checking..., I still cannot believe that what she told me wasn't true," she writes. "I would still find it more plausible to learn that she'd been hit by a bus than that she'd made the whole thing up."

Well, I bought it. Although I shuddered at the justifications and the deceit implicit in Susan's double life, her story didn't shock me. By the time I read it, I already knew a great deal about how women were conducting their affairs—both married women and single women who were sleeping with married men.

1) In Kinsey's time, significantly fewer married women cheated (25 percent by age forty) than married men (between 50 and 60 percent by the same age). While the proportion of married men having affairs since Kinsey's time has remained stable, the proportion of married women having them has risen. Now, the percentages may be almost neck and neck.

2) Because studies vary widely in methodology, it is difficult to say for certain exactly how many married women are having affairs, or even whether the majority of married people are unfaithful. In

1987, for instance, Shere Hite said in *Women and Love* that 70 percent of the women she'd interviewed who'd been married five years or more had had extramarital affairs. Of those, 76 percent didn't feel guilty about their infidelity. In 1988, British sociologist Annette Lawson authored a comprehensive study called *Adultery: An Analysis of Love and Betrayal*, in which she found that 60 percent of the women she interviewed had had affairs by age forty. The broad consensus among researchers, however, is that anywhere from one-quarter to one-half of married women have at least one lover in the course of any given marriage.

3) The fidelity span for men and women alike is shrinking, but women have particularly shortened the waiting period, and younger women (those married in the seventies) have passed men in the speed with which they begin to have affairs. Women are waiting, on average, four years after tying the knot, compared with men, who wait five. In the sixties, women waited just over eight years, while men waited slightly under that time period.

4) Women have appropriated behaviors previously perceived as male in the style in which they have affairs. For instance, more women are having affairs, not because they are in love, but because they seek a confidant, or because they wish to explore the possibilities of their own sexuality.

5) There has been a noticeable shift in thinking about infidelity. Before the sixties, men's attitudes about sex outside of marriage were consistently more liberal than women's. Women's attitudes began to loosen up in the seventies and now their views on infidelity are as liberal as men's. Women's magazines routinely run

non-judgmental articles today about the pros and cons of getting involved with a married man. Infidelity has become more tolerable among therapists and psychologists, some of whom currently subscribe to the view that, biologically speaking, lifelong monogamy may not be our destiny. Some therapists argue that increased life expectancy no longer makes it realistic, and that an affair may even be healthy for a marriage. As well, an affair is less likely to break up a marriage that it once was.

6) Men continue to take more lovers than do women, and to initiate liaisons more frequently. Increasingly, however, women are the ones to initiate the affairs.

7) Because of the perceived man shortage, single women are increasingly looking for sex and companionship and are willing to become involved with men already "taken" to get them. Today, however, the single woman who has an affair with a married man is less likely than her predecessor to want or expect him to eventually marry her.

8) If women are "catching up" sexually, they have a long way to go economically. Men, for the most part, still foot the cost of an affair.

9) Annette Lawson reported, in *Adultery: An Analysis of Love and Betrayal*, that the most popular locale for married women to consummate their affairs was in their own homes, in the matrimonial bed.

10) Men are likelier to confess to their indiscretions than they were twenty years ago. Women, however, are doing it more and confess-

ing to it less. Of the women and men who do confess, women report more serious consequences to their marriages. Lawson believes that for all their "progress" in emulating men, women still stand to lose a whole lot more if they confess. Cultural taboos and archetypes remain deeply embedded: a woman who "cuckolds" her husband is still largely viewed as guiltier than a husband who cheats on his wife. And when a wife tells, she grants her husband the traditional authority to punish; when a husband tells, he seeks from his wife the traditional forgiveness. What's more, for men the *sexual* betrayal of an affair is the unkindest cut—worse than the deceit of cover-up.

What Are Men Doing in the Extramarital Affairs of the Nineties? Women may be developing a comfy knack for emulating male behavior in their affairs, but when it comes to the finer points of justifying their infidelities, most of them still have a lot to learn from men. Indeed, moral ambiguity was the middle name of many of the men I met. If they'd had a fling, they had a rationalization. If they hadn't, it was less often out of a commitment to fidelity than because they just didn't have the energy or nerve. Deception takes time, organization, planning. Many simply aren't up to the challenge. Very few of these men said that they wouldn't have an affair because having an affair was wrong. And in inhabiting this late-twentieth-century moral limbo, they are no different from many of their "postfeminist" lovers.

"I know a lot of people who are having conventional extramarital affairs," one woman told me, "just as affairs have been going on for centuries. But now there's all this justification and talking layered into it. It's like a wolf in sheep's clothing. Now there are reasons, excuses. Now they're guilty but with an explanation. In the old days people had affairs but they knew it was wrong. If they chose to go ahead anyway, as people do, it was clear that by making that choice they were committing a transgression, a betrayal. And by committing that betrayal they were making a choice, and that choice had certain consequences, and they were aware of those consequences and prepared to deal with them. Now they have affairs and they talk and they talk and they analyze and they excuse, and if they are asked, down the road, to be accountable for what they've done, they're surprised, as if by all their talking they have somehow rationalized the dishonesty of their behavior, and through words made it right."

To be sure, I met both men and women who were equally adept at using moral ambiguity as an out, which allowed them to Kleenex themselves off with a clear conscience after a little recreational sex, and to stray without having to pay—unless, of course, they got caught.

What is singularly male, however, is to operate by a sliding moral scale—a mind-boggling system of rules and rationalizations. For instance, there is the argument that it doesn't count if you have a "nooner"—you aren't taking time away from the family. Then there's the argument that it doesn't count if you don't do it much; its proponents tend to talk in percentages or qualifiers, describing themselves as "95 percent monogamous" or "basically monogamous." Usually they believe they are entitled by virtue of their sex to a little something on the side. Often they run the "scientific" argument up the flagpole: unless a man (who, they insist, is genetically in need of constant sex) gets his rocks off when The Need strikes, he'll behave like a rabid dog, and since he's going to be hell to live with, he's actually doing his wife a favor by draining off his bestial impulses elsewhere.

I also encountered the argument that it doesn't really qualify unless you do the old in-out. Blowjobs don't qualify. One guy spent over two years feeling up and fingerfucking his Other Woman.

CONNECTION

They pawed each other in bars, necked and petted in public parks, but touching his bare pee-pee was off limits. He scrupulously refused to actually stick it in—that would have been disloyal.

Several men had convinced themselves that their wives knew and silently condoned their affairs—until someone blew the whistle, their wives went berserk and the men had to face the truth: they'd invented the Silent Assent Theory for their own convenience.

One of the most popular lines of reasoning is that it doesn't count if you do it on foreign turf. One professor carried on a five-year affair with a single woman who would travel with him to out-of-town lectures. He wouldn't do the deed in his own town, nor would he make separate plans for a weekend away. "He seemed to operate," said his lover, "on degrees of duplicity. He could have an affair, but not in the city—that was too close to home. He wouldn't invent a reason to go out of town, but if he had to go, I could go with him. That way he didn't have to 'lie'; he just didn't have to tell the whole truth. This situational morality that men seem to have is really baffling. I know women are duplicitous too, but I think they're more honest with themselves *about* their duplicity. There's less self-delusion and bullshit going on."

Although many men who fool around on business trips do it because they think it's one of the perks of the job, for some the occasional foreign affair is the only time they have sex. Said one recently separated man who'd spent ten years in a miserable marriage, "In the last five years of my marriage, sex was an annual event. But I wouldn't compromise my wife by screwing around in the same city. I didn't want her to hear about it from somebody else. As much as I hated her, I wouldn't do that."

Who Are the Repeat Offenders?
"I think it's a given that somebody who fools around on his wife will

242

be unfaithful to me," said one single woman who'd had affairs with married men but swore she would never marry a cheating man. "If he has the potential to be an ax-murderer and he's done it once, you can't be *sure* he'll do it again. But I think it's a safe bet."

The repeat-offender theory, although not necessarily substantiated in fact, is very common among single women who've had affairs with married men. While it's true that the first infidelity is often the toughest, and cheating gets easier for some people after that, repeat offenders are usually in a class by themselves.

The true repeat offender (speaking, for the moment, of the male repeater only) is the guy who never really takes the idea of commitment seriously, the guy who starts having affairs ten minutes into his marriage and then keeps on having them. One classic case was a man who'd been married for eleven years and said he'd "probably had fifteen affairs" during that time. Some were for sex, some for companionship, although he never "fucked them and walked out." Some lasted months, one a few years, and another ten years. (The latter relationship he brought with him into his marriage.) Some of his lovers were married (although none "happily") and some single. He got caught only once, when his lover's fiancé showed up at his door with incriminating pictures.

Women always wonder what it is that drives these guys, so I'll let him tell you himself: "I looked on my affairs as challenges, adventures," he told me. "I thrive on lying to some degree, and sometimes I was living three different lives. It's exciting to keep all the balls in the air at once. Sure, it's taxing, but the excitement always intrigued me and the conquests fed my vanity and prowess as a male.

"I think if you're not satisfied at home you have the right to be satisfied elsewhere, and having affairs was a good way to support a bad marriage. I lied to my wife, but I never lied to the woman I was having the affair with—she always knew my situation. It was the least I could do—be honest with her. I don't think it's anything to be proud of, but I'm not ashamed of it either."

Women can get dissatisfied at home too; and while conventional wisdom suggests that women who roam do it for love, such is not always the case. "We were living together five and a half years," one woman in a marriage-type relationship told me, "but after the first couple of years the sex leveled out. He wasn't as passionately engaged with me as I wanted him to be. I told him I needed more sexual involvement, but he told me that things were perfect for him the way they were, that he didn't want or need anything more. He also told me he wasn't prepared to change. I didn't put heat on him. I had affairs. Our relationship went on delightfully for another three years. Much later he found out that I'd been having affairs, and he was shocked and terribly angry. 'How could you?' he asked me. 'Well,' I answered, 'what the fuck did you think I was going to do?' He was dumbfounded. He said that what *I* was going to do had never crossed his mind. They treat us callously, you know, or neglect us, and then they expect us to be madonnas and forgive them. But we've got other priorities."

How Do Single Men Feel about Sleeping with Married Women?
On the whole, remarkably blessed to have the opportunity. In fact, single men often described to me the unique allure of a married woman. Above all, she is "safe." There is also a particular sense of power and ego-gratification in bedding her, since she is setting aside another man to partake. And of course the "sneaking around" is exciting. "Married women?" said one man. "Oy—they're the best. There's no pressure to call or commit and it's always quality time." Another told me that he had "discovered" older, married

women when he turned thirty. Most single women he was meeting at that time, he said, could not handle sex without promises—the only kind of involvement that interested him then. Married women, however, were remarkably undemanding. "They're so *neglected*," he observed. "Not to mention," he added, smiling with gleeful malevolence, "so *grateful*." He might have thrown in "bored to the point of comatose." And wonderfully hospitable, too; one recently separated man in his mid-forties related that when *he* split, several of his friends' wives called, inviting him to their beds. They were available, they said, for "a little nooky"; was he interested in some "extracurricular activity"?

Do Men Have Any Idea How Unfaithful Women Can Be?
Are you kidding? For the most part, men remain stubbornly blind to the possibility that their wives may be messing around, even when *they're* merrily cheating, themselves.

Many men I interviewed still believe that women don't need "variety" as much as men; they also subscribe to the view that most women (unlike most men, who are, as one put it, "all screwing around and lying about it") will not act on the main chance. Often I listened to stories of this or that casual encounter and afterwards inquired as to whether it had ever occurred to the man that his own wife, or the wives of his friends, might also be straying. Most were nonplussed at the mere idea. I sensed that, for many men, the possibility of a cheating wife—or, more to the point, of *their wife* cheating—had never even entered conscious thought. This is doubly ironic since a number of them are having it off with other men's wives. I heard statements such as "Most women would be content with just one man," and "I know women enjoy sex as much as men do, but they're not as horny," or—a personal favorite—"You'd know if she were unfaithful—a woman just reeks of it when she's been sexual."

What Draws People to an Affair, And Is It Likely to Have a Happy Ending?

People who have affairs will tell you that they do it because they're not getting any at home, or because what they're getting is nothing to write home about. Or they'll tell you that they're lonely, starved for companionship, understanding, romance, attention, intimacy and love. Sometimes they'll tell you they do it because everybody else is doing it, the opportunity presents itself and they crave a little adventure. Lisa Grunwald—the reporter who told Susan's story—theorized that Susan did it out of greed: "It seemed that the glorious normalness of life had never been glorious to her. She'd imported the men to give her life danger. Without it, her life would have lacked an edge. Perhaps she was...a symbol of the hungry decade in which nothing had ever been enough, in which all that anyone wanted was *more*."

Annette Lawson argues compellingly, however, that when people have extramarital affairs what they're really doing (although they don't know it) is playing out the ancient themes in the adulterous love myth of Tristan and Isolde. Lawson points out that, as erotically charged love stories go, the tale of Tristan and Isolde has all the right stuff: love and death, heroism and suffering, joy and sorrow, secrecy and passion.

Tristan is the talented nephew of the king and Isolde is the king's princess-bride-to-be. As fate will have it, they mistakenly drink a love potion intended for the king and his bride, and fall hopelessly in love. Since they can't very well carry on in the palace (what with all the courtiers whispering), they flee to the forest.

Eventually the king finds out what's going on, shows up at their humble hut and sullies their love-nest by placing his sword between the sleeping pair. This ruins everything, and they can't live on love anymore.

Tristan sets off for France and eventually marries, and Isolde goes back to the king, but their hearts aren't in it. Tristan is still so smitten with Isolde that he refuses to sleep with his wife.

Finally, lying on his death bed, Tristan sends for Isolde, telling her to hoist a white sail on the ship to announce her arrival. She shows up but Tristan's wife—who is out of her mind with jealousy by this point—gets revenge on her husband by telling him the ship has black sails. Tristan dies of a broken heart and Isolde is so anguished at this news that she too dies. Two briars with intertwining branches grow from their graves—which is a clue that adulterous lovers have to wait until eternity if they want to make it work.

What does this tragic legend have to do with an extramarital affair in the nineties? Lawson believes that in a democratic age you don't have to be a princess or a knight to have a magnificent adventure on a grand scale. You can have one that *seems* spontaneously invented but in fact springs from this myth, which for centuries has taught that the pursuit of passionate love is a noble quest. Lawson says that not only did her subjects create, live and narrate their own stories, it was "in living this story that so many...felt, sometimes for the first time, that they were 'really alive' and, even, *why* they were alive...."

In other words, since most of us live lives burdened by mundane schlock, an affair affords us a brief, heady moment to star in our own movie. As it turns out, however, people who are seeking to sustain a grand romance often discover the hard way that movies are the stuff of make-believe:

"I was forty-three when it happened. That was so central to my husband. That's what made it possible for him to survive the humiliation of it. He saw it as female menopause—one last fling. He didn't take it too personally, and that took tremendous ego-strength on his part. My lover was thirteen years younger than my husband, and he told himself I had fallen for a macho younger man.

"My attraction to my lover was largely based on sexual fascination. Through the early part of the affair, we only slept together twice. There was a lot of groping and kissing and petting, though. The whole energy of it was that we were being bad teenagers. We were rebellious, staying out late, running away from home. My lover used to say that he hadn't experienced those feelings since he was a teenager.

"We met at work and we began seeing each other six months after we met. We saw each other for almost a year. At that point I decided to leave my husband and I moved in with my lover eight months after I'd split.

"When we moved in together the fantasy broke down almost immediately. It was astounding. I realized that we had very little in common. He was an intense type and he wanted engagement with me almost every moment. I'm solitary and wanted to be off by myself a lot.

"We broke up after only twelve weeks of living together and there was a gradual period of withdrawal. I couldn't quite give him up. And of course, the minute he moved out, the fantasy took hold and he became quite interesting to me again.

"A few months after we broke up I got a call from a woman whom he had characterized to me as a crazie, someone he'd slept with twice one drunken night years ago, who wouldn't leave him alone. A *Fatal Attraction* thing. It turned out that he'd been keeping her on the hook. After we broke up, he actually took her to my apartment when I was away, and told her it was our place. That side of him didn't surprise me, but when I found out, it finished the affair off for me. Boy, did I ever not want to know this person.

"Throughout my affair, my husband kept the home fires burning. Through it all he remained my best friend. I can remember one weekend when my lover told me that he was going out of town to visit his parents. I was suspicious. So I met my husband for a drink and I told him my fears and suspicions and he sat there and listened and tried to put himself in my lover's shoes and advise me. There I am, talking to my husband, with whom I'm not living at the time, about my lover, with whom I am, and I am turning to my husband for advice about problems with my lover, and my husband is counseling me. He did that, and only later did I realize how extraordinary that was.

"This thing—commitment—is pretty fragile. The sixties fucked everything up because in the sixties you fucked everything in sight. It's hard to conceive of a good stable family and sex life after a history like that. There's always a part of you that sees yourself as that wild kid up for some new adventure. I don't think my head will be turned again, though. I'm very cynical about The Affair. There's a real falsity about it."

What Is the Postmodern Other Woman Really Like?
According to Hollywood, if you're male and you grab a little nooky while your wife's out of town, you could wind up with a psychotic on your hands.

Fatal Attraction—the second-highest-grossing film of 1987—was both a cautionary tale and a sexual parable. The film cleverly recast the adultery story with thoroughly modern archetypes: Dan is the feminized, morally wishy-washy cheating husband who suc-

249

cumbs to a steamy encounter with a single woman up against her kitchen sink. Beth is the forgiving stay-at-home wife, but a chic homemaker with a great perm. And Alex is the masculinized Other Woman with the big career who throws herself at Dan and then turns wacko when he won't commit. Just as in the old days, however, the Other Woman is a homewrecker. She gets it in the end.

How many Other Women think or behave vengefully like Alex? Most of the women I met, far from being desperate prisoners of their need for a man, share a pragmatism about their affairs, and a sense of power within them—power born of staying free agents, maintaining emotional distance, refusing to fall in love.

In some cases, that power is also fueled by a low-grade (and sometimes extremely bitter) hostility toward men. A man who doesn't "own" them, either symbolically, through marriage, or emotionally, through love, can't control them. So the woman is less likely to be a lovesick psychotic than a woman who won't commit. In fact, the single Other Woman often gets annoyed and winds the affair down when her married lover gets so comfy with the arrangement that he starts treating her like a wife.

"Yeah, the guys with the lousy marriages think they'll call and you'll be waiting there with the *coq au vin* in the oven," said one woman. "Instead you say, 'I can't see you. I've got plans.' Meanwhile, they're sitting there with their briefcases and hero sandwiches and craving companionship."

Another woman grew increasingly disenchanted when her lover, who used to tear her clothes off and jump into bed the minute he showed up, now only wanted to discuss his marital problems. "His wife is all depressed because her mother died," she told me, "and so he comes over and whines about how miserable things are at home. I tell him that his wife is making everybody crazy—

including me! So then I wind up giving him advice about how he should counsel his depressed wife. This is what I've become: his wife's therapist by proxy."

Not that the postmodern Other Woman no longer needs men. She does—for a little romance, companionship and carnal communion. She wants to be listened to, charmed, wooed, seduced...and then she wants to be fucked blind. What she does not want, in most cases, is a full-time gig.

Because of the repeat-offender theory, and because they've often already been wives, few of the single women I met harbored any desire to marry their lovers. "Why would you want to marry a guy you *know* is capable of having an affair?" several Other Women pointedly asked. "A man who has an affair is a man who has an affair is a man who has an affair," said one woman who had married and then divorced her lover-turned-husband after he cheated on her. "It's like a nasty virus."

Sooner or later, the conventional wisdom goes, a woman will want more than a married man can give her; inevitably she'll get burned. Most of the women I met don't fit those assumptions either. Rather than chafing at the bonds of an affair, they feel comfortably free with a part-time man. Furthermore, if the woman is single, she hasn't got time for the guilt either. Feeling guilty, she figures, is the man's job, since he's the one doing the cheating. If they know (and maybe like) the wronged wife, a few single women do feel a certain woman-to-woman empathy for her—sisterhood and all that—but not enough to call a halt to the proceedings if the affair is filling a gap in their lives.

An affair, many say, is a close-to-ideal solution to a modern dilemma: there aren't enough men and the ones who are out there won't come across. In an affair, the sex is astonishing, the clandestine trysts are thrilling and there is none of the grueling practical and emotional "work" of a standard relationship. Welcome to the 1990s: the illicit love affair as pragmatic bargain.

"It's a perfect situation," one woman told me matter-of-factly, "because you can spend time with them and get great sex. You don't have to worry about them moving in, because they won't be leaving their wives. To me, that's not a betrayal of the deal you have with them. If they got emotionally involved with you and started making demands—*that* would be a betrayal."

Sex—the kind of sex that makes you believe in God, hand over your kids if you think you'll be denied it, and go into long-term analysis if you are—is definitely a major drawing card for nineties women who have affairs. They *always* mention the sex. One woman said that when she and her lover got together they'd "go at each other on the floor like crazed animals." When he went home, she still had the diversions of a demanding career, her kids, her friends and her personal interests. She was adamant that she didn't want him to leave his wife and shack up with her. "When a man moves in—I don't care how progressive he is—it's always more work for a woman. I'm just not interested in picking his hairs out of the sink or saying, 'What do you want for dinner, honey?' "

Both of these women had previously been married, but many never-married women, too, seem to have settled for, rationalized or made peace with the fly-by-day nature of their dangerous liaisons. However they've worked it out, an affair serves their needs. Said one, "I get male companionship, the sex is outstanding and an affair allows me to be me. I can experience the epitome of a fabulous relationship that I know is out there somewhere. Until I can find it, this will have to do."

The view that an affair "allows me to be me," that it *empowers* rather than demeans, that it gives a woman control instead of reducing her to a yo-yo jerked at the end of a married man's string, is new—brand-new. As in most other realms, women are insisting on equality within their affairs. For some, this simply means demanding that their lovers meet them halfway: "I don't have time to scurry around dark corners and be on call," said one. "I have a tight schedule too. Either he makes plans with me and takes me out in the world, or no go." Perhaps the fact that she occasionally surprised her lover by arriving pantyless for their assignations, and regularly lauded him for having "the perfect penis," made these terms tolerable, for he did take her out—to baseball games, to his office watering-hole, to swank restaurants.

For others, autonomy simply means leaving themselves open to other options by continuing to date—and sleep with—other men. Some lay out the ground rules at the outset. Others simply carry on with double (or triple) lives, cheating, in a sense, on their cheating lovers.

Having concluded that she couldn't meet all of her needs with just one man, one divorced mother of two with an awesome sense of time-management was keeping three affairs on the go at once. She had a main squeeze who was divorced, and two occasional married suitors, about whom her main man knew nothing. From lover number one she got companionship and tender loving care. They did have sex, she said, "if you can call it that." Lover number two, however, was the stud. Lover number three was a long-time buddy with whom there'd always been "chemistry"; with him she enjoyed cuddling, "friendly sex" and a sense of history.

Although more and more women are taking the first step in initiating affairs, the predator is still likelier to be the man. "If you're single," one woman who had recently split told me, "married men suddenly come out of the woodwork. It's like I have an Open for Business sign on my forehead."

Not all women, however, are experts at controlling their emotional involvement in an affair—particularly when the affair is a long-term one. Such women discover that while a married man served their needs at the outset, and for the first year or more they were able to keep their emotions in a tidy little compartment, over time the affair wreaked havoc with their self-esteem. By that point, however, they were in so deep that ending the affair became a torturous proposition.

If you are—as one woman referred to herself—"alone, single and needy, raising three kids on my own with a high-powered job, no money and no time," even stolen moments with a man who gets to call all the shots function as "a little oasis in all the shit."

Even though the woman in question believed that her on-again, off-again three-year affair had destroyed her sense of self, even though she harbored no illusions that her lover, who had "screwed around from the third year of his twenty-year marriage," would leave his wife, even though, in the back of her mind, she viewed as weak a man who wouldn't leave a sham of a marriage, she still couldn't make the final break.

"I still see him and talk to him and I feel great immediately afterwards, but then the depression sets in because I have come to want so much more. He says he knows I'd never put up with what his wife puts up with, but I *am* putting up with it! He managed to find another woman to accept his self-centeredness. I joke with him and say, I'm too good for you. What I should say is, if you can't give me what I need, fuck off. And yet my actions speak louder than my words. It's all on his terms and I'm letting it be on his terms, so he's hanging in there. I'm willing to take whatever crumbs are thrown my way.

"I've realized that the solution is not a married man. An affair taught me that an affair is not enough. Oh, the sex was phenomenal at the beginning. And maybe that's all you can get. You can't sustain that kind of sexual connection without companionship and intimacy, though, and you need to build those things in a day-to-day way. You can have a fling once in a blue moon, because you can contain the sex and keep it separate from your emotions. But when a relationship becomes connected—as it inevitably does when there's more going on than just sex—it's way too painful to disengage."

What's the Sexual Etiquette of the Illicit Affair?

Like so many dynamics between the sexes, the illicit affair is developing a byzantine etiquette all its own. Most women I interviewed had, by their mid-thirties, entertained at least a few offers from married men, and they had worked up a highly opinionated viewpoint about the man who knows how to extend a below-board invitation stylishly.

Generally, women don't object to the married man who's up front about his marital status. They are, however, contemptuous of the "scumbags" (as one woman put it) who pretend they're not married and then show up at the door with a baby-seat in the car.

One woman reported that, after an "eyes-across-a-crowded-room situation," she met the object of her desires for a drink the next day. "I started hearing something in the conversation—something that clanged. It was that feeling you get sometimes—you know, like, what's wrong with this picture? Then I realized he kept saying 'we.' It turned out he was married. After I registered my displeasure at having to find this out when I was already in the middle of a date, he delivered the standard line: 'To tell you the truth, the sex isn't that great at home.' That pissed me off even more."

Another typical ploy, women report, is for a married man to invite them to lunch on the pretext of discussing business. Sometimes he neglects to mention his wife; sometimes he announces that he has an "arrangement" with her. This tactic is common enough these days to have become a cliché, but the man who dissembles about his marital status so incenses some women, they retaliate brutally by calling the man's wife and leaving the message that they "don't do mistress."

Many single women refer with annoyance to what one called "the availability factor"—the assumption a married man contemplating an affair sometimes makes, that single women are sitting at home in their lacy panties, their genitals ossifying from lack of use, ready to spring like wildcats at the first offer. Some married men who are in the mood to stray figure they don't have to seduce or court anymore; they just have to show up.

One woman who had virtually no moral objections to getting involved with a married man, and indeed had on a few occasions ("It's *his* problem, not mine"), became enraged when a married colleague (and friend) with whom she'd "scratched an itch" a few months earlier called her up at midnight one evening, drooling into the receiver, for telephone sex.

"Michael told me his wife was out of town, and his voice got all seductive and he said he was lying there on his bed and he was thinking about me...and, well, you know.... I told him I was tired and I was going to sleep. What really irks me is that we agreed, after we slept together that one time, that we weren't going to do it again, and we managed to get our friendship and working relationship back on a comfortable footing. I'm sure he called because one of his close friends has been having an affair for years and he keeps egging him on, telling him to go for it, saying an affair improves your marriage, revs you up. And I'm sure Michael thought of calling me simply because I'm single, and in his mind on call whenever he needs a little sexual diversion. I was turned off by two things: the weakness of a man who could be so easily manipulated, and the casual assumptions he made about me. He was horny or curious or bored or whatever and I guess he just figured I'd be waiting by the phone."

Single or married men who've been hit on by married women say that they too prefer the straightforward invitations, because at least then they can say yea or nay without feeling uncomfortable. They also prefer the invitations where the intention of the woman is clearly a little short-term pleasure as opposed to a long-term love affair. One man willingly went home with a married woman he met in a bar, because she made no secret of the fact that her husband was out of town for a few days, she found him attractive and she felt like getting laid.

How Is AIDS Affecting the Illicit Affair?

AIDS may be inspiring nervous second thoughts about having an affair, but it doesn't appear to be cramping the style of many would-be philanderers (or their female counterparts) in the moment of truth.

In *Men Who Can't Be Faithful*, author Carol Botwin reported encountering people for whom AIDS *was* a deterrent. But she met far more who were tempting the fates—as did I.

My favorite story in Botwin's book is that of the errant husband who says that he's narrowed his target group to married women with workaholic mates. The women are safe, he reasons, because they're married, while their husbands are safe because workaholics don't have time to fuck around.

What Mr. Market Research and his ilk ought to know is that, if chance smiles upon them, many workaholic male executives do indeed fool around—as do many workaholic female executives, married homemakers, lazy people, game-show hosts and Rhodes scholars. And, from what I can gather, many of them still don't use condoms. What this means is that—when they do indulge in an affair—they're laying two lives on the line (theirs and those of the spouses with whom they're presumably still sleeping).

The consensus among researchers is that while AIDS appears to be having little impact on the number of extramarital affairs, it may be affecting the choice of lovers and style of affairs. Women most often cheat with their workmates, their neighbors or their husbands' best friends. Availability and the thrill factor partly explain such choices, but quickie anonymous affairs may be down, researchers speculate, because AIDS has made people feel safer with those they know—or, more accurately, *think* they know.

What about Getting Caught?

Some people manage to carry on serial flings and/or affairs for years without their mates finding out. (Well, sometimes they're suspicious but they're unwilling to confront the issue, and life goes on more or less as usual.) Often, however, the law of averages prevails and luck runs out, or somebody gets jilted and squeals for revenge, or word gets around and somebody feels duty-bound to buy the wronged party lunch and tell them what's going on behind their back, or someone gets sloppy about concealing the evidence.

One guy, for instance, had a one-night stand with a woman he met through "heavy eye contact" while folding his laundry at the laundromat. He took her home while his mate was away; the next day, while rummaging in the garbage can for a dropped contact lens, his mate found the used condom.

And although we're supposed to believe that hell hath no fury like a woman scorned, in the nineties men are becoming extremely creative about the subtleties of revenge. One woman reported that she attended a wedding reception where the guests were just digging into the fruit cocktail when the groom stood up to make his speech. After a few gracious welcoming words, he announced in a jocular way that he was "going to leave now." Expecting a punch-line, the guests chuckled. Then they got it: "I just want to let everyone know," he went on, "that for the last five months my wife has been screwing my best man." After delivering his coup, he turned on his heel and walked out.

Finding out that someone you're married to is screwing some-body else, not to mention buying them expensive presents or writing them mushy letters, is one of life's lousiest experiences. It's so lousy, in fact, that it often hurts even if you *detest* the person you're married to. There's no telling what'll happen if you get caught, but chances are that if you are confronted, it won't be an upbeat occasion.

What's the Price of an Affair?

I did hear about one couple who met out of town, fell madly in love, gave themselves a year to attend to the annoying details of shedding their respective spouses, reunited in another city when the year was over, got married and remain blissfully married to this day. But, boy, was that story an anomaly!

How do affairs usually end? Rarely happily ever after. Some-times by creating more problems than they solve. Often not with a bang but a whimper. But often sordidly, too, in melodrama, disillusionment and pain—not unlike the dénouement of many modern marriages.

For, though some would rather not admit it, an adultery is a story of betrayal. Its plot, sooner or later, becomes tangled with the complications of duplicity and duplicity's emotional fallout. Even in the latter part of the twentieth century, when moral questions sometimes seem like quaint anachronisms, to enter into an affair is to face a moral question, and there's just no way of getting around that. Whether an infidelity is ever discovered or not, you have to lie to embark on it—to yourself or to another—and ultimately you'll have to make peace with those lies. Try as you may, it's impossible to avoid what Annette Lawson calls the "toxic" themes of adultery, and betrayal is one of the biggies.

One man I spoke to was trying to make sense of what infidelity meant. He was thirty-nine years old, had tumbled into the arms of another woman once, as a diversion from stress, and deeply regretted his actions. His wife didn't know, nor did he think she ever would, but the lie had become a terrible burden. It was there, chanting like an unrelenting Greek chorus, in the shadows of his marriage and his heart. He had confided in no one because he would be "dead" with his friends, he said, if they knew. They looked to his marriage as a model, you see.

Despite his guilt and sincere contrition, he was uncertain about the future, because he knew there were no guarantees that it would not happen again. He didn't think there was anything extraordinary about him. He was simply a human being. His wife traveled a good deal on business, he got lonely, he made plans and often he found himself in situations that could lead to something. And the women were more forward now, too, calling him up, inviting him to dinner. "You can become interested in people," he sighed, "and then the sexual thing is just there, hanging in the air. That male-female thing is always there—always—and it's difficult to deal with."

For instance, he'd recently met a 25-year-old woman with whom he was keeping company when his wife was out of town. "She's bright and different and strong and I really like her. She reminds me of my wife, actually. When I first met her I was aware of the fact that I was extremely attracted to her, but over time I decided that I wanted a friendship with this woman. I needed that.

"At first I thought, what's going on? She's fourteen years younger. Am I having a midlife crisis? Am I going to get a motorcycle next? All those clichés just sneak up on you and you think, oh Christ, I'm not immune from any of them!

"What's new about this relationship for me is that, while I'm attracted to her, I don't want to sleep with her. I want to work at developing a friendship with her. I think the fact that women have moved into the workplace has really helped men to start taking women seriously in other ways, to think of them, not just in sexual terms, but as peers and friends.

"There are incredible temptations out there, and I think whether you have an affair or not really comes down to coming to grips with what it means to be with another person over the long term. I was twenty-five when I got married, and I don't think I really knew in any deep sense then what it meant to be in a long-term relationship. What trust, respect, loyalty and fidelity actually meant. All these clichés you grow up with—about responsibility, and it's tough to be married, and you've got to work at a relationship—all that junk your parents told you—it's all true. You wake up one day and you're confronted by that."

———————

I could leave you with a tidy list of the pros and cons of having an affair—tell you that you're out of your mind to have one, or that you're out of your mind not to. But that would be pointless and you know it.

What I will tell you is that you're snowing yourself if you think you can deal with the decision in an ethical void. What you decide is a choice, and that choice has consequences not only for you but for others close to you—your spouse, certainly, the person you're involved with and, depending on how things turn out, possibly your kids and your friends. So if you choose to go ahead, you're gambling. Maybe you'll win, maybe you'll lose, but it's a pretty safe bet that someone else who didn't have any say in your gamble is going to be affected by your decision. I thought I should mention that, because it's the sort of thing people forget when they're thinking about ripping somebody's clothes off.

PART THREE:

CONCLUSION

Work in Progress

THEY'RE TRICKY THINGS, THESE SOCIAL REVOLUTIONS. PARTICULARLY when they start hitting people in their privates—or at least the way people *think* about their privates. That's a vulnerable place to get nailed, especially when you've been caught off guard. A lot of us have learned the hard way that a transformation in consciousness of the magnitude imagined in the sixties simply doesn't happen in one lifetime. The psychological price of social progress has been steep—we got more than we bargained for—but as men and women, mates and lovers, we're better off than our parents were. We now enjoy an astonishing diversity of choice in our lives, and I think too many of us have lost sight of that fact.

Even if we could put the genie back in the bottle, I suspect not many of us would. How many thinking women would choose to give up the options that now lie open to them? And how many thinking men would honestly wish to return to pre-feminist days when male and female roles were so narrowly defined?

Women feel that they've paid the higher price in this power struggle, and I think it's true that they have. What women tend to forget, however, is that they've also won most of the spoils. What they also forget is that men too have their scars to bear. Their weenies got roasted in the feminist fire, and that was no fun either.

We're still in the middle of a work in progress. Flexible, diverse social and sexual roles, freely chosen, are infinitely more rewarding, in the long run, than limited, rigidly prescribed ones. We're just weary at the moment, trying to cope while all the manners and mores filter down through the culture. "There have been times when I've just given up," one woman told me, "but the thing about giving up is that it too is susceptible to change. Change is the only thing we can be sure of in this crazy world. And I think more change is coming. Change and synthesis. Our relationships are in a dreadful state of transition now. It's as if someone has taken all the chemical elements and jumbled them up and we can't see our way clear to believe that the elements will ever find their separate levels again. It's terrifying and confusing and apt to send us all into despair. Yes, we're in a time of turbulence. But if we seize it and work it through to a more hopeful stage, we'll be okay. We can't just collapse and say we're powerless in the grip of history, lie down on our bellies and whimper and whine that it's not fair, it's not fair. We have to find a way to embrace living well, in the philosophical sense, with one another. And that's going to take some fortitude, some energy and some time."

As men and women, we stand now at a crossroads. We won some and we lost some; we're bored out of our gourds with the cussing and fighting, and we want to move on. Whether we'll go forward, mark time or immolate ourselves in recriminations—each sex in its own corner holding up a cross to the other as if to keep the vampires at bay—depends, I think, on whether we can come together to resolve our differences. If the bawdy politic is going to heal, the problems have to be tackled, and the solutions found-in twos. But making it, arm in arm, to safer ground depends on facing a tough question: *what does it mean to be a man and a woman in the nineties?*

For men, answering that question involves breaking a vow of silence and understanding their experience in the aftermath of feminism. Until men figure out who they are and who they wish to be, they can't possibly come back to women whole.

God knows they need some introspection time of their own! For the last twenty-five years or so, they've been doing more or less what women have been telling them to do, and a lot of them aren't handling it that well. Men are running scared, but retreating into avoidance is a cop-out. A no-commitment credo is a crock. Living and loving *is* complication. Engaging with another human being brings with it a responsibility. Acts do have consequences.

It's too early to tell whether the burgeoning men's movement, inspired by Robert Bly's *Iron John*, will awaken men to a new way of thinking about themselves, as the women's movement did for women. "Movement" may be a grandiose word for what's going on. *Iron John* is an unlikely bestseller, but Bly's mythopoeic treatise has struck a chord. Certainly the enormous response by a wide range of men to the ideas in the book suggests that men dearly want to understand the possibilities of manhood; it also suggests however, that, up until now, there's been a noticeable dearth of male voices guiding them toward understanding. The men's movement took off, I suspect, partly because a generation of men were eternally grateful to hear *a man* talk about manhood for once in their lives. And it took off because men were finally burned out and bummed out enough to listen.

The tremendous response to *Iron John* also suggests that men are far likelier to express what ails them if the atmosphere for self-revelation celebrates what's worthy about manhood, instead of denigrating what isn't. If men are craving some bonding with the guys right now, it's because they can find much-needed comfort in a male milieu, and they can leave it with their dignity intact. It's easy to ridicule the movement's more bizarre excesses, but someone who lived through the vanguard days of feminism well knows that social movements are apt to begin in strange ways. I worry, though, that the movement so far lacks political imperatives and a fundamental authenticity. The warrior costumes and masks are only superficial accoutrements, and I wonder how far passing around talking-sticks, sitting naked in sweat lodges, reenacting sacred Sioux rituals or smacking conga drums will take men along the road to self-awareness. I also question the movement's accent on the warrior-king, and its undervaluing of the guardian-protector—both, it seems to me, speak eloquently of manhood. And I wonder where men are supposed to go, and how the sexes are supposed to go forth hand in hand, once the Wild Man weekend is over. (How, for instance, do you ask a guy who's just found his Inner King to do the dishes?)

No, I think men are likelier to find what they're looking for with a little less dancing in the forest and a lot more serious thinking—about the kind of men they aspire to be, about the quality of relationships they wish to establish, and about the day-to-day ways in which they can realize those aspirations. I met many men who are doing just that. All I hope is that they'll be given the chance to talk freely about what's on their minds and in their hearts, uncensored by the Thought Police of political correctness, in the open arms of women who will listen.

For women, deciding what it means to be a woman in the nineties involves stepping down from the tightrope so many of them are walking between dogma and desire, sexism and sexiness, feminism and femininity; and having the courage, as Camille Paglia, author of *Sexual Personae* puts it, to "abandon the pretense of sexual sameness and admit the terrible duality of gender."

It may also mean acknowledging that it's empowering to be submissive in the bedroom once in a while, or admitting that men and women *like* being different and are most alluring to each other when they are, or saying out loud that doctrinaire feminism has, quite unwittingly, put women into a worse sexual straitjacket than men ever did.

But women can't know what it means to be a woman in the nineties without first addressing what it means to be a feminist in the nineties. The women's movement sprang from celebration, idealism and joy but for too long has been straining under the weight of self-righteous moral indignation, us-against-them sexual politics, and the tyranny of all those do's and dont's. Yes, men and women are different in many ways, and yes, those differences can be scary at times, but they can also be intriguing, mysterious and exhilarating. So focused has feminism been on the rifts between the sexes, it has forgotten the commonalities. For when it comes to matters of sex and love, men and women share a commonality far deeper than they're admitting.

If I accuse the younger generation of feminists of lacking a sense of history, of reaping the spoils of feminism without acknowledging their debt to it (for they owe feminism big), I must also acknowledge that too many of my own contemporaries have become feminist caricatures, feminists gone mad. "Men have a great fear that women don't like them," one woman told me, "and I think that fear is justified. I don't think anything is going to change until there's been a real recognition by women that men have been put through the wringer by us."

And so I think women will have to stop blaming men for being men. They'll have to find it in their hearts to give men some empathy, even when they don't always seem to deserve that empathy. Women must try to remember that a man who came of age somewhere in the latter part of the twentieth century is a stranger in a strange land, and he is doing what he can.

━━━━━━━━━━━━

We are making headway. I believe this for many reasons, but mainly because I set out to write a book about sex, and I wound up writing a book about intimacy. Sex passed for intimacy for a bunch of years because the sex that was fashionable for my generation was an amazingly convincing *approximation* of intimacy: it was all so new and exciting and we were such hungry kids. Let's face it, recreational sex has its own set of charms, and apparently it had a lot of us fooled. We thought all that messing around would create a new kind of intimacy; what we got instead was a new kind of alienation.

We tried to convince ourselves, when we took off our clothes and climbed into bed, that what we were indulging in was "just sex"—but now we know better. However shallow the deed may seem on the surface, in the cold light of day we usually discover that we've engaged in a powerful rite of connection, and eventually we have to deal with its ramifications. We can deny or avoid them, of course, but we can't escape them.

There are still people around who would kill for cheap sex, but most of the people I met are looking for something more refined. The way they see it, bookcases made of bricks and boards are okay when you're young, but when you mature you want something more stable, constructed of finer materials—something, shall we say, a little more esthetic. As one woman put it, "Sex is a lovely thing to do, but when I go to my grave, I don't think I'll be thinking about the greatest sex of my life. I think I'll be thinking about the greatest love."

In the nineties, sex worth writing home about sometimes means hot sex, sometimes means dirty sex, sometimes means tender sex, but almost always means honest, open, emotionally connected sex. In other words, people are looking for a friend they can sleep with. For what a lot of men and women have discovered traveling this long and winding road together is that sex is an *intimate, meaningful act*. That's probably the single most important thing I've learned about sex since the sixties. And it's taken me a long time and a lot of thrashing about—mental or otherwise—to figure it out, even though I don't think I'm abnormally stupid. The sad part of this story is that it took so many of us so long to find out.

I've also learned that a sense of humor will take a woman farther with a man, both in and out of bed, than a sense of superiority, that listening will take her farther than a lecture, and that honesty will take her farther than a lie. But I know too that even if all the women in the world started shooting straight with men tomorrow, little would change unless men started shooting straight with them. Intimacy is an exchange—a square deal—and it cuts both ways.

How will we achieve this precious intimacy so many of us yearn for? I see bellwethers that we're already achieving it, in the rich, rewarding friendships that men and women are forging—in the workplace, with former lovers, with the mates of dear friends—friendships that are sexy without being sexual, attractions that are friendly and flirtatious without being fatal. Through avenues other than the physical, men and women are learning to cherish the mysteries and joys and pleasures of the opposite sex—the sweet, sweet otherness.

I'm heartened too by the sincere introspection that is already percolating in many people. Men and women are starting to emerge from a long, troubled sleep, to acknowledge their foibles and failings, their need and desire for each other. They've developed an often funny, often wise, often staggeringly honest perspective only time and distance could have provided—a perspective that's so evident in the stories in this book. I remember, for instance, the man who told me that you have to behave with decency in a relationship and hope your will will be honored, or the man who said we'll have to put our heads together and work things out, because nobody likes this stuff that's going on. I think of the woman who couldn't get hot for a guy with a *Ms.* magazine in his bathroom, and what that incident forced her to confront about her own desires. And I remember too a woman who asked me to give men a message for her: "Men are always saying that women don't need them anymore," she said, "but we *do* need them—only not for the things they've traditionally provided, like a roof over our heads and three squares a day. We need them to be our protectors, our companions, our mates, our lovers and our friends."

I'm encouraged too by the many people who are formulating creative strategies so they can meet and mate well. In the absence of clear rules or codes, they're inventing their own. The most successful codes are based on moral fundamentals: decency, courtesy, integrity, honesty and sensitivity to the fact that there is another human being in the sexual equation. "I'm really coming up with a code of behavior," one man told me, "how I should and shouldn't act in a relationship. And I'd rather deal with loneliness than allow myself to be caught in lies and hypocrisy."

Such people are refusing to grow bitter and give up. But they're also refusing to settle for less than the vision of relationship they seek. Like everybody else, they dream of loving and being loved, but their days of pining for The One are over. Instead, they're leading multifaceted lives, becoming fully rounded human beings on their own, turning to their friends and families for solace in lonely times. They are uncoupled but they're not alone. They're staying tuned, connected and alive. Such people face the future with optimism—qualified optimism, perhaps, but optimism none-theless—because they believe that readiness is all. Only a whole person with an open, generous heart will be ready for love when it comes walking through the door.

"If people would only talk as openly and honestly about these issues as you and I are talking about them," one man said to me. "Having the courage to risk honesty—that's the most important thing. Getting close, getting near and telling the truth. That's what it's all about. I've never had a bad discussion with a woman lying down."

I think he may be on to something.

Notes on Sources

Introduction

"Sexual Etiquette for the '90s," *Toronto Life*, February 1989.

Chapter One: The State of the Heart

"The Eleventh Megatrend," *Time*, July 23, 1984.

For the discussion among six men see "Sex, Lies and Audiotape," *GQ*, November 1989.

"The New Scarlet Letter," *Time*, August 2, 1982.

"The Revolution Is Over," *Time*, April 9, 1984.

"Fear of Sex," *Newsweek*, November 24, 1986.

"The New Sexual Morality," *Ebony*, November 1987.

"Once Upon a Time, There Was a Thing Called Sex," *Cosmopolitan*, October 1989.

For Edward Cornish see "Moonlight, Violins, Briefs, and Bytes," *The Futurist*, January/February 1987.

For downplaying of gloomy predictions see "Sex in the '90s," *The Washington Post*, January 8, 1989.

For remarks on New York see "Wild in the Clubs," *The Village Voice*, December 20, 1988.

Chapter Two: Why Are Women Confused?

For review of *The Hite Report* see "Back Off, Buddy," *Time*, October 12, 1987.

For Yale-Harvard study see "Too Late for Prince Charming," *Newsweek*, June 2, 1986.

For Ron Powers see "The Beastie Girls," *GQ*, December 1989.

For study of life after divorce see "Recent Changes in Sex-Role Ideology among Divorced Men and Women: Some Possible Causes and Implications," *Sex Roles*, Vol. 12 Nos. 5/6, 1985.

For Linda Sunshine see "Neuroses Are a Girl's Best Friend," *Harper's Bazaar*, March 1989.

For college-student sex experience see "The Selfish Sex Standard," *Psychology Today*, July 1986.

For college survey see "How College Women and Men Feel Today about Sex, AIDS, Condoms, Marriage, Kids," *Glamour*, August 1987.

For Rebecca Sydnor see "A Fine Romance," *Harper's Bazaar*, April 1989.

For Club Med see "The New Sobriety," *The Village Voice*, December 30, 1986.

Chapter Three: Why Are Men Confused?

For Michael Blumenthal see "No Big Deal," *About Men*, edited by Edward Klein and Don Erickson (New York: Pocket Books, 1987).

For Ken Kesey and Robert Stone see "Blows to the Spirit," *Esquire*, June 1986.

For responses to poll on New Man see "Who Is the New Ideal Man?" *Psychology Today*, November 1989.

wife," *Esquire*, June 1990.

Witch-Hunt," *Playboy*, April 1985.

...ner see "Montreal Massacre," *Maclean's*, December 18, 1989.

For Andrew Dice Clay see "In Your Face," *Vanity Fair*, June 1990.

For random rage see "We So Horny," *The Village Voice*, October 16, 1990.

Chapter Four: Getting Men and Women Together

For James Bennet see "The Data Game," *The New Republic*, February 13, 1989.

For Thomas Murray see "The Language of Singles Bars," *American Speech*, Spring 1985.

For tongue down throat see "Snow Job," *Playboy*, December 1989.

For Cathy Smith see "After The Fall," *Mirabella*, August 1989.

For Saturday-night dating see "Love," *New York*, June 29-July 6, 1987.

For "bimbos" see "We Need Bimbos," *Chicago*, February 1990.

Chapter Five: Sexual Etiquette for the Nineties

For Phil Donahue see "And How Do Men Feel Now about Monogamy?" *Glamour*, July 1988.

For "Dr. Ruth" Westheimer see "The Munchkin of the Bedroom," *Time*, July 1, 1985.

For study re lying see "Sex, Lies and HIV," *The New England Journal of Medicine*, March 15, 1990.

For statistics on anal sex see *Erotic Wars* by Lillian B. Rubin, Ph.D. (New York: Farrar, Straus & Giroux, 1990) p. 125-126; "Desperately Seeking Sexual Statistics," *Science News*, July 8, 1989.

For John Leo see "On the Trail of the Big O," *Time*, March 3, 1986.

For survey on orgasm see "Sexual Pleasure: The Surprising Preferences of 100,000 Women," *Redbook*, September 1975.

For Ann Landers see "Finding Trouble in Paradise," *Time*, January 28, 1985.

Chapter Six: Sex and the Long Haul

For marriage study see "The Changing Relationship of Marital Status to Reported Happiness," *Journal of Marriage & the Family*, May 1988.

For marriage statistics see "The Postmarital Society," *American Demographics*, November 1988.

For sex and two-career marriages see "Enter Success! Exit: Sex," *Mademoiselle*, February 1988.

For sex and parenting see "Sex after Baby," *Parenting*, March 1988.

For Peter Wish see "Sex in the '90s," *The Washington Post*, January 8, 1989.

For X-rated video statistics see "Romantic Porn in the Boudoir," *Time*, March 30, 1987.

For John Money see "Doctor of Sexology," *Psychology Today*, May 1988.

Chapter Seven: Dangerous Liaisons

For "Betrayed" see *Esquire*, June 1990.